Imprints 11

VOLUME II

Essays
Media

Lori Farren
David Friend
Janet Hannaford
Cam MacPherson
Jeff Siamon

CONSULTANT
Marg Frederickson

GAGE EDITORIAL TEAM
Joe Banel
Diane Robitaille
Cathy Zerbst

 gage EDUCATIONAL PUBLISHING COMPANY
A DIVISION OF CANADA PUBLISHING CORPORATION
Vancouver · Calgary · Toronto · London · Halifax

Permissions Editor: Elizabeth Long
Photo Research: Karen Taylor
Design, Art Direction, & Electronic Assembly: Wycliffe Smith Design Inc.
Cover Image: Dave Robertson/Masterfile

IMPRINTS REVIEWERS
Patricia Ames, Rainbow DB, ON
Gerry Bartlett, School District #2, NB
Mike Budd, Greater Essex County DSB, ON
Michelle Coleman, Cape Breton Victoria Regional SB, NS
Kathy Coles, Langley SB, BC
Jennifer Connell, Eastern School District, PEI
Maria DeBerardinis, Dufferin-Peel Roman Catholic DSB, ON
Bryan Ellefson, Palliser Regional Schools, AB
Pat Kover, Calgary B of E, AB
Karen Montgomery-Jones, Algoma DSB, ON
Jane Prosser, Saskatoon B of E, SK
Catherine Reid, Avalon East SB, NF
Robert Riel, Winnipeg School Division #1, MB
Shelley Robinson, Rocky View School Div. #41, AB
Georgina Barbosa Tousignant, Dufferin-Peel RCSSB, ON
Harry Wagner, Parkland School Div. #70, AB

Gage would like to thank Marg Frederickson's Grade 12 students from Burnaby North Senior Secondary School for their significant contributions.

National Library of Canada cataloguing in publication data

Main entry under title:

Imprints 11

For use in grade 11.
Issued also in 1 vol.
Contents: v. 2. Essays and media / [compiled by] Lori Farren, Janet Hannaford, Cam MacPherson.
ISBN 0-7715-0942-1

1. Readers (Secondary). I. Farren, Lori.

PE1121.I536 2001a   428'.6   C2001-930047-6

We acknowledge the financial support of the Government of Canada through the Book Publishing Industry Development Program for our publishing activities.

The selections collected in *Imprints* are drawn from a wide variety of sources. To respect the integrity of these sources, Gage has preserved the original spelling, grammar, and punctuation used by each author. Gage editorial style, however, is used throughout for activities and other text generated by Gage writers.

ISBN 0-7715-0942-1
2 3 4 5 FP 05 04 03 02 01
Printed and bound in Canada

Table of Contents

Essays

Persuasive

It's Time to Think About Visors by Ken Dryden ✦ 8
The Importance of Being Earnest by Lynn Coady ✦ 12
Whose Lathe? by Ursula K. Le Guin 16
Alarm Bells for Civilization by Gwynne Dyer ✦ 20
Of Studies by Sir Francis Bacon 28
Progress by Alan Lightman 32
The Time Factor by Gloria Steinem 36

Literary

Joy by Molly Peacock 41
In Support of Nick Bantock's "Life Class" by Kristal Fung ✦ 50
A Comparison by Sylvia Plath 53
The Short Story Defined by Peter Hung 56

Personal

The Shack by Margaret Laurence ✦ 61
Doubletake by William DeKay ✦ 66
Arming the Spirit by George Faludy 71
Dis?Ability on the Internet by Heather Proud 75
Chicken-Hips by Catherine Pigott ✦ 79
What Colour Is a Rose? by Drew Hayden Taylor ✦ 83
Some Thoughts on the Common Toad by George Orwell 86

Expository

Homage to Barcelona by Marjorie Doyle ✦ 91
Lessons From a Walk in a Rain Forest by David Suzuki ✦ 98

Biography

In Memory of W.O. Mitchell by Fred Stenson ✦ 105
Mann and Machine from *Contemporary Canadian Biographies* ✦ 111
from *Long Walk to Freedom: The Autobiography of*
Nelson Mandela by Nelson Mandela 118

Media

Why Investigate Media?

Looking at the Media by Cam MacPherson (essay) ✦ 130
Classroom Without Walls by Marshall McLuhan (essay) ✦ 134

Radio

The Psychological Power of Radio by Tim Crook (essay) 138
Christmas Consumer Frenzy by Paul Moth (script) ✦ 143
One Ocean by Betty Quan (one-act radio play) ✦ 148

Advertising and Marketing
    People as Products by Jean Kilbourne (essay)   155
    The Trouble With People by Vance Packard (essay)   160
    All Part of Becoming Canadian by Al Pittman
        (autobiographical anecdote) ✦   167
    The Sea-Monkey Lady: Susan Barclay by Arthur Black
        (radio interview) ✦   169
    No News Is Bad News: Using Publicity to Your Advantage
        by Alexander Hiam (how-to article)   178
    Sports Logos an Insult by Noah Augustine (opinion piece) ✦   186
Television
    Television: The Collective Imagination
        by Derrick de Kerckhove (article) ✦   189
    The Quiz Show Format by David Halberstam (article)   197
Movies
    What Would You Change? by Claudia Puig (article) ✦   204
    Screen Scenes by various authors (scripts)   208
News
    Just the Facts by Sue Kanhai (diary) ✦   219
    Laughter Soothes His Soul by Paul Melting Tallow (profile) ✦   224
Computer-based Media
    "Cyberanchor" Delivers All the E-News That's Fit to Click
        by Ann Perry (newspaper article) ✦   230
    The Net Generation by Don Tapscott (article) ✦   234
    If I Can't Have Beer, at Least Give Me a Playstation
        by Rob Blizzard (essay) ✦   240
    Being a Woman in a Man's Game World
        by Samantha Peters (editorial) ✦   243

Glossary   247

Index of Titles and Authors   251

Acknowledgments   252

✦ indicates Canadian content

Alternate Table of Contents

Aboriginal Selections

What Colour Is a Rose?   83
Sports Logos an Insult   186
Laughter Soothes His Soul   224

Art and Music

In Support of Nick Bantock's
    "Life Class"   50
Doubletake   66
Laughter Soothes His Soul   224

Challenges

Arming the Spirit   71
Dis?Ability on the Internet   75
Long Walk to Freedom   118
One Ocean   148
Being a Woman in a Man's
    Game World   243

Conflict

Whose Lathe?   16
Alarm Bells for Civilization   20
Progress   32
The Time Factor   36
Arming the Spirit   71
Long Walk to Freedom   118
Sports Logos an Insult   186
Screen Scenes   208
Being a Woman in a Man's
    Game World   243

Environment/Nature

The Shack   61
Some Thoughts on the
    Common Toad   86
Lessons From a Walk in a
    Rain Forest   98
The Sea-Monkey Lady   169

Ethics

Progress   32
Lessons From a Walk in a
    Rain Forest   98
The Quiz Show Format   197
Screen Scenes   208

Humour and Satire

The Importance of Being
    Earnest   12
The Short Story Defined   56
Doubletake   66
In Memory of W.O. Mitchell   105
Christmas Consumer Frenzy   143
All Part of Becoming Canadian   167
The Sea-Monkey Lady   169
Laughter Soothes His Soul   224
If I Can't Have Beer, at
    Least Give Me a Playstation   240

Identity

The Shack   61
Chicken-Hips   79
What Colour Is a Rose?   83
People as Products   155
Laughter Soothes His Soul   224

Justice

Whose Lathe?   16
Arming the Spirit   71
Long Walk to Freedom   118
Screen Scenes   208

Media

Progress   32
Dis?Ability on the Internet   75
Chicken-Hips   79
What Colour Is a Rose?   83
Mann and Machine   111
See also the Media unit

Science and Technology

Progress   32
Dis?Ability on the Internet   75
Mann and Machine   111
Classroom Without Walls   134
The Psychological Power
    of Radio   138
The Sea-Monkey Lady   169
Television: The Collective
    Imagination   189
"Cyberanchor" Delivers All the
    E-News That's Fit to Click   230

The Net Generation   234
If I Can't Have Beer, at Least
    Give Me a Playstation   240
Being a Woman in a Man's
    Game World   243

Scripts, Speeches, and Interviews

Arming the Spirit   71
In Memory of W.O. Mitchell   105
Christmas Consumer Frenzy   143
One Ocean   148
The Sea-Monkey Lady   169
Screen Scenes   208

Survival

Alarm Bells for Civilization   20
Arming the Spirit   71
Some Thoughts on the
    Common Toad   86
Lessons From a Walk in a
    Rain Forest   98
Long Walk to Freedom   118
Laughter Soothes His Soul   224

World Views

Arming the Spirit   71
Chicken-Hips   79
Homage to Barcelona   91
Long Walk to Freedom   118
One Ocean   148

Essays

But words are things, and a small drop of ink,
Falling like dew, upon a thought, produces
That which makes thousands, perhaps millions, think.

Lord Byron

It's Time to Think About Visors

AFTER BRYAN BERARD'S INJURY, IT'S NOT JUST AN ISSUE OF ATHLETES' PERSONAL CHOICE

By Ken Dryden

I was at the March 11 game in Ottawa, sitting in the press box far from where it happened. I could see a Senators player near the Leafs' net spin quickly around to swing at a suddenly available puck. Then I saw Bryan Berard topple to the ice. The stick of Marion Hossa, the highly promising Senators left-winger, had struck Berard in the face with its full force. I looked at the TV monitor beside me. Berard was lying prone, his legs kicking at the ice. A dark spot formed beside him. Blood on ice is crimson; it splatters and streams. This was darker and thick.

I didn't think about his eye. I have seen so many pucks and sticks come threateningly close, then, with the tiniest reflexive twitch of a head, slam on the face's protective armature of cheekbones, eyebrows or nose. I wasn't ready for the news that came early the next morning. Bryan Berard, just a week after his 23rd birthday, was not likely to play again.

There is a sadness in Toronto that still hasn't lifted. And inevitably people are beginning to debate the mandatory use of face protectors in the NHL. The great majority of NHL players wore a full-face mask from the time they took their first strides on the ice at age 5 or 6 until they were 18. Most wore visors for a few more years until they reached the NHL and were given a choice. Then most decided to play as they never had before, with no facial protection at all.

In hockey's formative years, rules were created to protect what equipment didn't. Blows to the head were penalized; so were high-sticking and elbowing. In the past 20 years of minor hockey, with its helmets and masks, the head was as well protected as any other part of the body, and these penalties became obsolete even as they were still applied. Today's NHL players grew up knowing that a stick to the head might result in a penalty but not an injury. Sticks could be carried high or low and used with near impunity—it didn't matter.

Then, in the NHL, the players take their face masks off.

What Hossa did was an accident. That isn't the same, however, as saying it's merely an unfortunate part of the game. Some activities are riskier than others. Hockey's imaginable accidents are much more severe than those in basketball or soccer. It's not enough to find explanation in the inevitability of accident. We need to imagine accident as part of the game and generate plans to minimize it.

Would most available visors have saved Berard's eye? Not necessarily. Could a visor be designed that would have? Yes. Would wearing a visor have made most of today's eye injuries less likely? Yes.

Everything we do, sports included, is a compromise between safety and performance. Around the office we don't think of safety much. At the wheel of a car we do. Skiers can't ski down a hill fast until they learn how to control their speed and know they can stop if they have to. Hockey players will reach speeds of 40 km/h only when they know they can brake before the end boards. Safety doesn't need to straitjacket performance. Usually, it enhances it.

I know this from personal experience. When goalies first experimented with masks, they were distracted by all the differences they noticed. Masks are heavy; they're hot. When you try to see a puck at your feet, parts of them get in the way. I didn't wear a mask until an NCAA rule forced me to wear one. Then heavy and hot didn't matter, because you didn't have a choice. You learned to see through and past any obstructions. It was the same, years later, for skaters and helmets. It will be the same for visors.

Mandating visors will take more than a decree from the NHL. It will require the support of the players and the NHL Players' Association. It isn't the entire answer for a player to say, I don't want to wear a visor, and I shouldn't have to—it's my choice.

> ## Knowledge is power.
> Sir Francis Bacon

Sport depends on public acceptance. If it doesn't reflect the tastes and values of a time, players and spectators will seek out other activities. People are attracted to risk. Near misses are thrilling. Wipeouts at skiing or surfing; cars brushing a wall, turning broadside, sent catapulting into the air over other cars, that's exciting—when no one gets hurt, or really hurt.

But more hockey players are getting really hurt now. NHL players talk openly about a new lack of respect that players seem to have for one another. With this lack of respect, they are not only hurting one another, they are damaging the sport. This is what takes this beyond a matter of simple personal choice.

For the first 80 years of hockey's existence, no goalie wore a mask. It took nearly 40 more years before every skater was required to wear a helmet. From today's perspective, that doesn't seem possible, just as playing football without a helmet, then without a face mask, to us seems incredible lore. How could they do it? Ten years from now, maybe 20, but sometime, all hockey players will wear facial protection, and 20 years after that, it will seem just as incredible that they didn't always do it.

The question is not *if* but *when*. And the question for us is whether we drag out this time to its extreme or act sooner.

Hockey Hall-of-Famer **Ken Dryden** is president of the Toronto Maple Leafs. He was an NHL goaltender during the 70s, and during his career won the Calder Trophy, five Vezina Trophies, the Conn Smythe Trophy, six Stanley Cups, and was a five-time First Team All-Star.

1. *Response*

a. Drawing on your own knowledge and/or experience of hockey, generate your own list of the pros and cons of wearing a protective visor.

b. What is Ken Dryden's thesis in this essay? Where does it first appear?

The **thesis** of an essay is the main idea or argument that the author is attempting to prove.

c. Identify the places where Dryden inserted a personal element into the essay. What do you think he was trying to achieve? In your opinion, do the personal references make Dryden's essay stronger? Explain.

2. *Literature Studies* *Thesis and Supporting Details* In a persuasive essay, the writer wants the reader to accept a particular thesis. The writer does this by presenting supporting details (facts, statistics, examples, reasons, and so on) that help to prove the thesis. List the supporting details Dryden includes in his essay. Do you think Dryden proved his thesis convincingly? Explain. Based on the list you created in activity 1. a, what other details might Dryden have used to support his thesis?

3. *Critical Thinking* Should the wearing of visors be mandatory for professional hockey players? Give the reasons for your recommendation.

4. *Media* *Advertisement* Create an advertisement (a TV, radio, or magazine ad, or a poster or billboard) designed to convince a target audience to support the mandatory wearing of visors in the NHL. When you present your work to the class, describe the target audience and explain the specific techniques you would use to persuade that audience.

Where are all
the funny Canadian writers?

The Importance of
Being Earnest

By Lynn Coady

Every writer is familiar with the aggravation of rejection. And I'm not talking about photocopied slips initialed by an indifferent editor. I mean that really drawn out, knife-twisting kind of rejection where they've scrupulously tracked you down, solicited your work, thanked you profusely for your contribution, and then, at the last possible moment—sorry, we just don't think it's going to "fit" in with our "format." This has happened to me recently, as it probably has to every writer. But it got me thinking about why my work has been solicited and then rejected in the same sort of way by other editors. And when I say the same sort of way, I'm referring to the preface they always use: "It's hilarious, but…."

I would like to talk seriously about irreverence, and why, as a writer, I often find myself feeling like the class clown in a very dour religious boarding school. When you're a Canadian writer, people expect certain things from you. There are clichés that you feel expected, on some level, to live up to. Landscape, for example. You get the feeling people expect a hell of a lot of landscape in your work. Long, meandering descriptions of rivers and fields, as though our national prose must somehow reflect our geography.

True, many of the new generation of writers would seem to be sloughing off these traditional expectations. Urban-Canadian appears to be the new catch phrase. Readers can now enjoy gritty tales of the city, with all its attendant sordidness. Drug use, grimy alleyways, soulless, neurotic women and men having seedy Canadian sex in dingy boarding houses. It's all good. My only problem is that, as Canadians, we seem to be taking the urban landscape every bit as seriously as our pristine countryside. The one thing

Canadians can't seem to get out from under is this penchant for absolute earnestness in our writing. Rugged, noble country folk undergoing day-to-day hardships have been replaced by hip, dispassionate urbanites undergoing day-to-day hardships. It still doesn't make me laugh. If it weren't for Mordecai Richler's irony-rich novels, Canadian literature would have no equivalents to laugh-riots such as Roddy Doyle's *The Commitments*, or works of scathing, gleeful satire like *Catch-22* or *Breakfast of Champions*.

Maybe you think I'm frivolous, believing we should laugh at literature; perhaps you think this is somehow wrong of me. But I have a very legitimate reason for this: life makes me laugh, because life is stupid. If a work of literature is not able to get that sublime sense of stupidity across, at least in some degree, then I have to consider it a flawed work of literature. Because it simply doesn't represent, to me, a true picture of life in this world. Yes, even life in Canada.

It could be that I am more highly sensitized to this as a result of being from Atlantic Canada. The publication of my novel *Strange Heaven* came about, ironically, as a result of an editor's refusal to reproduce an excerpt of it in a Christmas anthology. It was a collection of Atlantic Canadian stories, the kind of book that seems part of an ongoing tradition of cloyingly sentimental renderings of life in the Maritimes. But should the sketches of your fictional little town become anything less than sunshiny, you're in trouble. You're breaking the rules. My story was about an ex-pregnant teenage girl with diarrhea sitting down to Christmas dinner with her senile, nonagenarian grandmother, her mentally handicapped uncle, her alcoholic other uncle, and her verbally abusive father. This may sound a little over-the-top to some, but to me it is nowhere near as outlandish and unbelievable as, say, an episode of *Road to Avonlea*. Basically, any time I see a depiction of a happy loving family enjoying a peaceful Christmas dinner—in the Maritimes or anywhere else—I call it bull.

So the editors were horrified, yet intrigued. They respectfully declined to include the excerpt in their anthology, but did ask to see the rest of the novel, and then published it. And weirdly, this particular story of Christmas dysfunction has become one of its most celebrated fragments.

The editor's words of rejection were that the story didn't "fit" with the rest of the collection. Why not? I'll tell you why not—because it wasn't hokey. To me, this implicit insistence that every story by every Maritime writer included in a Christmas anthology has to be hokey is nothing less than censorship. The smiley kind of censorship that hides behind a Pollyanna face of sentiment and dreary convention.

I had another experience of "not fitting" into an anthology recently. *Brick* magazine solicited contributions from authors across the country for a book called *Lost Classics*. Each author was asked to pen a short memory of some obscure book they remember from their past that ended up influencing them as adult writers. I came up with a book that had affected me profoundly right off the bat. The editors sent me some examples, however, and I knew at once that my excerpt would have to be nothing like the others. They were all very reverent and, yes, earnest.

My choice was actually a series of volumes, innocently titled *Uncle Arthur's Bedtime Stories*. These supposedly Christian morality tales had filled me with horror as a child, instilling the seeds of what developed into a distinctively warped relationship with God and religion. I couldn't think of any work of literature that had influenced me as deeply as that, so I set to work. Uncle Arthur's message was basically that God is out to get you, and it was reinforced with every story he told. Little Susie skips piano lessons to play hopscotch with her friends, and, *whammo!* From out of nowhere a brick falls, crushing her fingers so she can never play piano again. It's grotesque to think that somebody actually thought this was the way to raise good Christian children. It's *stupid*, and that's what I wanted to get across. People are stupid. We're all stupid. That's basically all I'm trying to get across in any of my writing. I don't think it's a particularly frivolous message, either.

Maybe it was naive to think I could get this past the editors of *Lost Classics*, but it boggled my mind that anyone would want to sit through page after page of absolutely humourless reminiscences of the cherished childhood tomes of Canadian writers. Surely, I thought, there are people like me out there, who would want to read the kind of thing I wanted to write.

But once again, the editors disagreed.

I have nothing against so-called "serious" writers who write "serious" books, essays, and articles. I just don't understand why I have to be one. Every nation boasting a mature literary tradition has its share of great ironists, so why are we permitted so few? Why are we consistently discouraged from poking fun at ourselves? Why does Mordecai Richler get to have all the fun?

> A good essay must have this permanent quality about it; it must draw its curtain round us, but it must be a curtain that shuts us in, not out.
>
> Virginia Woolf

Lynn Coady is a fiction writer and essayist. Born in Cape Breton, Nova Scotia, she received a BA from Carleton University, and an MFA from the University of British Columbia. Her novel *Strange Heaven* was published in 1998, and her collection of short stories, *Play the Monster Blind*, in 2000. Her second novel is due to be published in Spring 2002.

I. *Response*
a. Lynn Coady makes a number of controversial claims in this essay. What are they? For each one, explain your own position.
b. What approach does Coady use to convince readers that Canadian writers are too serious? Do you think that approach is convincing? Why or why not?
c. Give some examples of your favourite books and/or stories. Was humour an important component of any of them? Explain.

2. *Writing* Humour Try your own hand at writing something funny—a short story, anecdote, or skit, for example. When you've finished your first draft, reflect on the challenges of being humorous. What advice would you give to someone trying to write something funny?

3. *Vocabulary* Unfamiliar Words In the fifth paragraph of her essay, Coady uses the adjective *nonagenarian* to describe a character. Reread the sentence and speculate on what *nonagenarian* might mean. What strategies did you use to make your guesses? Consult a dictionary that contains etymologies to find out where the word comes from. Why would an author use a challenging word instead of one that most readers would know?

4. *Making Connections* Compare "The Importance of Being Earnest" with Drew Hayden Taylor's "What Colour Is a Rose?" Examine aspects such as intent, tone, and subject matter.

Whose Lathe?

"Of course we have to be sure about the kinds of books we want our kids to read in school. Don't we?"

By Ursula K. Le Guin

In a small town near Portland late this spring (1984), a novel, *The Lathe of Heaven*, was the subject of a hearing concerning its suitability for use in a senior high-school literature class. I took a lively interest in the outcome, because I wrote the novel.

The case against the book was presented first. The man who was asking that it be withdrawn stated his objections to the following elements in the book: fuzzy thinking and poor sentence structure; a mention of homosexuality; a character who keeps a flask of brandy in her purse, and who remarks that her mother did not love her. (It seemed curious to me that he did not mention the fact that this same character is a Black woman whose lover /husband is a White man. I had the feeling that this was really what he hated in the book, and that he was afraid to say so; but that was only my feeling.)

He also took exception to what he described as the author's advocacy of non-Christian religions and/or of non-separation of Church and State (his arguments on this point, or these points, were not clear to me).

Finally, during discussion, he compared the book to junk food, apparently because it was science fiction.

The English Department of the school then presented a carefully prepared, spirited defense of the book, including statements by students who had read it. Some liked it, some didn't like it, most objected to having it, or any other book, banned.

In discussion, teachers pointed out that since it is the policy of the Washougal School District to assign an alternative book to any student who objects on any grounds to reading an assigned one, the attempt to prevent a whole class from reading a book was an attempt to change policy, replacing free choice by censorship.

When the Instructional Materials Committee of the district voted on the motion to ban the book, the motion was defeated twenty votes to five. The hearing was public and was conducted in the most open and democratic fashion. I did not speak, as I felt the teachers and students had spoken eloquently for me.

Crankish attacks on the freedom to read are common at present. When backed and coordinated by organized groups, they become sinister. In this case, I saw something going on that worried me a good deal because it did not seem to be coming from an outside pressure group, but from elements of the educational establishment itself: this was the movement to change policy radically by instituting, or "clarifying," guidelines or criteria for the selection/elimination of books used in the schools. The motion on which this committee of the school district voted was actually that the book be withdrawn *"while guidelines and policies for the district are worked out."* Those guidelines and policies were the real goal, I think, of the motion.

Guidelines? That sounds dull. Innocent. Useful. Of course we have to be sure about the kinds of books we want our kids to read in school. Don't we?

Well, do we? The dangerous vagueness of the term "guidelines and policies for the district" slides right past such questions as: Who are "we"? Who decides what the children read? Does "we" include you? Me? Teachers? Librarians? Students? Are fifteen-to-eighteen-year-olds ever "we," or are they always "they"?

And what are the guidelines to be? On what criteria or doctrines are they to be based?

The people concerned with schools in Oregon try, with ever-decreasing budgets, to provide good, sound food in the school cafeterias, knowing that for some students that's the only real meal they get.

> To know one's ignorance is the best part of knowledge.
>
> Lao-Tsze

They try, with ever-decreasing budgets, to provide beautiful, intelligent books in classes and school libraries, knowing that for many students those are the only books they read. To provide the best: everyone agrees on that (even the people who vote against school levies). But we don't and we can't agree on what books are the best. And therefore what is vital is that we provide variety, abundance, plenty—not books that reflect one body of opinion or doctrine, not books that one group or sect thinks good, but the broadest, richest range of intellectual and artistic material possible.

Nobody is forced to read any of it. There is that very important right to refuse and choose an alternative.

When a bad apple turns up, it can be taken out of the barrel on a case-by-case, book-by-book basis—investigated, defended, prosecuted, and judged, as in the hearing on my *Lathe of Heaven*. But this can't be done wholesale by using "guidelines," instructions for censorship. There is no such thing as a moral filter that lets good books through and keeps bad books out. Such criteria of "goodness" and "badness" are a moralist's dream but a democrat's nightmare.

Censorship, here or in Russia or wherever, is absolutely anti-democratic and elitist. The censor says: You don't know enough to choose, but we do, so you will read what we choose for you and nothing else. The democrat says: The process of learning is that of learning how to choose. Freedom isn't given, it's earned. Read, learn, and earn it.

I fear censorship in this Uriah Heepish[1] guise of "protecting our children," "stricter criteria," "moral guidance," "a more definite policy," and so on. I hope administrators, teachers, librarians, parents, and students will resist it. Its advocates are people willing to treat others not only as if they were not free but were not even worthy of freedom.

---

[1] *Uriah Heepish:* Behaving in the manner of Uriah Heep, a servile character in *David Copperfield* by Charles Dickens

Ursula K. Le Guin, born in California, is a prolific writer best known for her science fiction and fantasy titles for young adults. She also writes poetry, children's books, novels, and short stories. A few of her over 30 titles include: *Going Out With Peacocks and Other Poems, Catwings, Always Coming Home, Rocannon's World,* and *The Wind's Twelve Quarters.*

1. *Response*

a. "Whose Lathe?" is divided into two distinct parts. What are they and how do they work together to develop the argument?

b. What specific biases does Ursula K. Le Guin bring to her essay? How do you know? What counter-arguments might someone use in debating the issue of censorship with Le Guin?

c. Have you seen any movies or listened to any recordings that you would not share with a nine-year-old? Validate your decision.

d. Do you practise censorship on yourself, avoiding materials that you think are inappropriate? Explain your position, giving examples if possible.

2. *Media* Censorship Survey Conduct a survey on community attitudes toward censorship. You'll need to draft a questionnaire that asks specific questions about the appropriateness of censorship and the creation of guidelines. Find out which media (movies, computer games, CDs, Web sites, TV shows, and so on) people think should be subject to censorship. When your questionnaire is ready, distribute it to various grades in your school and to teachers and parents. Analyse the findings. What conclusions can you make? Report your findings to your class using PowerPoint or overheads.

3. *Literature Studies* Organizational Patterns There are several ways of organizing an essay. These organizational patterns help a writer construct a powerful argument. Here are some of the most commonly used patterns:

- *Comparison and contrast:* investigation of the similarities and differences between two or more things
- *Classification:* division of a complex topic into smaller categories
- *Cause and effect:* exploration of why something happens and what the results will be
- *Chronological order:* examination of a situation or event in the order in which it occurred
- *Definition:* explanation of a series of key terms or concepts

Select the pattern that best describes the way in which "Whose Lathe?" is organized. Explain your choice.

Alarm Bells for Civilization

By Gwynne Dyer

"This ship is going down ..."

It would have taken quite a hardy soul to see a bright side to the First World War at the time, but it may have served a useful purpose nevertheless. Like the alarm bells of a stricken ship, it still rings insistently across the decades: do something decisive right now, or this ship is going down with all hands. The ship is civilization.

It would be another two and a half decades before the first nuclear weapon was dropped on a city, another four decades before Dame Barbara Ward began talking about "spaceship earth," another six before Carl Sagan and his colleagues stumbled onto the ironically unifying concept of a "nuclear winter." But the First World War gave people their first glimpse of the abyss.

People began responding to the message right away. The war literature of the twenties and thirties was quite revolutionary in its style and its sensibility: ordinary men writing extraordinary things. Humble men like British infantryman Frank Richards would never before have had the temerity to write about their experiences; *Her Privates We*, Richards called his book about infantrymen in war. Or consider the League of Nations, that first, foredoomed attempt to bridge the abyss that the First World War revealed. Even governments realized that everything had changed.

The problem, as people in 1914 did not understand but people in 1918 were beginning to, was basically one of scale. Governments and states were still behaving in ways that had hardly changed since the eighteenth century, and (apart from the exacerbating effects of popular nationalism) the political causes and the initial strategic moves of the First World War differed little from those of the War of the Spanish Succession two centuries before. But if you quintuple the population, increase the per capita GNP tenfold, and replace single-shot muzzle-loading muskets with machine guns that fire six hundred bullets a minute, then you have changed the very nature of the game.

Conscript armies millions strong, supported by huge industrialized economies, fight very different wars from those that were waged by small armies of professional soldiers. It is not just that the butcher's bill is a lot higher; the political consequences of going to war are also different.

To be precise, the European empires went to war in 1914 believing that the conflict would serve the traditional purpose of adjusting the pecking order among the great powers. Instead, it ended up by destroying the losers utterly. Whole empires vanished, more than a dozen new countries appeared, and radical political movements like fascism and communism rose to power in great states—which was not what the initiators of the war had intended at all.

We have drunk quite deep of the horrors of the First World War over the years, so there is little point in going over them again here. Besides, the horrors suffered by the soldiers in the trenches were largely the same as those experienced by soldiers in any major nineteenth-century war (give or take a couple of novel weapons like poison gas and flamethrowers), except that they went on for much longer and affected many more people. It is the question of scale, in the war's physical and political aspects alike, that should hold our attention, as indeed it drew the attention of those who actually fought the war.

The shocking discovery that old institutions produce different and highly unwelcome results when you multiply the inputs tenfold or a hundredfold was what drove the many determined postwar attempts to change or replace those old institutions, from the creation of the League of Nations to Lenin's victory in the Soviet Union. The shock of the First World War also killed the smug confidence of the late nineteenth century that "history" knew what it was doing when it gave the Europeans such enormous power: one of the characteristics of twentieth-century European consciousness is a sense that history is in deep trouble and needs help.

But one can expand the argument quite a long way beyond that. There is nothing unique in the twentieth century's view of itself as the vital turning point of human history, of course—half the ages of humanity have believed that they lived in the final days. But the peculiar twentieth-century version of this apocalyptic vision relies on some quite tangible evidence, and the fact that people have cried wolf many times before does not disprove the existence of wolves.

I believe that our times, broadly defined—say, the nineteenth through the twenty-first centuries—really are a critical era that will make or break the experiment of human civilization. We have lived with one model of civilization for around five thousand years, but our powers over each other, over weapons, over the balance of the environment have grown so great that the transition to a different model has become a question of survival.

The model that has predominated in almost all civilized societies since early in the third millennium BCE is one in which war was actually the centrepiece. So-called "patriarchal" civilizations, typified in the ancient Middle Eastern tradition by god-kings, elaborate hierarchies, rigid class systems, slavery, armies, and the systematic depoliticization and suppression of women, were so efficient at warfare that they eliminated virtually all rival models.

There was once a variety of such rival models, and the earliest civilized societies were mostly a good deal less warlike, less autocratic, less brutal in almost every respect. Some, like those of Egypt and Crete, retained that character as late as 1500 BCE, but in the parts of the Middle East that were less isolated by geography, the patriarchal model had triumphed everywhere by the early part of the third millennium BCE. Moreover, there is strong reason to suspect that this transformation, however regrettable, may have been inevitable.

It is significant in this regard that the civilizations that grew more or less independently in east Asia and the New World appear to have undergone a similar collapse into "patriarchal" value systems and social structures at approximately similar points in their development. The fact that the same lurch into the patriarchal model occurred in so many societies, and that we have no examples of significant movement in the opposite direction until quite recently, suggests strongly that this may have been a highly functional adaptation—and I suspect that this may have been related, once again, to the question of scale.

Imagine an early urban society struggling to maintain social cohesion and political purpose through the traditional means of kinship ties and personal friendship. As it grows from a few thousand to tens and then hundreds of thousands of individuals, the old rough democracy is less and less able to cope. Just once let a militarized hierarchy gain sway over this society, and it will never lose control again, for it is simply more efficient at running things, both internally and in relations with other states.

War does not determine who is right—only who is left.

Bertrand Russell

It is more efficient, among other things, at conquering neighbours, so that soon there are no nonmilitarized states left in the region. Thenceforward, militarized kingdoms and empires predominate everywhere, and warfare is chronic. Gresham's Law applied to whole societies: bad social models drive out good.

The resulting international system flourished for five thousand years (despite a steady toll of casualties among the member states, not to mention their inhabitants) because it was functional. It answered a variety of needs, it rewarded those who collaborated and punished those who defied it, and the warfare that was its constant accompaniment did not do enough damage to threaten the survival of civilization itself.

Neither, to be frank, did the First World War. Eight million military dead (or thirteen million total fatalities, or whichever figure you favour) is an awesome toll, but it is not the end of civilization. However, it felt like the end of everything to the participants, and the perception is as important as the fact: it set the alarm bells off.

The political leaders no less than the soldiers who survived the First World War were frightened by the implications of industrialized warfare, and quite rightly so. People could not have identified the specific threat of nuclear weapons in 1919, but they were only twenty-five years away from the first nuclear test, and in a broader sense they already knew, or at least suspected, what was coming next. Thus the revolutionary conclusion that was born as a propaganda slogan in the war and has been a constant theme of public discourse ever since: that it is now necessary to end not just some particular war, but the whole institution of war.

I am not suggesting that this was an entirely original thought that occurred to people only after the assassination of Archduke Franz Ferdinand and the events that followed. The traditional moral and philosophical arguments about just and unjust wars had already developed, in the late nineteenth and early twentieth centuries, into a critique of the institution itself: Marxists flogged their simplistic nostrums, the Tsar of Russia called conferences on the subject, and early peace activists (with the suffragists prominent among them) struggled to gain the public's attention.

Moreover, one can argue with the benefit of hindsight that this was part of a considerably broader erosion of the patriarchal model. The democratic revolutions in America and France had swept away the divine right of (god-)kings even before the end of the eighteenth century, and the nineteenth century saw the abolition of slavery, the spread of democracy and even the first stirrings of the women's emancipation movement. Other aspects of the patriarchal model were coming into question, so it was only natural that the central institution of warfare would also come under attack sooner or later.

Why, after five thousand years without any serious challenge, should the patriarchal institutions have come into question in this period? If we admit the hypothesis that the rise of patriarchy, including the institution of warfare, filled a need for strong hierarchy and central direction in newly formed mass societies that had no other means of articulating themselves, then the advent of alternative, more democratic means for deciding a society's values and goals was bound to challenge patriarchy.

From the invention of printing to today's CNN, the modern mass media have begun to supply those means and thus have restored the possibility of democracy in mass societies. As a result, all the patriarchal institutions are under threat—and hardly before time, for the change in scale has made them potentially lethal.

The people who fretted about patriarchal institutions (though they didn't use that term) in the late nineteenth century did not know one tenth of it, of course. They had no idea of how destructive warfare could become, of how calamitous the environmental consequences of massive industrialization might be, even of the implications of unlimited childbearing. Yet without knowing any of the specific projections that have obsessed people in the late twentieth century, some of them knew enough to be worried anyway, and worried aloud for the benefit of everybody else.

It had virtually no effect: we are a species that responds better to crises than to predictions. Before all these well-founded fears could coalesce into an analysis of the problem and a prescription for dealing with it, there had to be some apocalyptic event to focus people's attention. The First World War was that event.

Although that war frightened millions of people into thinking seriously about the prospects for civilization itself for the first time, it solved nothing. Seventy-three years later, we are still in the midst of a struggle to alter the characteristic behaviours of civilized societies in ways that will give human civilization a better chance of survival.

It is a struggle that will probably continue long past our own lifetimes, and it is clearly not a foregone conclusion that we will win it. We have both the United Nations and nuclear weapons, the environmental movement and global warming, the rapid spread of democracy and the widening North-South economic gulf. We must continue to regard civilization as an experiment in progress.

Easter Island by Abrams/Lacagnina. Photo

Research the Easter Island civilization that created these famous stone carvings. What are the parallels between the history of Easter Island and the history related in this essay?

But it is just as well that we had the First World War when we did. At a relatively modest cost, it gave us early warning of what kinds of perils we were about to encounter and caused us to start thinking about how to survive them a few decades earlier than we might otherwise have done. For all we know, that could be the margin between success and failure.

That is one of the speculations that can never be proved. But if you doubt that the margin is narrow, consider a twentieth century in which the old empires and the old complacency continued into the 1940s or 1950s, and acquired all the technology that accrued in the meantime, before they stumbled into their first fully industrialized war. We would probably be in a lot deeper trouble than we are—if, indeed, we were here at all.

Gwynne Dyer was born in 1945 in Newfoundland and Labrador. He is a journalist and historian now based in London, England, and writes a twice-weekly column that appears in over 150 newspapers in over 30 countries. He has worked in film and on radio, including the seven-part TV documentary series *War* in 1983. One episode of *War* was nominated for an Academy Award.

I. *Response*
   a. In point form, summarize what you know about World War I. To help fill in the gaps in your knowledge, compare your summary with those of several classmates.
   b. Gwynne Dyer says World War I "gave people their first glimpse of the abyss." In your own words, what is this abyss?
   c. After you first read "Alarm Bells for Civilization," how well did you feel you understood it? What aspects of the essay were the most challenging for you as a reader?

2. *Writing* Précis Condense this essay into a **précis** of 150–200 words. Begin your précis with a brief statement of Dyer's thesis. Your précis should provide the most important evidence that Dyer presents to support his main argument. Why do you think creating a précis might be a useful skill?

A **précis** is a concise summary of a text. It is written in full sentences, but contains only the most important information.

3. **Literature Studies** *Essay Structure* Many formal essays follow a traditional structure:

An *introduction* (usually the first paragraph) clearly states the thesis or controlling idea, engages reader interest, and previews organization or content.

The *body* (at least three paragraphs following the introduction) develops arguments and ideas to support the thesis, provides supporting evidence, mentions counter-arguments and disproves them.

The *conclusion* (usually the last paragraph of the essay) provides a logical follow-up to the thesis and arguments offered in the essay, summarizes key points, and includes an insightful conclusion related to the thesis.

Examine "Alarm Bells for Civilization," and identify each of the above components. Does this selection follow the above structure exactly? Would you consider it an example of a traditional essay? Explain.

4. **Language Conventions** *Sentence Structure* Skim "Alarm Bells for Civilization" to find two sentences that are three or more lines long. For each sentence, identify what punctuation is used and explain the function of each punctuation mark. Rewrite each sample sentence as two or more shorter sentences. Would you recommend that Dyer edit his essay to decrease the complexity of his sentences? Explain.

5. **Research and Inquiry** Using the Internet and other reference resources, research and prepare a brief written report on one of the following: Dame Barbara Ward, Carl Sagan, Frank Richards, the League of Nations, Archduke Franz Ferdinand, or the GNP.

**Reading makes a person complete.
Would you agree?**

Of Studies

By Sir Francis Bacon

Studies serve for delight, for ornament, and for ability. Their chief use for delight is in privateness and retiring; for ornament, is in discourse; and for ability, is in the judgment and disposition of business. For expert men can execute, and perhaps judge of particulars, one by one; but the general counsels, and the plots and marshalling of affairs come best from those that are learned. To spend too much time in studies is sloth; to use them too much for ornament is affectation; to make judgment wholly by their rules is the humor of a scholar. They perfect nature, and are perfected by experience: for natural abilities are like natural plants, that need pruning by study; and studies themselves do give forth directions too much at large, except they be bounded in by experience. Crafty[1] men contemn studies, simple men admire them, and wise men use them; for they teach not their own use; but that is a wisdom without them and above them, won by observation. Read not to contradict and confute, nor to believe and take for granted, nor to find talk and discourse, but to weigh and consider. Some books are to be tasted, others to be swallowed, and some few to be chewed and digested; that is, some books are to be read only in parts; others to be read, but not curiously;[2] and some few to be read wholly, and with diligence and attention. Some books also may be read by deputy, and extracts made of them by others; but that would[3] be only in the less important arguments and the meaner sort of books; else distilled books are, like common distilled waters, flashy[4] things. Reading maketh a full man; conference a ready man; and writing an exact man. And, therefore, if a man write little, he had need have a great memory;

The above image is the title page from *Instauratio Magna* by Bacon. The viewer sees a ship heading toward two pillars —the pillars of Hercules. These pillars represented the limits of human exploration for the ancients—and so Bacon uses this image of exploration by sea to symbolize human exploration into learning—learning that will surpass what the ancients taught. The Latin phrase at the bottom of the image means "Many will pass through and knowledge will be increased."

if he confer little, he had need have a present wit; and if he read little, he had need have much cunning, to seem to know that he doth not. Histories make men wise; poets, witty; the mathematics, subtle; natural philosophy, deep; moral, grave; logic and rhetoric, able to contend. *Abeunt studia in mores.*[5] Nay, there is no stond or impediment in the wit but may be wrought out by fit studies, like as diseases of the body may have appropriate exercises. Bowling is good for the stone[6] and reins, shooting for the lungs and breast, gentle walking for the stomach, riding for the head, and the like. So if a man's wit be wandering, let him study the mathematics; for in demonstrations, if his wit be called away never so little, he must begin again. If his wit be not apt to distinguish or find differences, let him study the schoolmen; for they are *Cymini sectores.*[7] If he be not apt to beat over matters, and to call up one thing to prove and illustrate another, let him study the lawyer's cases. So every defect of the mind may have a special receipt.

Notes

1. By *crafty* Bacon presumably means *sly*.
2. carefully
3. should
4. flat, or showy
5. Studies pass into (that is, form) manners.
6. Of the bladder or reins (kidneys)
7. Dividers of cuminseed; that is, hairsplitters. See St. Matthew 23:23.

Sir Francis Bacon (1551–1626) studied law and entered the House of Commons at the age of 23. In 1597 he published *Essays*, the first essays to be written in English. (The French writer Montaigne had originated the form in 1580.) Bacon is therefore often called the "father" of the English essay. Each of his essays was a concise exploration of a single topic, such as travel, truth, or friendship. Though the essay form has changed greatly since Bacon's time, his works are still admired for their brevity and cleverness, and as examples of Elizabethan values.

1. *Response*

a. Francis Bacon makes many claims in "Of Studies." Choose one of those claims and express it in your own words.
b. What "defect" of your own mind could you improve through study? Identify one specific book or other resource that would help you to increase your knowledge in that area.
c. "Some books are to be tasted, others to be swallowed, and some few to be chewed and digested ..." Make a personal list of books that fit each of the conditions described by Bacon in the preceding quotation.

2. *Language Conventions* Parallelism   Identify the **parallelism** in the opening two sentences in "Of Studies." Find other examples of parallelism in the essay, and suggest at least two reasons why parallelism is a useful writing technique.

Parallelism is the intentional use of identical or similar grammatical structure within one sentence or in two or more sentences.

3. *Writing* Persuasive Essay   Write a persuasive essay in which you consider three main functions or purposes of an activity you know about from personal experience. Sample titles are:

- Of Sport
- Of Extracurricular Activities
- Of Part-time Jobs

In your essay, be sure to express a clear point of view about your topic.

Is Lightman the "last holdout against the onslaught of unbridled technology," or just afraid of e-mail?

Progress

By Alan Lightman

Over the past several years, friends and colleagues have become increasingly irritated with me for not being on the electronic network. Scientists want to send me their data on E-mail. Secretaries for distant committees, forced to resort to the telephone, hound me for my E-mail address and lapse into stunned silence when I allow that I don't have one. University administrators, who organize meetings and send messages across campus at the push of a button, grumble about hand-carrying information to me or, even worse, putting paper in an envelope and sending it through the interdepartmental-mail system. I admit I'm a nuisance. But I resist getting on the Internet as a matter of principle, as a last holdout against the onslaught of unbridled technology galloping almost blindly into the twenty-first century.

For at least the past two hundred years, human society has operated under the assumption that all developments in science and technology constitute progress. According to that view, if a new metal alloy can increase the transmission of data from 10 million bits per second to 20 million, we should create it. If a new plastic has twice the strength-to-weight ratio as the older variety, we should produce it. If a new automobile can accelerate at twice the rate of the current model, we should build it. Whatever is technologically possible will find an application and improve us....

Today, at the end of the twentieth century, a crucial question before us is whether developments in technology inevitably improve the quality of life. And if not, we must ask how our society can employ some selectivity and restraint, given the enormous capitalistic forces at work. That is a terribly difficult problem for several reasons, not the least of which is the subjective nature of progress and quality of life. Is progress greater human happiness? Greater comfort? Greater speed in personal transportation and communication? The reduction of human suffering? Longer life span? Even with a definition of progress, its measurements and technological requirements are not straightforward. If progress is human happiness, has anyone shown that twentieth-century people are happier than nineteenth-century people? If progress is comfort, how do we weigh the short-term comfort of air-conditioning against the long-term comfort of a pollution-free environment? If progress is longer life span, can we ever discontinue life support for a dying patient in pain?

Only a fool would claim that new technology rarely improves the quality of life. The electric light has expanded innumerable human activities, from reading to nighttime athletic events. Advances in medicine—particularly the germ theory of disease, public-health programs, and the development of good antiseptics—have obviously reduced physical suffering and substantially extended the healthy human life span.

But one can also argue that advances in technology do not always improve life. I will skip over such obvious environmental problems as global warming, ozone depletion, and nuclear-waste disposal, and consider something more subtle: high-speed communications. We are already seeing people at restaurants talking into cellular phones as they dine. Others take modems on vacations, so they can stay in touch with their offices at all times. Or consider E-mail, the example I began with. E-mail has undeniable benefits. It is faster than regular mail and cheaper and less obtrusive than the telephone. It can promote conversations among far-flung communities of people, and it can encourage otherwise reticent talkers to speak up, via computer terminals. But E-mail, in my view, also contributes to the haste, the thoughtlessness, and the artificial urgency that increasingly characterize our world. The daily volume of E-mail communications is inflating without limit. A lawyer friend says he spends 50 percent of his time at work sifting through unimportant E-mail messages to arrive at the few that count. Some communications are invariably of the form "Please ignore my last message." Evidently, it has become so easy and fast to communicate that we often do so without reflection. When messages come in so quickly and effortlessly, we irresistibly and immediately respond in kind. Although I cannot document it, I suspect that bad decisions are being made because of the haste of transmitting and responding to E-mail messages.

> Progress lies not in enhancing what is, but in advancing toward what will be.
>
> Kahlil Gibran

But more to the point is the overall fast-food mentality at work in the rapid conveyance of our thoughts and responses. We are suffocating ourselves. We are undercutting our contemplative powers. We could even be, ironically, impeding progress.

E-mail, of course, is only one example. Its use or abuse is up to the individual. But E-mail is representative of other technological developments, such as genetic engineering, throw-away plastics, advanced life-support systems, and computer networks. Certainly, many of those developments will have good consequences. But that is not the point. Modern technology is racing forward with little examination or control. To be sure, a number of thinkers and writers have for some time expressed alarm over where unchecked science and technology might be taking us. Mary Shelley, in *Frankenstein* (1818), was certainly concerned about the ethical dilemmas of artificial life. So was H. G. Wells in *The Island of Dr. Moreau* (1896), wherein the evil surgeon, Dr. Moreau, synthesizes creatures that are half man and half beast. In *Walden* (1854), Thoreau wrote, "We do not ride on the railroad; it rides upon us." A more recent example is Don DeLillo's *White Noise* (1985), in which the hero is exposed to a cloud of poisonous industrial chemicals, and then suffers a far worse mental ailment because of a computerized medical system that constantly announces his fate. But those countervailing voices have, for the most part, been ignored. That is not just because of the considerable economic forces that are propelling today's ravenous technological engine. Rather, we seem to believe—perhaps at some subconscious level—that technology is our sacred future.

I am not in favor of squashing new developments in pure science, in any form. The act of understanding the workings of nature—and our place in it—expresses for me what is most noble and good in us. As for the applications of science, I am certainly not opposed to technology as a whole; I benefit greatly from it. But we cannot have advances in technology without an accompanying consideration of human values and quality of life.

How should this examination and questioning proceed? I don't know. It is not likely that government regulations would be effective. Our government, as well as other large institutions, understandably has an investment in allowing technology to develop unabated. The problem cannot be solved from the top down. It is a cultural problem. Perhaps we must regulate ourselves. Perhaps we each must think about what is truly important in our lives and decide which technologies to accept and which to resist. That is a personal responsibility. In the long run, we need to change our thinking, to realize that we are not only a society of production and technology but also a society of human beings.

Alan Lightman was born in Memphis, Tennessee, in 1948. He has worked in astrophysics at Cornell, as assistant professor of astronomy at Harvard, and as a research scientist at the Harvard-Smithsonian Center for Astrophysics. Lightman has published poems, essays, reviews, and short fiction, and his books have been translated into 30 languages.

I. *Response*
    a. Write a paragraph explaining what the word *progress* means to you. Did Alan Lightman's essay affect your view of progress? Explain.
    b. Read the author biography for Lightman (above) and, if possible, do some additional research to learn more about him. In your view, do his qualifications make him a credible spokesperson on the topic of technological progress? Draw on your experience as a reader to draft five guidelines that you can use to establish a writer's credibility.
    c. Prepare a brief rebuttal to one of the arguments Lightman offers in support of his thesis. Use a concrete fact or personal experience to make your rebuttal more convincing.

2. *Oral Language* *Speech* Lightman encourages each person to "decide which technologies to accept and which to resist." Prepare a short speech that argues in favour of either accepting or resisting one specific technology.

3. *Literature Studies* *Rhetorical Questions* In the third paragraph of his essay, Lightman asks a series of eight rhetorical questions. Given that he doesn't answer the questions directly, why do you think he includes them? How do they affect the reader? Would you call the question in the final paragraph a rhetorical question? Explain.

4. *Making Connections* Create a chart that contrasts Lightman's position in "Progress" with Heather Proud's position in "Dis?Ability on the Internet." Are Lightman and Proud equally credible in your view? Would you say that the two essays are in direct opposition? Explain.

The
T*ime* Factor

By Gloria Steinem

Are you the type of person who already has your whole life mapped out? In this essay, Gloria Steinem argues that forward planning is a function of class and gender.

PLANNING AHEAD IS A MEASURE OF CLASS. The rich and even the middle class plan for future generations, but the poor can plan ahead only a few weeks or days.

I remember finding this calm insight in some sociological text and feeling instant recognition. Yes, of course, our sense of time was partly a function of power, or the lack of it. It rang true even in the entirely economic sense the writer had in mind. "The guys who own the factories hand them down to their sons and great-grand-sons," I remember a boy in my high school saying bitterly. "On this side of town, we just plan for Saturday night."

But it also seemed equally true of most of the women I knew—including myself—regardless of the class we supposedly belonged to. Though I had left my factory-working neighbour-hood, gone to college, become a journalist, and thus was middle class, I still felt that I couldn't plan ahead. I had to be flexible—first, so that I could be ready to get on a plane for any writing assignment (even though the male writers I knew launched into books and other long-term projects on their own), and then so that I could adapt to the career and priorities of an eventual husband and children (even though I was leading a rewarding life without either). Among the results of this uncertainty were a stunning lack of career planning and such smaller penalties as no savings, no insurance, and an apartment that lacked basic pieces of furniture.

Allées Piétonnières by Jean-Pierre Stora

Examine and discuss this image. What kinds of lives do you
think the people in this imaginary landscape must lead? Identify
the specific visual elements that create this impression. What
message does this image send?

On the other hand, I had friends who were married to men whose long-term career plans were compatible with their own, yet they still lived their lives in day-to-day response to any possible needs of their husbands and children. Moreover, the one male colleague who shared or even understood this sense of powerlessness was a successful black journalist and literary critic who admitted that even after twenty years he planned only one assignment at a time. He couldn't forget his dependence on the approval of white editors.

Clearly there is more to this fear of the future than a conventional definition of class could explain. There is also caste: the unchangeable marks of sex and race that bring a whole constellation of cultural injunctions against power, even the limited power of controlling one's own life.

We haven't yet examined time-sense and future planning as functions of discrimination, but we have begun to struggle with them, consciously or not. As a movement, women have become painfully conscious of too much reaction and living from one emergency to the next, with too little initiative and planned action of our own; hence many of our losses to a much smaller but more entrenched and consistent right wing.

Though the cultural habit of living in the present and glazing over the future goes deep, we've begun to challenge the cultural punishment awaiting the "pushy" and "selfish" women (and the "uppity" minority men) who try to break through it and control their own lives.

Even so, feminist writers and theorists tend to avoid the future by lavishing all our analytical abilities on what's wrong with the present, or on revisions of history and critiques of the influential male thinkers of the past. The big, original, and certainly courageous books of this wave of feminism have been more diagnostic than prescriptive.

> Thinking gets you nowhere. It may be a fine
> and noble aid in academic studies, but you can't
> think your way out of emotional difficulties.
> That takes something altogether different.
> You have to make yourself passive then,
> and just listen. Re-establish contact
> with a slice of eternity.
>
> Etty Hillesum

We need pragmatic planners and visionary futurists, but can we think of even one feminist five-year-plan? Perhaps the closest we have come is visionary architecture or feminist science fiction, but they generally avoid the practical steps of how to get from here to there.

Obviously, many of us need to extend our time-sense—to have the courage to plan for the future, even while most of us are struggling to keep our heads above water in the present. But this does not mean a flat-out imitation of the culturally masculine habit of planning ahead, living in the future, and thus living a deferred life. It doesn't mean the traditional sacrifice of spontaneous action, or a sensitive awareness of the present, that comes from long years of career education with little intrusion of reality, from corporate pressure to work now for the sake of a reward after retirement, or, least logical of all, from patriarchal religions that expect obedience now in return for a reward after death.

In fact, the ability to live in the present, to tolerate uncertainty, and to remain open, spontaneous, and flexible are all culturally female qualities that many men need and have been denied. As usual, both halves of the polarized masculine-feminine division need to learn from each other's experiences. If men spent more time raising small children, for instance, they would be forced to develop more patience and flexibility. If women had more power in the planning of natural resources and other long-term processes—or even in the planning of our own careers and reproductive lives—we would have to develop more sense of the future and of cause and effect.

An obsession with reacting to the present, feminine-style, or on controlling and living in the future, masculine-style, are both wasteful of time.

And time is all there is.

Gloria Steinem is best known for her work as a feminist–activist. In 1968, she co-founded *New York* magazine, and in 1971, co-founded *Ms. Magazine*. She wrote the bestsellers *Outrageous Acts and Everyday Rebellions* and *Revolution From Within: A Book of Self-Esteem*.

1. Response

a. Identify five key terms in "The Time Factor" (for example, *class, caste*) and write brief definitions of them in your own words.

b. Gloria Steinem argues that females and males have different ways of viewing both time and life. Create a t-chart that shows those different ways. Do you agree with Steinem's analysis? Why or why not?

c. "The Time Factor" was taken from a *Ms. Magazine* from 1980. In your opinion, is the essay still relevant today? Explain.

2. Language Conventions *Transition Words* Steinem uses a variety of **transition words** to help the reader follow her argument. Identify words that you would classify as transition words. Where do they usually occur, and why might this be so? Select a piece of your own writing and either highlight the transition words you used, or insert transition words appropriately.

Transition words indicate relationships between ideas. Writers use them to suggest links between sentences or paragraphs.

3. Literature Studies *Fact Versus Opinion* It's important for a reader to distinguish between fact and opinion when reading persuasive writing. A *fact* is a statement that can be proved correct. An *opinion* is a statement that expresses a belief that is open to question. Though all opinions can be debated, some opinions are easier to defend than others. Analyse the evidence Steinem presents, classifying individual statements either as fact or opinion. Present your findings. Based on your analysis, would you say Steinem's essay is convincing? Explain.

4. Critical Thinking Make a personal five-year plan. It should present goals related to education, employment, living arrangements, relationships, personal growth, and so on. Outline some plans for achieving these goals, as well. Compare your plan with someone else's and discuss the similarities and differences. Explain whether you feel that creating the plan was useful to you.

Joy

By Molly Peacock

Filling Station
By Elizabeth Bishop

Oh, but it is dirty!
—this little filling station,
oil-soaked, oil-permeated
to a disturbing, over-all
black translucency.
Be careful with that match!

Father wears a dirty,
oil-soaked monkey suit
that cuts him under the arms,
and several quick and saucy
and greasy sons assist him
(it's a family filling station),
all quite thoroughly dirty.

Do they live in the station?
It has a cement porch
behind the pumps, and on it
a set of crushed and grease-
impregnated wickerwork;
on the wicker sofa
a dirty dog, quite comfy.

Some comic books provide
the only note of color—
of certain color. They lie
upon a big dim doily
draping a taboret
(part of the set), beside
a big hirsute begonia.

Why the extraneous plant?
Why the taboret?
Why, oh why, the doily?
(Embroidered in daisy stitch
with marguerites, I think,
and heavy with gray crochet.)

Somebody embroidered the doily.
Somebody waters the plant,
or oils it, maybe. Somebody
arranges the rows of cans
so that they softly say:
ESSO—SO—SO—SO
to high-strung automobiles.
Somebody loves us all.

When you can't make sense of the world in any other way, merely to describe what you see before you leads to understanding. That is the lesson of the watching way of life, whether you are a detective tailing a suspect, or a bird-watcher, or a child. The clue to the life understood is observation. When Elizabeth Bishop was eight months old, her father died. Her mother's mental breakdowns and eventual institutionalization meant that by the age of five the young Elizabeth was shuttling back and forth between one set of grandparents in New England and the other in Nova Scotia, the beginning of a life in perpetual transit. For this poet, life was a tangle of travel due to mysterious circumstances; she developed a poetic art out of getting her bearings. After all, when you are at a complete loss as to how you came to be where you are, to describe what is before you is the beginning of restoration. This the lesson of fictional sleuths like Miss Jane Marple and Nero Wolfe, of naturalists like John James Audubon and Roger Tory Peterson: to describe, describe, describe the world, recording scrupulously, and thus also to watch a theory emerge. Description becomes knowledge. Details inform you of the shape of the world. Shape means perspective. If you are in a state of disorientation, you will gain a point of view. A point of view makes a sense of humor possible. And humor not only saves us from confusion, it paradoxically gives us the camera eye we need for sharp description. Not only is Elizabeth Bishop a noticing type of poet, she is funny. Capable of being amused, she amuses us, and it is a joy to read her. Joy is the inadvertent apotheosis of observation. The unexpected result of training your eye on detail is that the world becomes beautiful simply *because* it is noticed, and therefore appreciated. To have a sense of humor in an approving world—there is no fuller definition of enjoying where you are. And here we are with Bishop at a "Filling Station."

> *Oh, but it is dirty!*
> *—this little filling station,*
> *oil-soaked, oil-permeated*
> *to a disturbing, over-all*
> *black translucency.*
> *Be careful with that match!*

Oh, but it is dirty! she exclaims in the present tense. It seems we will be perennially in the filling station, getting gas, liquid nourishment to drive us forward—as vehicles for existence. The present tense, not the future tense, is the tense of forever because it pulses a current of "now" into all activity. *Be careful with that match!* she warns us. Bishop assumes her readers are her traveling companions, and by the end of the first stanza we share the intimacy of fellow travelers, passing through the world as witnesses. (Everything is interesting to observers; they are never bored.) Here we find ourselves at a place that is *oil-soaked, oil-permeated/to a disturbing, over-all/black translucency.*

Bishop revises what she says as she deepens what she sees. At first the station is *oil-soaked,* but then, as she notices more, it's *oil-permeated.* The oil is so embedded it changes the surfaces of things *to a disturbing, over-all/black translucency.* Each stage is ever more carefully scrutinized —and not neutrally. We are Bishop's chosen companions, after all; she claims us as her familiars—the sort of people who would find the oiliness *disturbing*—then pokes us in the ribs with her joke about the match. This is a place to escape from immediately!

Yet observers never escape; they see things through, instead. (That's the watching way.)

> *Father wears a dirty,*
> *oil-soaked monkey suit*
> *that cuts him under the arms,*
> *and several quick and saucy*
> *and greasy sons assist him*
> *(it's a family filling station),*
> *all quite thoroughly dirty.*

Within two stanzas, she's told us that the place and its inhabitants are *dirty* three times. Why, when the world is so exquisitely detailed, does she insist on that same word over and over again? Reusing the *dirty* word makes us feel that nothing seems to be happening. And so we learn the necessary patience of the watcher. When you are tailing a subject, the subject's world takes a lot of establishing. We have to trust, as Bishop does, that the closer the look, the greater the distance you possess—and the greater possibility for humor. When she says *Father* in her generic way, referring to the owner, we are in her confidence, sharing her point of view, and yet it is a point of view we would never have except for her. She's the one who catches the way his over-all *cuts him under the arms,* and how the black gold keeps embedding itself, now in the *oil-soaked monkey suit.* There's that exact phrase, *oil-soaked,* again. With all her discriminating powers, why use it again? Because the return to the phrase, as to the word *dirty,* is a return to the key note. Bishop's recapitulation refocuses attention. The describer's eye returns to *clues,* Jane Marple's technique of understanding what happened.

The standard wisdom of the literary detective says that varied vocabulary is the key to sharp notation; a true scrutinizer rarely repeats. Yet Bishop's repetition is keen because it is reorienting—the way bird-watchers sweep the binoculars to the same tree in order to make sure of their bearings. Once gotten, descriptive precision is necessary again, and that's where Bishop's satisfyingly individual adjectives appear. The man's sons are *several quick and saucy/and greasy*. Those adjectives could be the names for the sons: Several, Quick, Saucy, and Greasy. Jaunty and cartoonish, they stand as if she had outlined them in Magic Marker. After she pokes our ribs *(it's a family filling station)*, she purses her lips as her grandmother might have done and spurns the joint: *all quite thoroughly dirty*. Not only does the refocusing on *dirty* reemphasize how grimy the place is, it deepens the judgment of those adverbs *quite thoroughly*. My own grandmother would have pursed her lips in the same way—and at a similar sight. The inescapability of the dirt teases out a question: *Do they live in the station?*

Yes, of course they do, I thought immediately when I first read this poem. My grandfather Gilbert Wright built one of the first gas stations in his part of upstate New York, a jerry-built structure, somewhere between house, store, and garage—and it was all three, presided over by our blind guard dog, Pal. The garage was a mishmash marvel of boxes of Model A parts stacked beneath a farmer's daughter calendar. The store wafted a heaven of smells: the dry sneeze-inducing flour, sugar, and laundry soap, the syrupy smell of root beer, Coca-Cola, and toffee, the rubbery whiff of windshield-wiper blades, and the smooth, crude smell of engine oil over all. The house behind, my grandmother's realm, smelled of molasses cookies and the starch of the embroidered doilies on the upright piano and the davenport. My grandmother Ruth battled the grease and dirt of La Grange Garage till her dying day; she would have hated Bishop's filling station.

> *It has a cement porch*
> *behind the pumps, and on it*
> *a set of crushed and grease-*
> *impregnated wickerwork;*
> *on the wicker sofa*
> *a dirty dog, quite comfy.*

Even though I suffered at first from Bishop's put-down of the station and the men in it, I soared at the idea that she wrote the poem at all. That a comfy dog, just like Pal, could be the subject of a poem made me recognize the value of this hearty dirtiness. La Grange Garage was an Esso station.

The ambivalence I feel reading this poem comes from the special conjunction of the facts that my grandparents shared the same values as Bishop but were in the very circumstances she describes. At first I felt ashamed to have La Grange Garage belittled, and elated that she also knew about those spots where filthy happiness prevails. Bishop herself must have experienced terrible shame at her own background. Having to tell people that your mother was in a mental hospital couldn't have been easy in 1916—it's difficult to pop into conversation today. Bishop's biographer, Brett Millier, tells us in *Elizabeth Bishop: Life and the Memory of It* that the poet saw her mother only a few times after the mother's breakdown and institutionalization. The story of her mother may have felt to Bishop like a secret too dirty to wash away. Yet as the oil-hyphenated words become doused with grease in the second stanza, and the wicker in the third becomes *grease-impregnated*, we begin to know that this place is so dirty it will never be clean; and this becomes the peculiar source of its happiness.

Often when an ebullient and self-possessed entity saunters into Bishop's poems, it seems to be in the shape of an animal. Toward the end of her life Bishop would write a poem called "Pink Dog," and in that poem would describe a mongrel mother dog at carnival time, out among the revelers. (Bishop lived for many years in Brazil.) When the speaker asks the dog where her babies are, the shadow of Bishop's mother seems to fly through the poem. The hairless pink dog, like a batty bag lady, conveys maternal presence, out among the crazies at carnival. The filling station seems also like a kind of benign nuthouse, where the *dirty dog is quite comfy*, right at home. The filling station itself is like a greasy Mardi Gras where everything is upside-down and saucy people can do exactly what they want, the whole scene held perennially in a comic moment.

> *Some comic books provide*
> *the only note of color—*
> *of certain color. They lie*
> *upon a big dim doily*
> *draping a taboret*
> *(part of the set), beside*
> *a big hirsute begonia.*

Part of the watching way of life is watching *again*. Bishop notes, then *renotes* what she studies. *Some comic books provide/the only note of color,* she begins, then qualifies—*of certain color.* The poet models changing her mind, deepening her description, like a bird-watcher, wincing through her binoculars, narrating what she sees at first, second, third, and fourth glances. These lookings entail revisions, modifications, and corrections as the focus sharpens. She sweeps us into the process of observation; we are with her as she checks, then checks again. To us, her readers and intimates, Bishop displays a kind of imperfection because, quite transparently, she lets us see her re-visioning, re-noticing, getting it right.

Bishop doesn't produce a perfect surface of exact word in precise place; she works at correcting, if not mistakes, then the wrongness of immediate impressions. It's not that the comic books are the *only* color, it's that the place is so greasy you can't exactly tell what colors things *really* are. The comic books are placed, as the dog is in its chair, on *a big dim doily*, entirely out of place in this masculine world. It *drap[es] a taboret*. There, on an end table (an end table!) on the porch (a porch?) of a gas station is a doily (!) on which squats a huge, hairy houseplant— *a big hirsute begonia*. That hairy begonia is as fuzzy as Father and his sons. *Hirsute* is my favorite moment in the poem, because the use of this word next to *big*, *dirty*, and *pumps* is just like the appearance of the doily in the gas station to begin with. It is entirely unlikely, as bizarre as the noun *taboret* in this *oil-soaked* place. Now the subject of the poem reveals itself: unlikeliness. Isn't the world made up of peculiarly unlikely things—and isn't this what we have to explain to ourselves? Think of the orphaned Elizabeth explaining to herself why she lives with her grandparents, why others have parents who make a home, but she doesn't.

Unlikelihood always leads to the child's question, Why? And a series of why's composes the next three lines:

> *Why the extraneous plant?*
> *Why the taboret?*
> *Why, oh why, the doily?*
> *(Embroidered in daisy stitch*
> *with marguerites, I think,*
> *and heavy with gray crochet.)*

Each *Why* makes the incongruities all the more obvious, the vocabulary increasingly heightened and intellectualized. The plant is extraneous—a word people use for correcting compositions, not for describing filling stations. And this stanza rhymes *taboret* with *crochet* at the end. The utterly female order (I think of my own grandmother's variegated embroidery floss) against the male dishevelment (and my grandfather's grease-stained coverall and cap) is even a further disjuncture. Why are the yin of the world and its yang the way they are? The demands for understanding pile up and up, even as the descriptive words flood the stanza. Parentheses reappear. And inside them Bishop meditates on the type of embroidery—*daisy stitch/with marguerites, I think*—and the type of edging, *gray crochet.* The dirty and the clean mix up to form the unlikely world.

In forty-one lines, Bishop manages to use every type of punctuation we traditionally have. Punctuation lies entirely in the realm of the system of the sentence. It is what modulates the storyteller's voice; it is what unravels the sentence to our ears and reveals its rhythms. In the first line, she uses the most and the least frequently occurring types of punctuation, a comma and an exclamation point. With breezy confidence, she dares to open the poem with an exclamation, as if she were jotting down a postcard to us. Writing is a lonely art, and no one is lonelier than a writing orphan—or more befriended by an audience. Perhaps we, her future readers, are her imaginary friends.

Immediately after that daring exclamation, Bishop throws on another mark of punctuation before she utters another word—the dash. Letters and postcards, those vehicles of intimacy, are littered with them. Dashes mark a special kind of aside (different from the parentheses she will use three times later in the poem), and she poises a dash like a magnifying glass in the fourth stanza. In both cases, the dash ensures a closer look at the world. Though dashes in a sentence modify perception, they don't alter tone of voice. What lies on the other side of a dash is equally important—even though it is separate from the rest of the syntax. The dash is like the line between yin and yang in the familiar symbol: ☯ . The sentence, like a river, flows around the island contained within dashes.

On the other hand, parentheses are much more like a stage whisper, where an actor turns to address us, her audience, in confidence. Inside parentheses Bishop makes her jokes—*(part of the set)*, she says, raising an eyebrow. Parentheses are like two raised eyebrows set side by side to contain in print the very comment that the eyebrows would accompany in speech.

Many poets argue that the line stopping gives enough of a pause without adding a comma, but Bishop punctuates her poems exactly like prose. The tale she tells—like a dinner table anecdote—requires attention fine-tuned to the sentence. And so she brings the commas to show how likenesses and disparities hinge and attach, or separate and reattach. Semicolons are her great equalizers. Detaching the link of "and," they maintain the equal importance of the information on both their sides. The semicolon is like the balancer in the middle of a see-saw. Commas distribute weight, making the seesaw go up and down, allowing the balance to swing back and forth, readjusting always. But semicolons come to a balance point.

In the final stanza, Bishop uses a colon. A mystery is often solved by the words placed after a colon. The colon implies an opening out, a realization. It is used where information leads to understanding, where the clues all add up. And that is exactly what happens in Bishop's last stanza:

> *Somebody embroidered the doily.*
> *Somebody waters the plant,*
> *or oils it, maybe. Somebody*
> *arranges the rows of cans*
> *so that they softly say:*
> *ESSO—SO—SO—SO*
> *to high-strung automobiles.*
> *Somebody loves us all.*

When *the rows of cans/ … softly say:/ESSO—SO—SO—SO/to high-strung automobiles*, a newly resolved voice enters the poem. The whispery ss's of the cans, as carefully arranged as lines on a page, are artfully revealed as the answer to the way one goes about living a life—in search of what we will find on the other side of a conjunction, *so*, which means therefore and also is the first syllable of *Somebody* with a capital S. Here is the joining, after which materializes … the name of God, the comforter. After Bishop's three *so's* the Somebody who acts like God enters the poem. God is an arranger, like an artist, and positions the world. Somebody is the prime mover of a domestic life, the godly person who *waters the plant* and *arranges the rows of cans* and, finally, is the one who *loves us all*.

A comforting hand seems to be on Bishop's forehead, perhaps uttering the words *don't be afraid*. Bishop's hands, in turn, are on either side of her reader's head, turning it, directing our gaze. The reward of description—the tactic of noticing details when nothing in the world makes sense—is lucidity. As intelligibility comes from specifics, so does humor. Humor never exists *in general*. It is present only *in details*. And Bishop's saving humor is also godly. It emanates from an oil can that mutters *so* what? There's a *Somebody*, like a huge grandmother in the sky, who's looking out for us. And make no mistake, it's our own inner motors that make us high-strung automobiles.

So, whatever is bothering you doesn't matter. Whatever it is, is OK.

Kick down your motor. Somebody loves us all. Bishop's gesture is so complete it traces a kind of circle, like the letter of the alphabet in the middle of jOy.

Molly Peacock is the author of four books of poems— including *Original Love* and *Take Heart*—as well as a memoir— *Paradise, Piece by Piece*. Peacock is a contributing writer and poet to journals such as *The New Yorker* and *The Paris Review*. She works closely with new poets.

1. *Response*
a. Why is "Joy" an appropriate title for Molly Peacock's essay? What different things should a good title do? Give an example of titles (of essays, stories, poems, movies, CDs, et cetera) that you think are especially effective, explaining why.
b. Does "Joy" have a formal or informal style? Use quotations from the essay to support your opinion.
c. When you study a poem, what steps do you take to understand it? Reflect on the different methods you use and describe each one.
d. Did Peacock's essay help you to understand "Filling Station"? Why or why not?

2. *Literature Studies* *Literary Essay* A **literary essay** usually considers both *content* (what the work says: its message and meaning) and *form* (how that meaning is expressed). Reread "Joy" and summarize the main points Peacock makes about the poem's content and the main points she makes about its form.

A **literary essay** presents an interpretation or explores some aspect of one or more works of literature.

3. *Language Conventions* *Punctuation* Review Peacock's discussion of Bishop's use of punctuation. ("In forty-one lines, Bishop manages to use every type of punctuation we traditionally have …") Did this discussion help you to appreciate punctuation in a new way? Do you think that this is an effective section of the essay? Explain.

In this essay, Kristal Fung, a student, explains why a favourite piece of literature should be included in a high school anthology.

In Support of Nick Bantock's "Life Class"

By Kristal Fung

"Life Class," an excerpt from *The Artful Dodger: Images and Reflections*, by Nick Bantock, is laced with humorous first-person anecdotes. Bantock, who moved to Vancouver with his wife and young son in 1988, began to work on his own books ten years ago. As his skills as a writer developed, he unexpectedly found himself being swept along by the *Griffin & Sabine* phenomenon. Since then he has continued to expand and develop a genre of narrative books that integrate both text and images.

I found this excerpt, entitled "Life Class," to be both refreshing and amusing. In fact, this excerpt reminded me a little of the short story "A & P" in that it explores the workings of a young teenaged boy's mind when it comes to the opposite sex or, in this case, "a beautiful woman in her early twenties." Although this excerpt holds "less" literary merit when compared to works by Shakespeare or Margaret Atwood (such a highly acclaimed and honoured Canadian author), I found Bantock's take on his own life to be surprisingly witty and humorous.

"Life Class" addresses timeless idiosyncrasies of adolescent life and that is why it should be included in a new Grade 11 Anthology for academic students. Bantock's work would readily serve as great comic relief and, to be honest, every reader needs to have a good laugh in between readings of *The Rime of the Ancient Mariner* and *Paradise Lost*, as grand as these works may be. In addition, the author is immediately able to enrapture his audience through the use of sharp wit and uncanny humour. Furthermore, I am sure that teenagers around my own age would empathize with the characters as I did, upon reading this excerpt.

Nick Bantock's open approach to writing is invigorating and I was completely taken away by this humorous short story.

I was not at all offended by the fact that the narrator is openly excited by the prospects of seeing a naked woman for the first time in his life, for Bantock does not objectify the young woman. Robbie, however, who "frankly didn't know what all the kerfuffle was about" is able to successfully embarrass himself in front of the entire class and, of course, in front of the "truly celestial body." At this point, the reader is left hungry for more; yet Bantock forces the reader to draw his or her own conclusions.

Life Class
Excerpt from *The Artful Dodger: Images and Reflections*
by Nick Bantock

The really big event in my early days at art college was our first life-drawing class. I was barely sixteen and I'd never seen a naked woman before. I was both excited at the prospect and scared stiff that I'd find some way of embarrassing myself. I'd discussed the matter with my friend Steve, who was also suffering from heavy attacks of conflicting expectations. He and I used to travel on the train together, and on the morning of the great event, we noticed a beautiful woman in her early twenties sitting at the other end of the carriage. We laughed and joked about "Wouldn't it be fantastic if she was the model instead of some Bessy Bradock." (Bessy Bradock was an amiable but pudding-faced, rotund, middle-aged politician, who, for a pair of teenaged boys, has grown to symbolize the sexually unappealing.)

At college, we got into a conversation about the impending life class with Robbie, a big Scottish lad who was a couple of years our senior. According to Robbie, he'd been there, done that, and frankly didn't know what all the kerfuffle was about.

When the moment was finally upon us, we filed into the life room with our heads bent low and our smirks tucked carefully into the shadows of our collars. Needing a security blanket, I immediately went over and stood by my favorite easel. Steve took up a similar position on the other side of the room. Robbie, meanwhile, perched himself right next to me astride a donkey, a kind of long, low stool with a drawing board cradled at one end.

After a couple of minutes, our drawing teacher came in with, of all people, the beauty from the train. She had bare feet and was wearing a Chinese silk robe. It took me a few seconds to come to grips with the implications of this momentous occurrence. I shot

Steve a glance and could see that he was wearing a look of panicked ecstacy similar to my own. I snatched up a pencil and started sharpening it for all it was worth. (Funny: Back then, I never noticed how blatantly phallic that gesture was.) I was trying to compose myself, knowing that she still had to go behind the screen and undress. I told myself that I had plenty of time to prepare for the oncoming shock to my senses. But, as it turned out, things didn't quite go the way I'd imagined. Our model's conversation with the teacher ended abruptly. Instead of stepping over to the screen, she simply pirouetted, and, with a flick of her delicate thumbs, unhinged the robe. Even without comparison, I knew I was gawking like a guppy at a truly celestial body. For long seconds the room filled with an unearthly silence. Then, from my right, there came a faint creaking noise that was followed by the awesome vision of Robbie's spasticated arms and legs beating in futility at the air as he and his donkey keeled over and crashed to the floor, spraying the room with a shower of pencil shavings, drawing board chips, and charcoal dust.

Kristal Fung was born in Vancouver, British Columbia. She was first drawn into the world of art and literature at the age of five. Her passions include writing poetry, drawing, snowboarding, and eating sushi. Fung plans to continue her studies at the University of British Columbia.

1. *Response* Do you agree with Kristal Fung that this excerpt from Nick Bantock's book makes a good addition to a Grade 11 anthology? Why or why not? Discuss her assessment of it.

2. *Research and Inquiry* Kristal Fung found Bantock's anecdote and wrote this essay as part of an assignment. Your assignment is similar: Find a piece of literature you like—a short story, poem, or autobiography, for example—and that you think would appeal to a Grade 11 audience. Write a one-page rationale explaining the reasons for your choice.

3. *Making Connections* Kristal Fung and Lynn Coady ("The Importance of Being Earnest") both present arguments in favour of humour. What similarities and differences do you see in their positions?

In this essay, poet Sylvia Plath compares
being a poet to being a novelist.

A Comparison

By Sylvia Plath

How I envy the novelist!

I imagine him—better say her, for it is the women I look to for a parallel—I imagine her, then, pruning a rosebush with a large pair of shears, adjusting her spectacles, shuffling about among the teacups, humming, arranging ashtrays or babies, absorbing a slant of light, a fresh edge to the weather and piercing, with a kind of modest, beautiful X-ray vision, the psychic interiors of her neighbors— her neighbors on trains, in the dentist's waiting room, in the corner teashop. To her, this fortunate one, what is there that *isn't* relevant! Old shoes can be used, doorknobs, air letters, flannel nightgowns, cathedrals, nail varnish, jet planes, rose arbors and budgerigars; little mannerisms—the sucking at a tooth, the tugging at a hemline— any weird or warty or fine or despicable thing. Not to mention emotions, motivations—those rumbling, thunderous shapes. Her business is Time, the way it shoots forward, shunts back, blooms, decays and double exposes itself. Her business is people in Time. And she, it seems to me, has all the time in the world. She can take a century if she likes, a generation, a whole summer.

I can take about a minute.

I'm not talking about epic poems. We all know how long *they* can take. I'm talking about the smallish, unofficial garden-variety poem. How shall I describe it?—a door opens, a door shuts. In between you have had a glimpse: a garden, a person, a rainstorm, a dragonfly, a heart, a city. I think of those round glass Victorian paperweights which I remember, yet can never find—a far cry from the plastic mass-productions which stud the toy counters in Woolworths. This sort of paperweight is a clear globe, self-complete, very pure, with a forest or village or family group within it. You turn it upside down, then back. It snows. Everything is changed in a minute. It will never be the same in there—not the fir trees, nor the gables, nor the faces.

So a poem takes place.

And there is really so little room! So little time! The poet becomes an expert packer of suitcases:

The apparition of these faces in the crowd;
Petals on a wet black bough.

There it is: the beginning and the end in one breath. How would the novelist manage that? In a paragraph? In a page? Mixing it, perhaps, like paint, with a little water, thinning it, spreading it out.

Now I am being smug, I am finding advantages.

If a poem is concentrated, a closed fist, then a novel is relaxed and expansive, an open hand: it has roads, detours, destinations; a heart line, a head line; morals and money come into it. Where the fist excludes and stuns, the open hand can touch and encompass a great deal in its travels.

I have never put a toothbrush in a poem.

I do not like to think of all the things, familiar, useful and worthy things, I have never put into a poem. I did, once, put a yew tree in. And that yew tree began, with astounding egotism, to manage and order the whole affair. It was not a yew tree by a church on a road past a house in a town where a certain woman lived … and so on, as it might have been, in a novel. Oh no. It stood squarely in the middle of my poem, manipu-lating its dark shades, the voices in the churchyard, the clouds, the birds, the tender melancholy with which I contemplated it—everything! I couldn't subdue it. And, in the end, my poem was a poem about a yew tree. That yew tree was just too proud to be a passing black mark in a novel.

Perhaps I shall anger some poets by implying that the *poem* is proud. The poem, too, can include everything, they will tell me. And with far more precision and power than those baggy, disheveled and undiscriminate creatures we call novels. Well, I concede these poets their steamshovels and old trousers. I really *don't* think poems should be all that chaste. I would, I think, even concede a toothbrush, if the poem was a real one. But these apparitions, these poetical toothbrushes, are rare. And when they do arrive, they are inclined, like my obstreperous yew tree, to think themselves singled out and rather special.

Not so in novels.

There the toothbrush returns to its rack with beautiful promptitude and is forgot. Time flows, eddies, meanders, and people have leisure to grow and alter before our eyes. The rich junk of life bobs all about us: bureaus, thimbles, cats, the whole much-loved, well-thumbed catalogue of the miscellaneous which the novelist wishes us to share. I do not mean that there is no pattern, no discernment, no rigorous ordering here.

I am only suggesting that perhaps the pattern does not insist so much.

The door of the novel, like the door of the poem, also shuts.

But not so fast, nor with such manic, unanswerable finality.

Sylvia Plath (1932–1963) was an American poet described as sensitive, intelligent, and compelled toward perfection. *Ariel, Crossing the Water, Winter Trees,* and *The Collected Poems of Sylvia Plath* were all published after her death.

1. *Response*
   a. Look at the first two sentences of the essay. Do you think they make an effective beginning? Explain.
   b. In your own words, state the thesis Sylvia Plath expresses in "A Comparison." At what point in the essay does the thesis become clear to the reader? How does this compare with the placement of the thesis in other essays you have read?
   c. Reread the essay and find an example of figurative language that you think is especially effective. Why do you like it?

2. *Literature Studies* Comparison If you were asked to write a comparison of two methods of transportation, what kind of structure might you use for your essay? Create a diagram or outline that shows how that essay might be put together. Now reread "A Comparison." Is Plath's approach similar to, or different from, yours? In your opinion, did Plath use a sensible structure for her essay? Explain.

3. *Language* **Conventions** Pronouns and Gender Plath uses feminine pronouns (*she, her*) to refer to her imaginary novelist. What other options did she have? Do you think it would be fair to say her choice of pronouns is *sexist?* Why or why not?

4. *Writing* Poetry Take a story you have read or written this year and condense its essential meaning into a poem. When your poem is finished, briefly describe how you approached this task. What challenges did you face?

The Short Story

Defined

By   Peter   Hung

Check several dictionaries for definitions of the term *short story*. How precise are these definitions? Which definition do you find the most useful?

In the following essay, student writer Peter Hung explores why it is not that easy to create a definition that truly captures the essence of the short story form.

zymurgy (zī ′ mər jē) n. [ZYM (O) - + URGY] the branch of chemistry dealing with fermentation, as in making wine, ale, etc. **While in college, Mr. Budweiser got an "A" in Zymurgy 101.**

There. It was done. The last entry of my new, updated *Dictionary of the English Language, Thirty-Fifth College Edition* was finished. Even I was impressed. It contained over a billion lexicographical entries, spanned a thousand volumes, and would take up more than four hundred feet of shelf space. Best of all, it would be the first dictionary of mine to be bound in genuine Naugahyde, which looks like leather, but at a fraction of the cost. Yes, I was impressed. I, the lexicographer's lexicographer. I, Webster.[1]

I settled back in my chair, feeling quite content. But wait— something wasn't quite right, something I couldn't identify. It was not unlike the insistent buzzing of an invisible fly that is trapped in a room and cannot find its way out. Pensively, I reached for a chocolate-chip cookie from the plate of goodies I always keep on my desk. Eating helps me to think clearly, and in my line of work you do a lot of thinking.

"Ah, yes," I mumbled through cookie crumbs. I opened the rough copy of Volume 768 and flipped some pages. Scanning page 393, I found what I wanted:

---

[1] **Noah Webster:** (1758–1843). American educator, author, and lexicographer. It took him 27 years to prepare the original edition of *An American Dictionary of the English Language.*

shortstop (shôrt′stäp′) n. Baseball **1** the infielder stationed between second and third base **2** the area covered by a shortstop. **I hate baseball, and I absolutely detest playing shortstop.**

short straw (shôrt′strô′) n. The bad end of a deal, usually obtained through the process of drawing straws (see **draw straw**) or through some other lottery system. **Tom got the short straw; he, out of all the new prisoners at San Quentin, would be executed first.**

I had almost forgotten that I hadn't yet defined "short story." I had left a blank space between "shortstop" and "short straw," intending to fill it in later on. I have a habit of postponing the hardest terms, and "short story" is as hard as they come.

I went to the kitchen, got another plate of cookies, and returned to my desk. Picking up a pencil, I began writing.

short story (shôrt′stôr′ē) n. A kind of story that is short.

Well, it was a start. But I had to be more specific. After all, the dictionary might be consulted by, say, a high school student who must write an essay defining the short story. People around the world depend on me to shed light on all manner of topics, and I mustn't let them down. I bit into a cookie and continued.

short story (shôrt′stôr′ē) n. A kind of story that is short (i.e., no longer than thirty pages) with a simple plot and no more than ten characters.

Now that was more like it. I rewarded myself with another cookie. Munching steadily, I came up with another idea. I grabbed Volume 359, turned to page 410, and located the desired entry.

Hemingway (hem′in wā′), **Ernest** 1899–1961. U.S. novelist and short-story writer whose writing is characterized by the use of short, simple, declarative sentences (e.g., "Ad stood up," as in "The Battler"). Two of his favorite themes are man's internal struggle (as in "The Snows of Kilimanjaro") and trout fishing. Two interesting facts about Hemingway's short stories are that "The Short Happy Life of Francis Macomber" is thirty-five pages long, and "The Light of the World" has more than ten characters in it.

Hmp. This discovery was somewhat of a mixed blessing. Here I was reminded that the style of the short story is simple, and that its themes are man's internal struggle and trout fishing. Unfortunately, I was also reminded that short stories can have more than ten characters and thirty pages.

I erased my definition and started again.

short story (shôrt ' stôr ' ē) n. A
kind of story that is short and deals with man's internal struggle or trout fishing; stylistically, it consists primarily of short, simple, declarative sentences, such as "Ad stood up."

This definition was, I felt, lacking something, so I chose a large molasses cookie from the diminishing pile and shoved it into my mouth. It had just the right consistency and texture, but not quite enough molasses. Just the same, it cleared my head, and I was able to delve into my memory for another appropriate reference. I pulled out Volume 299 and opened it to the right page.

Ellison (el ' i sen), **Ralph** 1914– .
U.S. writer who won acclaim with his novel *Invisible Man*. Also wrote short stories of note, such as "Battle Royal," in which a single event serves to illustrate the struggle of black Americans against racial discrimination and mistreatment. Ellison tends to use more complex sentences than Hemingway, as well as more adjectives, adverbs, and similes to produce vivid images; e.g., "The boys groped about like blind, cautious crabs crouching to protect their mid-sections, their heads pulled in short against their shoulders, their arms stretched nervously before them, with their fists testing the smoke-filled air like the knobbed feelers of hypersensitive snails."

This couldn't be happening. Ellison and Hemingway were as different as authors can be, and yet they both had produced these "things" that are categorized as short stories. Despite an increasing sense of vertigo, I swallowed my last cookie and turned to another entry, this time from Volume 745.

Salinger (sal ' iŋ jer). **J(erome)**
D(avid) 1919– . U.S. novelist and short-story writer. Salinger blends overtones of love and squalor in his brilliant short story "To Esmé— with Love and Squalor." He separates the squalid part from the rest by dividing the story into two distinct sections, with completely different settings and characters. The structure is very different from that of stories by Hemingway or Ellison, which develop in a continuous, unbroken manner.

I stared blankly down at my plate, now devoid of goodies except for a few crumbs. I licked up the crumbs in desperation. My head was fairly spinning, and I was, for the first time in my illustrious career, at a loss for words. "Get a grip on yourself, Web," I told myself. Putting down my pencil, I got up from my chair, walked slowly over to the couch, and sat down heavily, feeling lost and bloated.

I don't know when I fell asleep, but I did, which was a good thing, because I tend to think better when I am asleep than when I am awake, except when I'm eating cookies. So my mind subconsciously mulled over the various ways of defining "short story." Hemingway, Ellison, Salinger, Hemingway, style, simple, plot, Salinger, short, Ellison, complex, Battle of Snows and Squalor, J(erome) D(avid) Waldo, character, theme, Ernest, earnest, any earnest, some Salinger, every Esmé, Royal Macomber, Short Happy Story of Life, Love, and Light of, dark.

Somewhere along the line, I came to the conclusion that the short story could not be defined, for it was all these things and more. It was strange, but I saw the Short Story there. No, not the spirit of the short story, or the embodiment of the short story. But just the Short Story there. It was like a candle in the darkness, or the flash of a firefly at night, shining brightly and then gone. Yes, it was gone. But that moment of light revealed a part of life that had gone unnoticed before. Or perhaps had been noticed, but ignored.

At any rate, it wasn't anything you could put into a dictionary, even Webster's *Dictionary of the English Language, Thirty-Fifth College Edition.* I woke up, no longer at a loss, but still feeling bloated by an overdose of thought-provoking cookies. I returned to my desk, erased my definition of the short story, and began to write again.

short story (shôrt ′ stôr ′ ē) n. A section of a building that extends from the floor to the ceiling and is lower than usual in height. **My, that building has a short story!**

Peter Hung was a senior at San Diego High School in San Diego, California, when he wrote this story. After reading a lot of short stories, Peter concluded that this particular genre is not easy to pin down. To make his point in an imaginative and amusing way he shows us Webster—"the lexicographer's lexicographer"—struggling to define "short story" in an updated edition of his dictionary.

1. Response
  a. Peter Hung, the student who wrote "The Short Story Defined," chose a humorous tone for his essay. What details and techniques create the humour?
  b. Did you like the humour? Do you think the humour strengthened or weakened the essay? Give reasons for your point of view.
  c. Despite the light tone of this selection, what are the serious points it makes about the short story?

2. Literature Studies *Exploring Genre* Is "The Short Story Defined" more of an essay or a short story? In a group, develop a series of convincing arguments supporting the view that it is an essay. Then develop other arguments suggesting that it should actually be classified as a story. Present your arguments to the class.

3. Language Focus *Definitions* A good definition is short, precise, and easy to understand. With a partner, brainstorm three words that you will attempt to define. Try to choose words that are not yet in the dictionary—good candidates are specialty words related to a sport or hobby. Write the definitions. How can you test the quality of your definitions?

4. Research and Inquiry Three famous short story writers are mentioned in this selection—all of them male. Needless to say, female authors could also have been included in this attempt to define a short story. Research two classic female short story writers, such as Katherine Mansfield, Toni Cade Bambara, or Alice Munro, and write biographical entries similar to those the author created for Hemingway, Ellison, and Salinger.

"For now, I'm content to be alone, because loneliness is something that doesn't exist here."

The Shack

By Margaret Laurence

The most loved place, for me, in this country has in fact been many places. It has changed throughout the years, as I and my circumstances have changed. I haven't really lost any of the best places from the past, though. I may no longer inhabit them, but they inhabit me, portions of memory, presences in the mind. One such place was my family's summer cottage at Clear Lake in Riding Mountain National Park, Manitoba. It was known to us simply as The Lake. Before the government piers and the sturdy log staircases down to the shore were put in, we used to slither with an exhilarating sense of peril down the steep homemade branch and dirt shelf-steps, through the stands of thin tall spruce and birch trees slender and graceful as girls, passing moss-hairy fallen logs and the white promise of wild strawberry blossoms, until we reached the sand and the hard bright pebbles of the beach at the edge of the cold spring-fed lake where at nights the loons still cried eerily, before too much humanshriek made them move away north.

My best place at the moment is very different, although I guess it has some of the attributes of that long-ago place. It is a small cedar cabin on the Otonabee River in southern Ontario. I've lived three summers there, writing, bird-watching, river-watching. I sometimes feel sorry for the people in speedboats who spend their weekends zinging up and down the river at about a million miles an hour. For all they're able to see, the riverbanks might just as well be green concrete and the river itself flowing with molten plastic.

Before sunup, I'm awakened by birdvoices and, I may say, birdfeet clattering and thumping on the cabin roof. Cursing only slightly, I get up temporarily, for the pre-dawn ritual of lighting a small fire in the old black woodstove (mornings are chilly here, even in summer) and looking out at the early river. The waters have a lovely spooky quality at this hour, entirely mist-covered, a secret meeting of river and sky.

By the time I get up to stay, the mist has vanished and the river is a clear ale-brown, shining with sun. I drink my coffee and sit looking out to the opposite shore, where the giant maples are splendidly green now and will be trees of flame in the fall of the year. Oak and ash stand among the maples, and the grey skeletons of the dead elms, gauntly beautiful even in death. At the very edge of the river, the willows are everywhere, water-related trees, magic trees, pale green in early summer, silvergreen in late summer, greengold in autumn.

I begin work, and every time I lift my eyes from the page and glance outside, it is to see some marvel or other. The joyous dance-like flight of the swallows. The orange-black flash of the orioles who nest across the river. The amazing takeoff of a red-winged blackbird, revealing like a swiftly unfolded fan the hidden scarlet in those dark wings. The flittering of the goldfinches, who always travel in domestic pairs, he gorgeous in black-patterned yellow feathers, she (alas) drabber in greenish grey-yellow.

A pair of great blue herons have their huge unwieldy nest about half a mile upriver, and although they are very shy, occasionally through the open door I hear a sudden approaching rush of air (yes, you can hear it) and look up quickly to see the magnificent unhurried sweep of those powerful wings. The only other birds which can move me so much are the Canada geese in their autumn migration flight, their far-off wilderness voices the harbinger of winter.

Many boats ply these waterways, and all of them are given mental gradings of merit or lack of it, by me. Standing low in the estimation of all of us along this stretch of the river are some of the big yachts, whose ego-tripping skippers don't have the courtesy to slow down in cottage areas and whose violent wakes scour out our shorelines. Ranking highest in my good books are the silent unpolluting canoes and rowboats, and next to them, the small outboard motorboats putt-putting along and carrying patient fishermen, and the homemade houseboats,

> Literature is the last banquet between minds.
>
> Edna O'Brien

unspeedy and somehow cosy-looking, decorated lovingly with painted birds or flowers or gaudy abstract splodges.

In the quiet of afternoon, if no boats are around, I look out and see the half-moon leap of a fish, carp or muskie, so instantaneous that one has the impression of having seen not a fish but an arc of light.

The day moves on, and about four o'clock Linda and Susan from the nearby farm arrive. I call them the Girls of the Pony Express. Accompanied by dogs and laughter, they ride their horses into my yard, kindly bringing my mail from the rural route postbox up the road. For several summers it was Old Jack who used to drive his battered Volkswagen up to fetch the mail. He was one of the best neighbours and most remarkable men I've ever known. As a boy of eighteen, he had homesteaded north of Regina. Later, he'd been a skilled tool-maker with Ford. He'd travelled to South America and done many amazing things. He was a man whose life had taught him a lot of wisdom. After his much-loved wife died, he moved out here to the river, spending as short a winter as possible in Peterborough, and getting back into his cottage the first of anyone in the spring, when the river was still in flood and he could only get in and out, hazardously, by boat. I used to go out in his boat with him, later afternoons, and we would dawdle along the river, looking at the forest stretches and the open rolling farmlands and vast old barns, and at the smaller things close by, the heavy luxuriance of ferns at the water's rim, the dozens of snapping turtles with unblinking eyes, all sizes and generations of the turtle tribe, sunning themselves on the fallen logs in the river. One summer, Old Jack's eighty-fourth, he spent some time planting maple saplings on his property. A year later, when I saw him dying, it seemed to me he'd meant those trees as a kind of legacy, a declaration of faith. Those of us along the river, here, won't forget him, nor what he stood for.

After work, I go out walking and weed-inspecting. Weeds and wildflowers impress me as much as any cultivated plant. I've heard that in a year when the milkweed is plentiful, the Monarch butterflies will also be plentiful. This year the light pinkish milkweed flowers stand thick and tall, and sure enough, here are the dozens of Monarch butterflies, fluttering like dusky orange-gold angels all over the place. I can't identify as many plants as I'd like, but I'm learning. Chickweed, the ragged-leafed lamb's quarters, the purple-and-white wild phlox with its expensive-smelling free perfume, the pink and mauve wild asters, the two-toned yellow of the tiny butter-and-eggs flowers, the burnt orange of devil's paintbrush, the staunch nobility of the huge purple thistles, and, almost best of all, that long stalk covered with clusters of miniature creamy blossoms which I finally tracked down in my wildflower book—this incomparable plant bears the armorial name of the Great Mullein of the Figwort Family. It may not be the absolute prettiest of our wildflowers, but it certainly has the most stunning pedigree.

It is night now, and there are no lights except those of our few cottages. At sunset, an hour or so ago, I watched the sun's last flickers touching the rippling river, making it look as though some underwater world had lighted all its candles down there. Now it is dark. Dinner over, I turn out the electric lights in the cabin so I can see the stars. The black sky-dome (or perhaps skydom, like kingdom) is alive and alight.

Tomorrow the weekend will begin, and friends will arrive. We'll talk all day and probably half the night, and that will be good. But for now, I'm content to be alone, because loneliness is something that doesn't exist here.

Margaret Laurence was born in Neepawa, Manitoba, in 1926. After attending the University of Winnipeg she became a reporter for the *Winnipeg Citizen*. Along with her husband, she lived in England, Somalia, and Ghana, before returning to Canada. Her novel *The Stone Angel* became the first of five novels set in the fictional Manitoba town of Manawaka. Laurence was awarded the Governor General's Award twice for her writing.

1. Response

a. What does the term *personal essay* suggest to you? In what ways might a personal essay differ from a persuasive essay?

b. What do you think Margaret Laurence set out to accomplish in "The Shack"? Provide evidence from the essay to support your view.

c. What three words do you think would best describe the mood of "The Shack"?

d. Does Laurence's cedar shack sound like a place where you would like to spend some time? Explain what does or does not appeal to you about it.

e. Reread the last line of the essay. What does Laurence mean? Do you think the sentence makes a good conclusion to "The Shack"? Why or why not?

2. ***Literature Studies*** *Description* Reread the essay, paying special attention to the techniques Laurence uses to create a strong sense of place. Find examples of simile, metaphor, specific nouns and verbs, and vivid adjectives and adverbs. Choose one sentence or phrase that presents a particularly effective description, and explain why it appeals to you.

3. ***Writing*** *Descriptive Paragraph* Review what you learned in activity 2 above, and apply the same techniques in a paragraph of your own writing. Your paragraph should capture the essence of a favourite place or pastime. Was it challenging to use the techniques you observed in Laurence's writing? Suggest some strategies you could use to improve your ability to write descriptively.

4. ***Media*** *Storyboard* Assume that The National Film Board is planning to make a short film documenting Laurence's experiences at the shack. Create the storyboard that would be the first stage in producing the film. What aspects of the essay will you include and what will you omit? Develop at least ten frames for the storyboard, including the opening and closing shots of the film. Beneath each frame, include notes about the shot, narration, lighting, sound effects, music, and so on. Share your storyboard with peers, explaining what you have done and the choices you have made.

Photographer William DeKay's travels in rural Canada have produced thousands of pictures and the discovery that, geography or subject matter aside, many photos seem to pair off naturally. They form a study of life and times beyond the cities and a tribute (by a southern Ontario farmboy) to the people of country Canada.

Doubletake

Photos and captions by William DeKay

Top TWIN BUTTE, ALBERTA While their parents attend the Shoderee Ranch's Red Angus bull sale, kids play baseball on the sort of field dreams are made of.

Above EDDIES COVE, NEWFOUNDLAND I wonder if a baseball game has ever been called on account of icebergs.

Top TWIN BUTTE, ALBERTA Blaine Marr rolls a metal feeder
across snow-covered pastureland. Slipped over a hay bale,
it will provide a moveable feast for his hungry yearlings.

Above WHITEHORSE, YUKON Two boaters head upstream past
Moccasin Flats, a more or less permanent community that survives
despite the efforts of city council, which has for years been threatening
to annex the land. I visited John Hutch, one of the squatters, in his home.
A notice on the wall proclaimed: "I Do Precision Guesswork Based on
Vague Assumptions and Unreliable Data of Dubious Accuracy Provided
by Persons of Questionable Intellectual Capacity."

Top TELEGRAPH CREEK, BRITISH COLUMBIA Young girls play with a sockeye salmon, netted at Six-Mile Camp along the Stikine River.

Above POINTE AU BARIL, ONTARIO Andrew Dampeir looks like I felt. His hardier friend, Mark Madigan, gets an assist from his sister Heidi.

Top SYDNEY RIVER, CAPE BRETON, NOVA SCOTIA Darren and Keith
Chomyn join their father Don atop their vacation home. They'd headed
east from Alberta and had been on the road for three months. I asked if
the amazing pile of goods strapped to the car had attracted the attention
of the police. Don said that as long as the "stuff" was secured, it posed no
problem. He'd had lots of double-takes, but no tickets. He went on to
explain that his wife had died of cancer a short while back. "The boys
really miss their mother," he said. "We're still hurting badly."

Above QUEEN CHARLOTTE CITY, BRITISH COLUMBIA Annick Blais and
Francis Madore, two young Quebeckers, were taking a week's vacation
from their summer job, planting trees for a forestry firm. I was glad
to have company, and agreed to drive them to Masset, where they
planned to camp on the beach.

William DeKay is a freelance photographer from London, Ontario. A graduate of Ryerson University, he has worked at the *London Free Press, National Geographic,* and the *Detroit Free Press.* He has won many state and national awards for his photojournalism.

1. *Response*
   a. Photographer William DeKay says that "many photos seem to pair off naturally." Identify the similarities in each pairing of photos. Consider both content (subject matter) and form (colour, line, shadow, shape, and composition).
   b. Which single photo do you like best, and why?
   c. If you were going to photograph one thing, place, or person that would capture your perception of the essence of your community, what would it be? Explain the reasons for your choice.
   d. A photo essay develops a thesis or point of view through a combination of photos and text. Identify the thesis of DeKay's essay.

2. *Visual Communication* Photo Essay Create your own photo essay, preferably using photos you take yourself. (If you don't have access to a camera, you can create your photo essay with print or digital photos you obtain through research.) Explore subject matter that interests you, and do not be afraid to be experimental with your photography. Remember that the artistry of the photo essay lies not only in taking the photographs and writing the captions, but also in arranging the photos in sequence, and in positioning photos and text on the page.

3. *Critical Thinking* Consider the relationship between text and photos in "Doubletake." Obviously the photos are central, but would they be as interesting or effective if presented on their own? What functions are served by the text?

The poet George Faludy recalls his experiences
in Hungary's concentration camps,
and how he survived.

Arming
the Spirit

By George Faludy

Some years ago in Hungary I found myself, for the second time in my life, in a concentration camp. There were some thirteen hundred inmates: democrats, Catholics, liberals, socialists and people without any political preferences, most sentenced to hard labor on trumped-up charges, though a few were there without having been sentenced or even charged. We could neither write nor receive letters or parcels; we had no books, newspapers, radios, or visitors. We cut stones from dawn to dusk 365 days a year, except for May Day. We did this on a diet of 1200 calories a day. Our situation was thus better than in a Nazi concentration camp, but much worse than in the present-day [1978] Soviet camps recently described by Bukovsky and others.

At first we returned to the barracks at night deadly tired, with no strength even to pull off our army boots and fall asleep on the rotten straw sacks. Our lives seemed not to differ from those of the slaves that built the pyramids, and our futures seemed equally bleak. But already on the day of my arrest, in the Black Maria that took me away, I had met young friends who had been denied a university education because of the war. Their faces had lit up: "You can lecture us in the camp," they said, "and we'll get our university education that way." After about a week in the camp two of them approached me and insisted that I start my lectures immediately after lights-out.

We were by then even more exhausted than on the day of our arrival. At first four men sat beside my pallet, and we were jeered at by the others. Eventually twelve prisoners gathered beside my straw sack every night for an hour or two. We recited poems, Hungarian poems, and foreign poems in translation. Among the English ones the "Ode to the West Wind" became the favorite. Then I would speak on literature, history or philosophy and my lecture would be discussed by all.

I was by no means the only prisoner to deliver such lectures. A former member of the short-lived democratic government knew *Hamlet* and *A Midsummer Night's Dream* by heart, and recited both to an enthusiastic audience. There were lectures on Roman Law, on the history of the Crusades, narrations of large parts of *War and Peace*, courses in mathematics and astronomy avidly listened to, sometimes by men who had never entered a secondary school. There was even a former staff colonel who whistled entire operas. Those of us who lectured ransacked our memories to keep alive a civilization from which we were hopelessly—and, it seemed, permanently—cut off.

There were prisoners who looked on all this with disgust, maintaining that we were insane to spend our sleeping time in lectures when we were all going to die anyway. These men, intent on survival, retreated into themselves, becoming lonely, merciless with others, shutting out thought and even speech.

By the second winter of our imprisonment it began to happen when we were at work that once, twice or even three times in the course of a day a prisoner would suddenly stop work and stagger off through the deep snow. After twenty or thirty yards of running he would collapse. In each case the man would die a day or two later, usually without regaining consciousness. Those who died in this way were always the men who had been most determined to survive, those who had concentrated on nothing but food, sleep and warmth. For my part, owing perhaps to large doses of pragmatism and positivism in my youth I was reluctant to admit the obvious: that delighting in a good poem or discussing Plato's Socratic dialogue could somehow arm the spirit to the point that it could prevent the body's collapse.

But then I was presented with proof. While I was washing myself in the snow before the barracks one evening, one of my pupils, a former government official, a strong young man, came up to tell me that he would not attend the lecture that night, nor indeed any other night. He wanted to survive and was going to sleep rather than talk; he was going, he said, to live the life of a tree or a vegetable. He waited before me as if expecting my objection. I was indescribably tired, and closing my eyes I saw scenes from my childhood, the sort of hallucinations one has in a state of semi-starvation. Suddenly it occurred to me that I must dissuade the man. But he was already gone. He slept perhaps twenty yards from me, but I never summoned the strength to argue with him. Five days later we saw him stop work, begin to run towards the trees, and then collapse in the snow. His death has been on my conscience ever since. But without exception all those who lectured, and all those who listened, survived.

It does not seem to me far-fetched to apply this lesson in the infinitely more pleasant society of this country. It justifies, I think, the Platonic view that man as given by nature owes it to himself to obey the dictates of his higher nature to rise above evil and mindlessness. Those in the camp who attempted this, survived; although physical survival had not been their aim. And those who for the sake of physical survival vegetated, perished in large numbers. It seems to me that the mentality of these latter is, *mutatis mutandis,*[1] analogous to the mentality of the consumer societies of the world, of those who seem obsessed with producing and consuming an ever-growing mountain of things to ensure comfort and survival; who have addicted themselves to energy as if to morphine until they are ready to destroy all nature to increase the dosage; who have, indeed, increased our life span but have failed to mention that the brain requires jogging even more than the heart if that life span is to mean anything.

The other conclusion I have drawn from my camp experience, and have tried to embody in my own poetry, is that our whole fragile tradition of art and thought is neither an amusement nor a yoke. For those who steep themselves in it, it provides both a guide and a goal for surpassing all the half-baked ideologies that have blown up at our feet in this century like land mines. Sitting comfortably in the present and looking forward to longevity in an unknown future does nothing to ensure our survival nor even to make it desirable. In any case we do not live in the future; we live in the present, and all we have to guide us in this present is the accumulated thought and experience of those who have lived before us.

For all the deficiency of my own learning, then, this is what I have attempted to voice in my work, and at this point in my life I feel safe in echoing the words of Petronius: *Pervixi: neque enim fortuna malignior umquam eripiet nobis quod prior hora dedit*—I have lived, and no evil fate can ever take away from us what the past has given. I believe we will do ourselves a favor if we extend the meaning of the author of the *Satyricon* to include the past of all humanity.

[1] *mutatis muntandis:* Latin phrase meaning "with the necessary changes"

George Faludy is a Hungarian-born poet. His book *Selected Poems 1933–80*, edited and translated by Canadian Robin Skelton, was published in 1985.

1. *Response*
   a. Why might "Arming the Spirit" be described as a personal essay?
   b. This speech was given as a convocation address to students at the University of Toronto in 1978. Why would the topic of the essay have been appropriate for that audience? Describe your own response to "Arming the Spirit."
   c. Do you think George Faludy is right to feel guilty about the young man who died? Explain.
   d. In the third-last paragraph of the essay, Faludy broadens the scope of his argument. Paraphrase the point he is making. Do you think the essay is strengthened by this paragraph? Why or why not?
   e. The editors of this anthology chose the title "Arming the Spirit" for this selection, which was untitled. Discuss this title. What else could it have been called?

2. *Critical Thinking* In a group, discuss Faludy's theory that "the brain requires jogging even more than the heart if that life is to mean anything." Do you agree with this theory? How could it be tested, and what evidence might provide convincing support? Present your ideas to the class.

3. *Oral Language* *Speech* Faludy uses his own experience to inspire others in this speech. Develop an inspirational speech based on your own experiences, or the experiences of someone you know. Rehearse your speech in front of a small group, getting feedback on presentation—body language, projection, pacing, and tone. Once you have delivered your speech, assess your oral communication skills and how they might be improved.

4. *Research and Inquiry* Using resources in your library, select one important work of art (literature, music, or visual art) created before 1900 and conduct research to learn why that work is culturally important. Present your findings to the class.

The Internet: "… a bright new window into a room that traditionally has been very dark."

Dis?Ability

on the

Internet

By Heather Proud

Over the past twelve years I have learned much by working, counselling, socializing, studying, advocating, observing, playing, and interacting with individuals with disabilities (IWD). It is still amazing to me that I have adjusted to being paralyzed for over half of my young life, and yet I feel so fortunate to have a good quality of life. I am excited and interested to learn about the Internet—the ways it has opened up vast new worlds to IWD by greatly increasing our interactivity and functionality in the world. We are using the Internet to be productive in countless creative and therapeutic ways.

People with disabilities face an ongoing and unique set of issues and challenges that many able-bodied individuals do not understand or are even aware of. As a person living with a disability for the last 18 years, I have gained tremendous experience and insight regarding the daily problems IWD face on so many levels. I've worked in the local disabled community for many years as an advocate, fundraiser, peer counsellor, educator, and case manager, and as director of a small spinal cord injury support group. From this experience I have learned about the physical, emotional, mental, spiritual, and economic challenges that IWD face.

The physical challenges vary widely for every individual,

according to their disability, from those who can live independently to those who are completely unable to take care of their physical needs. The physical limitations may not be obvious when you see someone in a wheelchair, yet even someone who is independent will generally find something in the "able-bodied" world which is a barrier to their accessibility. Even two or three stairs into a building or home means an individual in a wheelchair is excluded. In addition to the obvious barriers there are also hidden physical problems, such as chronic pain, which can make participating in ordinary life very difficult.

We all face mental, emotional, and spiritual issues as we live out our lives. We struggle with our inner conflicts and the need for love and acceptance from our world. For the individual with a disability, many issues such as self-esteem, optimism, and faith in ourselves, God, and our fellow humans are much more challenging. One reason for this is the physical separateness which leads to loneliness and a feeling of personal isolation. Relationships, both personal and romantic, become harder when the individual with a disability has so many needs. It can be overwhelming to a partner, making it more difficult to create and maintain healthy romantic relationships. Marriages often fail after disability occurs.

Adding to the personal physical limitations, IWD face societal limitations in order to be successful and reach their goals financially, educationally, professionally, and creatively. Not only are there fewer jobs and professions in which IWD can participate, there is often an inability to accommodate their needs. On the brighter side, advocacy groups, individuals, and family members have brought about the Americans with Disabilities Act and have been dramatically increasing the overall awareness of the need for accessibility, accommodation, and integration of IWD into mainstream life.

The Internet has also changed and expanded the capacity of IWD to function in the world. A wide variety of assistive technology devices have been developed, creating easy access to both computers and the Internet. Unfortunately these devices are still very expensive and continue to disenfranchise a large percentage of the disabled community who cannot afford them. I have been lucky. After researching what is available and what would make it possible for me to continue my education and become more employable, I received a state-of-the-art computer system from the State of Hawaii that allows me, as a quadriplegic, to go to school. I have never had a computer before or spent more than a couple of hours on the Internet at a friend's house. My experience with this class over the past two months has shown me the incredible vastness of information and ability to interact that one can experience while on the Net. I've come to realize that for IWD, this environment offers amazing freedom. The Internet is exceptionally supportive to those IWD who have always experienced so many limitations in the able-bodied world. It's like a bright new window into a room that traditionally has been very dark.

In a disabled person's world, the concept of space and time is very different. Most are often unable to devote the large chunks of continuous time that our society demands of its participants in employment/school/social settings. I personally cannot sit comfortably in a wheelchair for more than a few hours at a time. Until recently, I have not been able to "work" because of this. The fact that the Internet opens up new possibilities to work and go to school from one's home is an outstanding development for the disabled community who has been waiting a very long time for just such an opportunity to participate in mainstream/cutting edge life.

The Internet not only creates quality business and educational connections, but also healthy personal support systems. Networking through the Internet allows thousands of connections to be made which enhance our awareness that others are coping with the same situation. Knowing that someone is out there to talk with about a variety of disability issues helps ease the sense of isolation. A feeling of belonging combats loneliness. The disabled community has a strong presence on the Internet with numerous chat rooms and news groups available to discuss issues. I've been exploring now for two months and still feel that I have barely scratched the surface of what's out there. I want to know more!!

Individuals with disabilities are using the Internet to produce better lives for themselves both personally and economically. Many of these individuals have Web sites. They are sharing their personal stories of how they became disabled and how they have adjusted and accepted living with their disability. Their stories are inspiring and poignant. These people are addressing their issues and challenges in positive ways that encourage excellence within the global disabled village. By doing this they are an inspiration to others and are able to express their own personal creativity. This information is particularly helpful to people who have recently become disabled.

As I have been writing this essay, my awareness of IWD on the Internet has been radically broadened; a learn-as-you-go project. It has been enlightening and inspiring beyond my imagination. The Internet in no way takes away from my personal real-life interactions, but has enhanced and expanded my perspective of the unlimited possibilities and opportunities in the virtual world.

1. Response

   a. What is Heather Proud's thesis and how does she support it? Summarize her main argument.

   b. The body of Proud's essay can be divided into two sections. Where would you put the dividing line? Why?

   c. How does Proud's perspective on disability compare with your own? What knowledge and insight did you gain from her essay?

   d. Proud says that "a large percentage of the disabled community" is *disenfranchised*. What specific problem is she emphasizing at that stage of her essay? In a group, brainstorm some possible solutions to that problem.

   e. Explain the possible meanings of the title, and its use of typography.

2. *Writing* *Personal Essay* Proud uses this essay to explore the potential of the Internet for individuals with disabilities. Develop a short personal essay that describes your own experience with the Internet (or another technology). Remember that your introduction should engage the reader's interest, introduce your thesis, and preview the essay's organization. The body of your essay should develop your arguments logically, and include relevant supporting evidence. Your conclusion should summarize your key points and present a closing insight that is related to your thesis.

3. *Language Focus* *Preferred Terminology* Examine the language Proud uses to refer to those with disabilities. Why might the term *individuals with disabilities* be preferred to the expression *disabled individuals?* Provide some other examples of terminology that is preferred by a certain group or community. Do you think it is right for a community to encourage the general public to accept its preferred terminology? Explain your position.

4. *Media* *Web Sites* Investigate the Internet to find out what sites are designed for or targeted at individuals with disabilities. Describe any special features you find on these sites. What suggestions would you make to someone who wanted to design a Web page that is accessible to individuals with disabilities?

Chicken-Hips

By Catherine Pigott

When you look in the mirror, what do you see? In this essay, Catherine Pigott explains how a visit to Africa raised questions about her image of herself.

The women of the household clucked disapprovingly when they saw me. It was the first time I had worn African clothes since my arrival in tiny, dusty Gambia, and evidently they were not impressed. They adjusted my head-tie and pulled my *lappa*, the ankle-length fabric I had wrapped around myself, even tighter. "You're too thin," one of them pronounced. "It's no good." They nicknamed me "Chicken-hips."

I marvelled at this accolade, for I had never been called thin in my life. It was something I longed for. I would have been flattered if those ample-bosomed women hadn't looked so distressed. It was obvious I fell far short of their ideal of beauty.

I had dressed up for a very special occasion—the baptism of a son. The women heaped rice into tin basins the size of laundry tubs, shaping it into mounds with their hands. Five of us sat around one basin, thrusting our fingers into the scalding food. These women ate with such relish, such joy. They pressed the rice into balls in their fists, squeezing until the bright-red palm oil ran down their forearms and dripped off their elbows.

I tried desperately, but I could not eat enough to please them. It was hard for me to explain that I come from a culture in which it is almost unseemly for a woman to eat too heartily. It's considered unattractive. It was even harder to explain that to me thin is beautiful, and in my country we deny ourselves food in our pursuit of perfect slenderness.

That night, everyone danced to welcome the baby. Women swivelled their broad hips and used their hands to emphasize the roundness of their bodies. One needed to be round and wide to make the dance beautiful. There was no place for thinness here. It made people sad. It reminded them of things they wanted to forget, such as poverty, drought and starvation. You never knew when the rice was going to run out.

I began to believe that Africa's image of the perfect female body was far more realistic than the long-legged leanness I had been conditioned to admire. There, it is beautiful—not shameful—to carry weight on the hips and thighs, to have a round stomach and heavy, swinging breasts. Women do not battle the bulge, they celebrate it. A body is not something to be tamed and moulded.

The friends who had christened me Chicken-hips made it their mission to fatten me up. It wasn't long before a diet of rice and rich, oily stew twice a day began to change me. Every month, the women would take a stick and measure my backside, noting with pleasure its gradual expansion. "Oh Catherine, your buttocks are getting nice now!" they would say.

What was extraordinary was that I, too, believed I was becoming more beautiful. There was no sense of panic, no shame, no guilt-ridden resolves to go on the miracle grape-and-water diet. One day, I tied my *lappa* tight across my hips and went to the market to buy beer for a wedding. I carried the crate of bottles home on my head, swinging my hips slowly as I walked. I felt transformed.

In Gambia, people don't use words such as "cheating," "naughty," or "guilty" when they talk about eating. The language of sin is not applied to food. Fat is desirable. It holds beneficial meanings of abundance, fertility and health.

My perception of beauty altered as my body did. The European tourists on the beach began to look strange and skeletal rather than "slim." They had no hips. They seemed devoid of shape and substance. Women I once would have envied appeared fragile and even ugly. The ideal they represented no longer made sense.

After a year, I came home. I preached my new way of seeing to anyone who would listen. I wanted to cling to the liberating belief that losing weight had nothing to do with self-love.

An essay is a work of literary art which has a minimum of one anecdote and one universal idea.

Carol Bly

Family members kindly suggested that I might look and feel better if I slimmed down a little. They encouraged me to join an exercise club. I wandered around the malls in a dislocated daze. I felt uncomfortable trying on clothes that hung so elegantly on the mannequins. I began hearing old voices inside my head: "Plaid makes you look fat.... You're too short for that style.... Vertical stripes are more slimming.... Wear black."

I joined the club. Just a few weeks after I had worn a *lappa* and scooped up rice with my hands, I was climbing into pink leotards and aerobics shoes. The instructor told me that I had to set fitness goals and "weigh in" after my workouts. There were mirrors on the walls and I could see women watching themselves. I sensed that even the loveliest among them felt they were somehow flawed. As the aerobics instructor barked out commands for arm lifts and leg lifts, I pictured Gambian women pounding millet and dancing in a circle with their arms raised high. I do not mean to romanticize their rock-hard lives, but we were hardly to be envied as we ran like fools between two walls to the tiresome beat of synthesized music.

We were a roomful of women striving to reshape ourselves into some kind of pubertal ideal. I reverted to my natural state: one of yearning to be slimmer and more fit than I was. My freedom had been temporary. I was home, where fat is feared and despised. It was time to exert control over my body and my life. I dreaded the thought of people saying, "She's let herself go."

If I return to Africa, I am sure the women will shake their heads in bewildered dismay. Even now, I sometimes catch my reflection in a window and their voices come back to me. "Yo! Chicken-hips!"

Catherine Pigott has worked as a print journalist at the Kingston *Whig Standard*, a teacher in a Gambian college, and an editor for *CBC Radio News*. She has also worked as a producer of CBC's radio broadcasts *Morningside,* and *Sunday Morning.*

1. Response

a. In your own words, state the implicit thesis of this essay. Compare your wording with that of some classmates and discuss the differences.

b. Refer to the description of organizational patterns in "Whose Lathe?" What pattern has Catherine Pigott used in "Chicken-Hips"? How is this pattern appropriate to her topic?

c. Pigott describes some differences between life in Africa and life in Canada. Summarize those differences. In your opinion, how accurate is her portrayal of each place? Explain.

d. Do you think that teenagers' perceptions about their bodies are strongly influenced by media images and peer attitudes? Explain your answer. Would you say that you are more or less susceptible to these pressures than other teens? Why?

e. Do you think Canadians have changed their views about ideal body shape over the past 50 years? What kind of evidence could help you to answer this question, and where could you find it?

2. Vocabulary

Pigott says, "In Gambia, people do not use words such as 'cheating,' 'naughty,' or 'guilty' when they talk about eating." In a group, discuss the good or bad connotations that many food words (for example, *chocolate, dessert, butter, carrots, tofu,* and so on) have. Design and administer a survey that will help you to investigate the connotations of some specific food-related words. Present your findings to the class.

3. Oral Communication

Debate Soon after she returned to Canada, Pigott joined a health club. Brainstorm the most compelling arguments for and against that decision. Prepare for an informal debate in which you will either defend or attack Pigott's decision. During your preparation you should seek evidence to support your arguments, and you should practise delivering your position in a forceful way. After the debate, assess whether brainstorming arguments on both sides was a valuable first step.

4. Media

Image Analysis With a small group, choose one medium—TV, movies, or magazines, for example—and analyse the messages about body type and body image. What seem to be the most common explicit messages, and how do they compare with the implicit messages? What conclusions can you draw? Provide concrete examples to support your view.

"I write for my dying cactus."

What Colour Is a Rose?

By   D r e w   H a y d e n   T a y l o r

As a Native writer there are always three questions I get asked, *ad nauseam*, whenever I give a lecture or a reading for a non-Native audience. Question one: "What do you feel about cultural appropriation?" My answer: "About the same as I feel about land appropriation." Question two: "When you write your plays or stories, do you write for a specifically Native audience or a White audience?" My answer: "I'm usually alone in my room when I write, except for my dying cactus. So I guess that means I write for my dying cactus." The final, and in my opinion, most annoying question I often get asked is: "Are you a writer that happens to be Native, or a Native that happens to be a writer?"

I was not aware there had to be a difference. I was always under the impression that the two could be and often were, synonymous. But evidently I am in error. Over the past few years of working as a professional writer, I have slowly begun to understand the rules of participation in the television and prose industry in terms of this difference. It seems there is a double standard. Surprise, surprise.

It is not uncommon, though deemed politically incorrect, for White writers to write satires about Native people quite freely, particularly on television. Notice many of the "people of pallor" script credits on such shows as *North of 60* (which, granted, does have one talented Native writer), *Northern Exposure* (I guess I'll have to move to the North since it seems that's where all the Native people live), and movies like *Where the Spirit Lives* or *Dance Me Outside*. All these shows have strong, identifiable Native characters created by non-Natives.

However, should a Native writer want to explore the untrodden world outside the Aboriginal literary ghetto, immediately the fences appear, and opportunities dry up. Evidently, the Powers That Be out there in the big cruel world have very specific ideas of what a Native writer can and can't do. Only recently, a friend of mine submitted a story to a new CBC anthology series in development, about Native people, called *The Four Directions*.

His story outline was soon returned with an explanation that the producers thought the story wasn't "Native enough" for their purposes. I myself submitted a story to the producers, and during our first story meeting, I received a stirring and heartfelt lecture about how they, the producers, were determined to present the Native voice as authentically and accurately as possible, and how committed they were to allowing us Native-types the chance to tell our stories our way. I was then asked if I could cut the first eight pages of my twenty-seven-page script. Oddly enough, they seemed puzzled by my sudden burst of laughter.

I once wrote an episode of *Street Legal* and accidentally caught a glimpse of a memo from the producer to a story editor asking him to rewrite the dialogue of my Native Elder to "make him more Indian." I guess as a Native person, I don't know how real "Indians" talk. Bummer. These are just a few examples of the battle Native writers often face.

I hereby pose a question to these people who judge our stories. I personally would like to know by what set of qualifications these people examine Native stories. Is there an Aboriginal suitability quotient posted somewhere? If there is, I would love the opportunity to learn more about how I should write as a Native person.

For a story to be "Native enough," must there be a birch bark or buckskin quota? Perhaps there are supposed to be vast roaming herds of moose running past the screen. Oh geez, I guess I'm not Native enough. I momentarily forgot, moose don't herd, they just hang out with flying squirrels that have their own cartoon show.

Or maybe I's got be good writer like dem Indians whats W.P. Kinsella writes about. It no sound like any Indian I ever hears, but what the hell, I maybe win bunch of awards. On second thought, you never mind. I get headache trying write like this.

So what's a writer to do? Damned if he does, damned if he doesn't. And what if I want to write stories about non-Native people? It's possible, but will I be given a chance? I'm sure I could do it. I've learned enough about how White people really live from watching all those episodes of *Married With Children* and *Baywatch*.

This all brings us back to the original question. Am I a writer who happens to be Native, or a Native that happens to be a writer? Do I have a choice? I think that the next time I get asked that, I'll ask the equally deep and important question: "Is a zebra black with white stripes, or white with black stripes?"

Just watch. They'll make that into a racial question.

Scriptwriter **Drew Hayden Taylor** has written *The Bootlegger Blues*, which won the Canadian Authors Association Award for Drama, and *Only Drunks and Children Tell the Truth*, which won the Dora Award for most outstanding new play. Taylor also writes essays and commentaries for *The Globe and Mail*, *The Toronto Star* and *This Magazine*.

1. *Response*

    a. In your own words, state the "double standard" that Drew Hayden Taylor is commenting on in his essay.

    b. Taylor uses the term *cultural appropriation*. What does it mean? Give an example of a situation that could be described as cultural appropriation.

    c. What is the tone of the essay? Select three quotations that provide good examples. As a reader, how did you respond to this tone? Did it appeal to you? Do you think Taylor's approach is effective? Explain.

    d. Did you find Taylor's anecdotal evidence convincing? Why or why not?

2. *Language Conventions* Language Level "What Colour Is a Rose?" is written in an informal, conversational style. Identify the specific techniques Taylor uses to create this style, providing one or two examples of each. Pay attention to aspects such as sentence structure, punctuation, and diction. Using a conversational style yourself, write a paragraph that tells about the advantages and/or disadvantages of using informal language in an essay.

3. *Making Connections* The title of Taylor's essay may be a literary allusion to two famous quotations that also contain the word *rose*. How could you find out what they are? Try to identify what those quotations might be. How does the title of Taylor's essay relate to the main point of his essay? Are the quotations also appropriate to this message? Explain.

Have you ever considered the beauty of a toad?
In this essay, George Orwell explores what makes toads
such a wonderful sight.

Some Thoughts on the Common Toad

By George Orwell

Before the swallow, before the daffodil, and not much later than the snowdrop, the common toad salutes the coming of spring after his own fashion, which is to emerge from a hole in the ground, where he has lain buried since the previous autumn, and crawl as rapidly as possible towards the nearest suitable patch of water. Something—some kind of shudder in the earth, or perhaps merely a rise of a few degrees in the temperature— has told him that it is time to wake up: though a few toads appear to sleep the clock round and miss out a year from time to time—at any rate, I have more than once dug them up, alive and apparently well, in the middle of the summer.

At this period, after his long fast, the toad has a very spiritual look, like a strict Anglo-Catholic towards the end of Lent. His movements are languid but purposeful, his body is shrunken, and by contrast his eyes look abnormally large. This allows one to notice, what one might not at another time, that a toad has about the most beautiful eye of any living creature. It is like gold, or more exactly it is like the golden-coloured semi-precious stone which one sometimes sees in signet-rings, and which I think is called a chrysoberyl.

For a few days after getting into the water the toad con- centrates on building up his strength by eating small insects.

Presently he has swollen to his normal size again, and then he goes through a phase of intense sexiness. All he knows, at least if he is a male toad, is that he wants to get his arms round something, and if you offer him a stick, or even your finger, he will cling to it with surprising strength and take a long time to discover that it is not a female toad. Frequently one comes upon shapeless masses of ten or twenty toads rolling over and over in the water, one clinging to another without distinction of sex. By degrees, however, they sort themselves out into couples, with the male duly sitting on the female's back. You can now distinguish males from females, because the male is smaller, darker and sits on top, with his arms tightly clasped round the female's neck. After a day or two the spawn is laid in long strings which wind themselves in and out of the reeds and soon become invisible. A few more weeks, and the water is alive with masses of tiny tadpoles which rapidly grow larger, sprout hind-legs, then forelegs, then shed their tails: and finally, about the middle of the summer, the new generation of toads, smaller than one's thumb-nail but perfect in every particular, crawl out of the water to begin the game anew.

I mention the spawning of the toads because it is one of the phenomena of spring which most deeply appeal to me, and because the toad, unlike the skylark and the primrose, has never had much of a boost from the poets. But I am aware that many people do not like reptiles or amphibians, and I am not suggesting that in order to enjoy the spring, you have to take an interest in toads. There are also the crocus, the missel-thrush, the cuckoo, the blackthorn, etc. The point is that the pleasures of spring are available to everybody, and cost nothing. Even in the most sordid street the coming of spring will register itself by some sign or other, if it is only a brighter blue between the chimney pots or the vivid green of an elder sprouting on a blitzed site. Indeed it is remarkable how Nature goes on existing unofficially, as it were, in the very heart of London. I have seen a kestrel flying over the Deptford gasworks, and I have heard a first-rate performance by a blackbird in the Euston Road. There must be some hundreds of thousands, if not millions, of birds living inside the four-mile radius, and it is rather a pleasing thought that none of them pays a halfpenny of rent.

As for spring, not even the narrow and gloomy streets round the Bank of England are quite able to exclude it. It comes seeping in everywhere, like one of those new poison gases which pass through all filters. The spring is commonly referred to as "a miracle", and during the past five or six years this worn-out figure of speech has taken on a new lease of life. After the sort of winters we have had to endure recently, the spring does seem miraculous, because it has become gradually harder and harder to believe that it is actually going to happen. Every February since 1940 I have found myself thinking that this time winter is going to be permanent. But Persephone, like the toads, always rises from the dead at about the same moment. Suddenly, towards the end of March, the miracle happens and the decaying slum in which I live is transfigured. Down in the square the sooty privets have turned bright green, the leaves are thickening on the chestnut trees, the daffodils are out, the wallflowers are budding, the policeman's tunic looks positively a pleasant shade of blue, the fishmonger greets his customers with a smile, and even the sparrows are quite a different colour, having felt the balminess of the air and nerved themselves to take a bath, their first since last September.

Is it wicked to take a pleasure in spring and other seasonal changes? To put it more precisely, is it politically reprehensible, while we are all groaning, or at any rate ought to be groaning, under the shackles of the capitalist system, to point out that life is frequently more worth living because of a blackbird's song, a yellow elm tree in October, or some other natural phenomenon which does not cost money and does not have what the editors of left-wing newspapers call a class angle? There is no doubt that many people think so. I know by experience that a favourable reference to "Nature" in one of my articles is liable to bring me abusive letters, and though the key-word in these letters is usually "sentimental", two ideas seem to be mixed up in them. One is that any pleasure in the actual process of life encourages a sort of political quietism. People, so the thought runs, ought to be discontented, and it is our job to multiply our wants and not simply to increase our enjoyment of the things we have already. The other idea is that this is the age of machines and that to dislike the machine, or even to want to limit its domination, is backward-looking, reactionary and slightly ridiculous. This is often backed up by the statement that a love of Nature is a foible of urbanised people who have no notion what Nature is really like. Those who really have to deal with the soil, so it is argued, do not love the soil, and do not take the faintest interest in birds or flowers,

> Over increasingly large areas of the United States, spring now comes unheralded by the return of the birds, and the early mornings are strangely silent where once they were filled with the beauty of bird song.
>
> Rachel Carson

except from a strictly utilitarian point of view. To love the country one must live in the town, merely taking an occasional week-end ramble at the warmer times of year.

This last idea is demonstrably false. Medieval literature, for instance, including the popular ballads, is full of an almost Georgian enthusiasm for Nature, and the art of agricultural peoples such as the Chinese and Japanese centres always round trees, birds, flowers, rivers, mountains. The other idea seems to me to be wrong in a subtler way. Certainly we ought to be discontented, we ought not simply to find out ways of making the best of a bad job, and yet if we kill all pleasure in the actual process of life, what sort of future are we preparing for ourselves? If a man cannot enjoy the return of spring, why should he be happy in a labour-saving Utopia? What will he do with the leisure that the machine will give him? I have always suspected that if our economic and political problems are ever really solved, life will become simpler instead of more complex, and that the sort of pleasure one gets from finding the first primrose will loom larger than the sort of pleasure one gets from eating an ice to the tune of a Wurlitzer. I think that by retaining one's childhood love of such things as trees, fishes, butterflies and—to return to my first instance—toads, one makes a peaceful and decent future a little more probable, and that by preaching the doctrine that nothing is to be admired except steel and concrete, one merely makes it a little surer that human beings will have no outlet for their surplus energy except in hatred and leader worship.

At any rate, spring is here, even in London N.1, and they can't stop you enjoying it. This is a satisfying reflection. How many a time have I stood watching the toads mating, or a pair of hares having a boxing match in the young corn, and thought of all the important persons who would stop me enjoying this if they could. But luckily they can't. So long as you are not actually ill, hungry, frightened or immured in a prison or a holiday camp, spring is still spring. The atom bombs are piling up in the factories, the police are prowling through the cities, the lies are streaming from the loudspeakers, but the earth is still going round the sun, and neither the dictators nor the bureaucrats, deeply as they disapprove of the process, are able to prevent it.

George Orwell was the pen name of British author, Eric Blair, who was born in India in 1903. During World War II, Orwell was a war correspondent for the BBC and the *Observer*. Best-known for his satire, Orwell wrote non-fiction, essays, criticism, documentaries, and novels, including *Animal Farm* and *Nineteen Eighty-Four*.

1. Response
   a. Who was George Orwell and what were his politics? When and where is the essay set? Explain how this contextual information can help a reader better appreciate "Some Thoughts on the Common Toad."
   b. Orwell makes a reference to Persephone, a figure from Greek mythology. Who was she and why is she often associated with spring?
   c. How does this work differ from a typical essay about politics? In your view, are these differences strengths or weaknesses? Why?
   d. Who do you think was the audience Orwell was writing for? Is the essay relevant to a wider audience? Explain.

2. Language Focus *Simile* Identify the unusual simile that Orwell introduces in the fifth paragraph. In what way is this simile surprising? Why is it appropriate to the context and topic of the essay? Create three similes of your own that could have the effect of surprising the reader.

3. Literature Studies *Satire* "Some Thoughts on the Common Toad" could be classified as a gentle satire. What features of the work support that classification? Express Orwell's satirical message in your own words. If you were going to write a satire, what would be your target?

4. Writing *Monologue* Take the toad's point of view and write a monologue about Orwell, as he is taking notes in early spring. Your monologue could be satiric. Read your monologue aloud for an audience. Use your voice expressively in order to convey the tone of your writing.

*In this expository essay Marjorie Doyle describes
her experience in Barcelona; her description brings
the city and its people to life.*

Homage to Barcelona

By Marjorie Doyle

Barcelona. No wonder it's madness, with four million people trying to squeeze into a comparatively tiny space. Here is a city emerging from a long dictatorship; that may explain the resentment towards any law that hints at impinging on individual rights. Or it may be a deep-rooted love of anarchy that goes back to long before Franco. In any event, there is a pervasive scorn for anything that inconveniences the individual for the collective good. A request to a neighbour to lower his stereo at 4:00 a.m. is greeted with outrage. Not only is this a denial of basic rights, but where's the problem? You're free to play your stereo louder and later tomorrow night. And so it goes.

Take parking, for example.

The accepted system—which works, sort of—is to park where you want, when you want. If you find yourself hemmed in on all sides, you simply sit in your car and blow your horn until the guilty parties come forth. Except they're not guilty parties here. No apology; not even a glance or nod is exchanged. It's a problem, then, only for a foreigner who's reluctant to add more decibels to what must surely be the noisiest city on earth. An *extranjera* doesn't feel comfortable sitting with her hand glued to the horn for, say, twenty minutes. But this is a city in which volume is a virtue. How noisy is it? Imagine that city council is working on your street with a jackhammer, there's a house under construction next door, every youngster on the street has just been given a ghetto blaster and a motorcycle, and the muffler's gone on your car, your neighbour's car and your neighbour's neighbour's car. That would be a quiet moment in Barcelona.

Louder is better, the motto seems to be, and everyone does his best to live up to it. On the street there's the continual blare of horns as cars park and unpark, and there are thousands of muffler-less scooters. In the *bodegas* (cafes or bars), there are TV sets, gambling machines and coffee grinders that seem especially designed to rub your nerves raw. I retreat to my flat in grateful anticipation of a few moments' solitude with my electric piano. But even with top volume I still hear only the neighbour's radio, the schoolchildren playing next to my terrace, and the Andalusian singing floating down seven flights from the maid upstairs. I begin to accompany her—it's good practice for my ear—but eventually I give up. I don't know then that the real noise doesn't begin until the hot summer nights when everyone eats (late, as the Spanish do) on their terraces. There'll then be countless sleepless nights with a clashing of cutlery that sounds like one big swordfight. In retrospect, this will seem a quiet time.

So you can't be in and you can't be out. Maybe the parks are quiet, and there'll be grass, a precious commodity in a dry climate. I think there are two patches: one is in a little English garden tucked inside the walled protectorate of the British Consulate; the other is here, in the park. Your poor hardened toes are just beginning to sink into the soft stuff when the shrill whistle of the Guardia Civil suggests that grass is only to be seen. One look at his hat, more persuasive than his weapons, and concrete doesn't seem so bad. When you've reached the noise saturation level, you head back to your apartment building and descend three floors below sea level. But you can only hide out so long in a parking garage.

So you climb around the jungle city, crossing six lanes of traffic to get your morning croissant at the neighbourhood bakery. Not a bad life, really. It's just that when you find yourself in a crowd of fifty waiting to brave the crossing, you suddenly notice there's an equal number ready to attack from the other side. Experience in the Metro has taught you a law of physics you didn't know before—two people can occupy the same place at the same time. Or, at least, there's a strong conviction here to that effect. With the vague hope that tackle football can be learned on the job, you hunch your shoulders, duck and charge. The lucky ones make it to the other side. If you had a *peseta* for every person you touched and tackled along the way, you could even buy a second croissant—chocolate, maybe. So you return from the battlefield for a little reprieve, sit and contemplate. The thought of the fruit and vegetables finally wins out, and off you go again.

And here, in the *fruteria*, you come face to face with one of the peculiar ironies of Barcelona. In the midst of a city of madness and anarchy, there is an orderliness that would challenge a Swiss. You enter the store and call out, who's last? I, someone answers, and you fix your eyes on her, anxious not to miss your turn. It would be easy to in the scramble—there are two or three shopkeepers continually calling, who's next? who's next? and you've also got your responsibility to shout "I" to the person who enters the store after you. If by chance you do miss your turn, there's nothing for it but to leave and enter again. As with most things, this system is learned the hard way. It's easy for a foreigner to violate the order. War erupts, in two languages. In Catalan (the language of this region) and Castellano (Spanish) there are cries of: this lady was before that old man, that old man was before this young girl, that handsome young one was before that woman there, I was before her, she was before him, he was before me ... The shopkeepers remain silent. Whose fault is this anyway? the customers are shouting. Somewhere in the corner is a quiet Newfoundlander admiring the size of the avocados and noting that lettuce *is* green. *La inglesa*, they finally notice, *es la inglesa*. Ah well, so the Brits take the rap.

The sense of propriety continues when you are served. A kilo of oranges, half a kilo of bananas and four apples, you rush to tell her. You quickly learn all requests are ignored except the first. After your oranges are brought from the bin, weighed, priced and placed ceremoniously in your shopping basket, you're asked, what more? And on it goes, item by item. If you want one apple and one orange and they are next to each other in the bins, you learn to tell only about the apple at first. The apple is carried to the scale, priced and deposited. Then, and only then, is the subject of the orange addressed.

This sense of concentrated devotion to the activity is even more pronounced at the butcher shop, where you go to buy, say, a rabbit. You wait at least twenty minutes to be served, but then you are given the butcher's fullest attention; she will carefully and wholeheartedly do anything you want with the poor little thing in front of you. The butchers are usually raised on a rostrum behind the counter; this, and the fact that all eyes are on her, turn the activity into a show. The requests are thorough and varied: a chicken or rabbit will be skinned, boned, quartered, shredded, turned into patties, prepared for stew, the liver for this, the kidney for that; every conceivable direction is given. By the time you get your little rabbit home, you're intimate with it. Underneath this procedure in all the shops there is the continuous rhythm of: *Ultimo? Yo. Quien es? Que más? Algo más?* Who's next? What more? Something more? You eventually get the hang of the system.

You don't waste much time worrying about your performance in the *fruteria* as another reality of Barcelona hits you on the way home. This is the sight of the countless poor rummaging through the huge dumpsters that stand on every corner. You try to convince yourself at first that they're scrounging for odds and ends, but before long you have to face it: they are hunting for food. This, and all the begging in Barcelona, is something you never get used to. Poverty and unemployment manifest themselves here in various ways. There are the hundreds of homeless who huddle in shop doorways at night, carefully guarding their few possessions—usually more scraps of thin clothing. Then there are the men, in their twenties and thirties, who frequent the public plazas. Some sit on the sidewalks with a sign placed in front of them: I am hungry, I have no work, I have six children. Others kneel and hang the same sign around their necks, a posture that is disturbing as much for its self-abasement as for the confused sense of guilt it seems to suggest. And it's not uncommon for a pair of small boys to enter the Metro. One stands still and cries out a prepared speech: my mother is sick, my father has no work, I have seven brothers and sisters, we are hungry. The other walks through the car with his hand cupped. At the next station, they hurry onto the next car, and so they pass the day. Sometimes one boy will have an accordion; he can't play it (he's barely big enough to carry it), but he opens and closes it and some sort of wail comes out. One night, walking up the famed Ramblas, I literally tripped over a baby bottle, nipple up. I looked down to find a young woman sitting on the pavement with an infant in her arms and a baby (maybe ten months older?) lying across her lap. She and others are there every night, right in the path of Barcelona's wealthiest, the opera patrons pouring out of the opulent Liceo, dressed in furs it's never cold enough to wear. There is money in this city, a lot of it. Money is made, and money is saved. (A local joke says that copper wire was invented by two Catalans fighting over a *peseta*.) The Catalans pride themselves on their industry and are always careful to make the distinction between themselves and the Spanish.

Yes, indeed, the Catalans are separatist. When my choir was in France performing with a local choir, the conductor asked at the first rehearsal, where is the French choir? and they identified themselves. A moment later, where is the Spanish choir? I hauled my hand back just in time. Silence. After the conductor repeated his question, a strong, clear voice announced: *Nous sommes Catalans.*

In Barcelona, a Spaniard means someone from Spain; this is Catalunya. It's easy to understand the Catalan position. During the *dictadua* (the Franco regime of about 35 years), their language and culture were suppressed. Most Catalans over a certain age can't read or write their language. In an office, for example, in which nearly everyone is Catalan, the memos and correspondence will inevitably be in Spanish. On the other hand, there are some Catalans (usually women who've never worked outside the home) who haven't spoken Spanish since their school days. A few women whom I saw regularly told me they never speak Spanish. They did it with me as a concession, although I was asked more than once why I was learning Spanish when I wasn't living in Spain.

The Catalans are proud of their language and insist that foreigners learn it. But they are a warm and indulgent people and they'll never refuse to speak Spanish. In fact, they'll tolerate any mistake and struggle to understand the wildest attempt at pronunciation. (It's only when you cross the border to France that you remember what linguistic snobbery is—if you're one shade off one vowel sound in an otherwise respectable sentence, they look at you uncomprehendingly, making you wonder if you've slipped into some rare Beothuk dialect.) Nevertheless, trying to learn Spanish in a Catalan city is not easy. When I first arrived in Barcelona I heard enough vaguely familiar sounds to think I could fall back on my old church Latin, but relationships are somewhat limited when all you can do is confess and praise.

Barcelona, you thought: skiing trips to Andorra, weekends in the Pyrenees and wonderful *menus del dia* (those three-course meals, with wine, offered for $5 at midday in all restaurants), sitting on the Ramblas sipping cool *sangria* and nibbling on *tapas* it takes you months to work off. Yes, that too is life in Barcelona, and the joys of the city are not to be underestimated, as the initiated well know. But the pleasure pales when your status turns from tourist to *livyere*.

After a few months home to breathe clean air and bask in quiet (cold quiet, I might add), I returned to the insanity known as Barcelona. Before there was time to be defeated by the city's noisy madness, I realized what it was that had made my time there enriching. It isn't easy to move from an island like Newfoundland to a city as dense as Barcelona (second to Calcutta, they say), but when you break down the dreaded crowds and seek out the individuals, you find a generous, tolerant, humane people. And to add to their charm, some of them now speak broken English with traces of a St. John's accent.

"So, you come back," a former student smiles at me over lunch.

"Yes," I say, delighted that we can now converse at a comfortable level of English. This is the student who always told me on rainy days to put my umbrella in the chicken. (It was one of those attractive mistakes I never had the heart to correct, knowing that my Spanish was just as colourful.)

"I say me today, how is doing Marjorie?" she tells me warmly.

"I've been thinking about you, too," I respond.

She raises her cup of champagne in a welcome back toast and I follow suit.

"Cheese," she smiles at me, proudly.

"Cheese," I echo, my teaching days over.

Marjorie Doyle was born in Newfoundland and Labrador shortly after it joined Canada, which fostered her later interest in the study of that province. She holds an M.A. from Memorial University. Her first book, *A View of Her Own*, was published in 1996, followed by *Newfoundlander in Exile*, in 1997. Doyle has worked on various CBC Radio programs, including *Arts National, The Doyle Bulletin,* and *That Time of the Night.* Her columns have appeared in *The Globe and Mail, The Ottawa Citizen,* the *Evening Telegram,* and *This Magazine.*

1. *Response*

   a. How does Marjorie Doyle create the feeling of what it is like to live in Barcelona? In your answer, refer to both the content and the form of her writing.

   b. Doyle frequently uses the second-person point of view ("But you can only hide out so long in a parking garage.") What might be some reasons for doing this? In what other kinds of writing might you find the second-person point of view?

   c. Did Doyle's essay spark your interest about Barcelona? Would you visit Barcelona if you had the chance? Explain.

   d. Comment on whether travel is a means of understanding one's self and the world at large. Reflect on how your attitudes about travel have been shaped—through personal experience or in some other way?

2. *Language Conventions* *Parentheses* Parentheses ( ) can serve a variety of purposes. Explain some of those purposes, using quotations from "Homage to Barcelona" as examples. How does Doyle's use of parentheses contribute to the style of the essay? Rewrite some of the quotations so they contain no parentheses. Describe the difficulties you faced and your solutions.

3. *Drama* *Improvisation* In a group, improvise one of the scenes that Doyle describes. Try to represent all the details she records in that scene. Before you present your scene, have a group discussion to assign roles and decide generally what will happen during your improvisation.

4. *Media* *Brochure* Use the Internet or library resources to learn more about Barcelona. Use your findings to design and write a travel brochure that promotes Barcelona as a desirable travel destination. Before you create your brochure, decide on a specific audience (families or business travellers, for example); then use visuals and language that are appropriate to that audience. How does the Barcelona depicted in your brochure compare with Doyle's Barcelona? Which one do you think is closer to the "real" Barcelona? Explain.

> *"It is a terrible irony that as formal development reaches more deeply into rain forests, deserts and other isolated environments, it tends to destroy the only cultures that have proved able to thrive in these environments."*

Lessons From a Walk in a Rain Forest

By David Suzuki

FROM CHOCO FOREST, COLOMBIA— To most Canadians the name Colombia conjures up images of coffee. But to biologists, Colombia is home to one of the richest ecosystems on the planet, the Choco tropical rain forest pinched between the Pacific Ocean and the Andes mountain range. It extends from Panama through Colombia to Peru.

Chugging from Bahia Solano to Utria National Park on the *Jestiven*, a wooden boat, I am accompanied by Francis Hallé, a French expert on tropical forests. Hallé is famous for having created a huge, pneumatic platform that can be erected on the canopy where researchers can explore 600 to 800 square metres of the treetops.

Hallé points out the thick cloak of trees extending to the water line. "The first thing people do when they invade such a virgin forest," he says, "is to clear the trees along the shore." Despite the difference in vegetation, the tree-covered mountains and pristine bays remind me of British Columbia.

Utria National Park was formed in 1987 and covers 54,300 hectares of spectacular forest. In a heavy rain, I set off alone to walk across a peninsular saddle along a thin path that is a slimy ribbon of red mud. Serpentine tree roots coil along the forest floor to suck nutrients from the thin topsoil and anchor the immense trunks in place. Though impediments on level ground, the roots provide welcome hand and footholds on the steep hills.

In the forest, temperature and light intensity immediately drop. Thirty metres overhead, the canopy blocks out the sky, preventing growth of the heavy underbrush we think of as jungle. The steady rainfall is intercepted by foliage so the water doesn't pound onto the soil. Even though it has rained constantly, the water in the creeks is crystal clear.

The ground is littered with leaves. In Canada, we classify

trees as deciduous or evergreens, but here the trees shed leaves year round. However, instead of building up to form thick humus, they quickly become food for insects and fungi and thus are recycled back up into the forest biomass.

It's easy to walk along creek beds or through the trees with little vegetation to hamper movement. The noise is constant, a cacophony of buzzing, clicking, and humming of insects and frogs. Walking quietly and slowly, eyes adapting to the shadows and shapes, one begins to notice movement that betrays a frog, a butterfly, a bird. A cosmos of complexity opens up.

Back on the boat, Hallé informs me that "jungle" is a word from India referring to the tangle of secondary growth that results after the initial forest is cleared. It is an insult to call a primary forest a jungle, he says. He draws my attention to trees with special properties—the hard white "tagwa" seeds, six to a cluster within an armoured shell, that can be carved like ivory; fruit trees; parasitic air-breathing plants, lianes, orchids. But when I bring a seed or leaf, he often admits he has no idea what it is. When I ask how much taxonomists know of the species residing in tropical rain forests, Hallé makes a gesture of futility and replies: "It's an impossible mess." He tells me individuals of one species are usually spaced far apart and each may house different spectra of associated species. A lifetime could be spent studying the organisms in a few square metres while an adjacent section could take another lifetime. That's the reason our ignorance is so vast.

Hallé believes the fabled diversity within a tropical rain forest gives it its stability. When one or a few trees are removed, the opening in the canopy allows light to reach the forest floor and stimulates a succession of plants. Over time, like a small nick in the skin, the opening is healed and filled in. But remove a large section of trees and like a mortal wound, the forest cannot repair itself.

Here a destructive parasite is controlled because its target species is not concentrated in an area the way species are in temperate forests. "There's no need for pesticides," Hallé tells me, "because the forest is too diverse to allow an outbreak." Similarly, an introduced exotic species can't explode like rabbits in Australia or purple loosestrife in Canada because there are too many predators able to attack them. So biodiversity is not just a descriptive property of tropical rain forests, it is the very mechanism of its stability for survival.

World demand for lumber and pulp continues to rise while forest plantations cannot deliver wood of quality or quantity. That's why deforestation continues to claim the great forests of the planet and threatens the Choco.

The Choco is the traditional home of perhaps 30,000 aboriginal people belonging to three main groups—Embera, Waunana, and Cuna—who continue to live as they have for thousands of years, depending on the forest for their food, medicines, and materials.

From the airport at Bahia Solano, we take a bus up the coast to the village of El Valle, which is populated by descendants of African slaves who were brought to mine gold more than 400 years ago. We rent a dugout with a motor and guide to take us up the Boro Boro River. After about three hours, we finally leave the plantations, cleared fields, sugar cane, and breadfruit trees to enter primary rain forest. As the river narrows, we drag the dugouts across shallow riffles and around fallen trees and logjams. At one point, we unload the boat and sink it to push it under a huge log blocking the river.

Night falls early and quickly in the tropics and as the light fades, we know we are still hours away from our destination, the Embera village of Boro Boro at the junction with the Mutata River. Five hours after nightfall, we finally reach the settlement, exhausted, wet, but exhilarated by the adventure. Hammocks and mosquito nets are slung in the tiny school, and we soon join the frog calls with snores.

Boro Boro is home for eighty-four people living under thatched huts built on supports two metres above the ground. The tiny cluster of buildings is surrounded by small fields of domesticated plants. Life here revolves around the river for bathing, laundry, food, and transportation. A three-hour hike up the Mutata ends at spectacular falls that drop 400 metres into a huge pool that is considered the source of life and power in the river. The people of Boro Boro fear the power of the place and stay away. Only the shaman goes to the pool to perform rituals to ensure the fecundity of the river and forest.

The villagers tell us they want to keep their culture and way of life. They have heard of proposals to develop the area, which one prime minister referred to as Colombia's "piggy bank." The Pan American Highway, nearly finished, was stopped only when the minister of the newly formed

> The challenge of nonfiction is to marry art and truth.
>
> Phyllis Rose

environment ministry threatened to resign if it wasn't. There are other proposals to build super-ports on the coast, a network of highways to link the ports to cities, and huge dams to deliver electricity to isolated villages. The familiar notion of "development" by extracting the resources of the forest is irresistible in Colombia too.

Colombia's forests, of which Choco is an important part, have the most known bird species (19.4 percent of all the world's known species compared to 17.6 percent in Brazil and 15 percent in Africa) and orchids, the second most amphibians, the third most reptiles, and one of every five bats. This rich tapestry of living things is beyond any scientific comprehension and, if destroyed, will never be duplicated or recreated.

There are people who have had the knowledge and expertise to make a living from these forests for millennia, but their futures are as uncertain as the fragile ecosystems that are their homes. The 1987 United Nations report *Our Common Future* stated: "It is a terrible irony that as formal development reaches more deeply into rain forests, deserts and other isolated environments, it tends to destroy the only cultures that have proved able to thrive in these environments."

Indigenous people throughout Colombia are organizing to resist incursions into their land.

In the Choco, OREWA was formed to represent the Embera, Waunana, and Cuna. But in the government discussions about the future of the Choco, the indigenous people who have always occupied the forests are seldom involved.

The predicament is complicated by an Afro-Colombian population that outnumbers the aboriginal people by ten to one. After escaping slavery, they were able to survive in coastal villages for 200 to 300 years. Lacking the indigenous culture and knowledge base built around the forest, the blacks have eked out a living and are desperate for the material benefits of modern life.

In negotiations with the government, OREWA has included Afro-Colombians as stakeholders in the forest lands. But impoverished people are easy prey to the blandishments of developers. Promises of jobs, electricity, and television tempt them to welcome roads and ports. To them, the forest is a resource that can be converted to money. If we in Canada haven't been able to resist the siren's call of development, why should people who start out with far less?

Environmentalists in industrial nations of the North are concerned about the fate of tropical rain forests that have been labelled the "lungs of the planet" and the "wellsprings of biodiversity." Here in Colombia, Latin

Americans demand to know why they are expected to save the forests when countries in the North haven't protected theirs. In the debate over vanishing forests, the people who live in them are often forgotten.

Travelling through the Choco rain forest along mud tracks, one can't help but wonder why magnificent forests like this are being traded for squalid towns and villages of impoverished people and of scrawny cattle grazing on barren hills. Is there no other way to create income for the human residents while preserving the forest ecosystem?

According to Francis Hallé there is. He has spent his life studying plant growth in the canopy of tropical rain forests. When I ask him whether we know enough to cut down the likes of the Choco and regrow it, he replies, "Absolutely not!" He points out that a tree plantation is not a forest and that rapidly growing species like eucalyptus or pine imported from other parts of the world seldom perform as expected. Hallé says ideas developed from northern temperate forests are inappropriate for the tropics, where vegetation and soil are completely different.

The secret to the resilience and productivity of a tropical rain forest is its tremendous variety of living forms. As long as the forest is intact, people can cut into it as the indigenous inhabitants have for thousands of years, and the cut will heal. But if the clearing is large, then like a spider web that loses too many threads, the system collapses.

Throughout tropical countries of Africa, South America, and southeast Asia, Hallé finds a sophisticated human practice called agroforestry (AF) that has sustained communities for hundreds, if not thousands, of years. Hallé has observed carvings on Indonesian temples depicting AF practices about A.D. 1000.

AF requires a profound knowledge of plants that can be used for a variety of needs. Useful plants are collected from intact primary forests and deliberately planted in a surrounding AF Buffer Zone. Here one finds small shrubs, medicinal plants, parasitic lianes for rope and furniture, and large trees that yield wood, edible leaves, and fruits.

Fifty percent of the biodiversity present in the primary forest can be found in an AF Buffer Zone. In fact, says Hallé, it has only been in the past century that foresters recognized that the AF Buffer Zone is human-created and not a natural forest. Domesticated animals are grazed in the Buffer Zone, where the huts and villages are also located. The primary forest remains intact to provide new material during collecting expeditions.

Hallé says, "Agroforesters are true capitalists; their capital is biological and it is constantly growing." Usually, they live off the interest but when they are confronted with an emergency, they may harvest more than they usually take, sure in the knowledge that over time, the forest will grow back.

Hallé's description of agroforestry makes one wonder why it isn't being pushed everywhere as a sustainable alternative to massive clearing of tropical forests. Hallé's explanation is: "AF is always local and small-scale. People are constantly coming out of the villages with baskets of fruits, vegetables, meat, and plant products for trade or sale, but that doesn't yield the large and quick profits that governments and multinational companies want."

Since all useful organisms are harvested from the Buffer Zone, the primary forest is protected as a priceless source of genetic material. Communities practising AF don't need outside help or expertise because they depend on their own time-tested indigenous knowledge.

Hallé observes that practitioners of AF are always women. Men may be recruited to cut trees down or lift heavy things, but women are in charge. He believes it reflects women's concerns with food and children's health. "Large-scale monoculturing seems to be more of a male impulse, while diverse, small-scale ventures seem more feminine," Hallé says.

AF exposes the insanity of destroying tropical forests for a one-time-only recovery of cash. AF rests on the fundamental capital of nature, which, if protected, can sustain communities and ecosystems indefinitely. But that flies in the face of the current suicidal path of global economics that glorifies human creativity and productivity above all.

Dr. David Suzuki was born in Vancouver, B.C., in 1936. He is an award-winning scientist, broadcaster, and environmentalist, and Chair of the David Suzuki Foundation—a charity concerned with environmental issues. Suzuki is well known as the host of CBC's science TV series, *The Nature of Things,* and is the author of over 30 books. He has received numerous awards for his work, including the Order of Canada, and is internationally recognized for his work in the field of ecology.

1. Response

a. Create a map that would be a useful accompaniment to David Suzuki's essay.

b. What did you know about David Suzuki before you read "Lessons From a Walk in a Rain Forest"? Summarize your prior knowledge. Do you regard Suzuki as a credible commentator on ecological issues? Explain.

c. In point form, note the factual information about rain forests contained in the essay. What steps could you take to establish the reliability of this information?

d. Make a list of environmental issues (local, national, or global) that interest you. Choose one of the issues and write a brief explanation of why that issue is important generally, and to you in particular.

2. Literature Studies Expository Writing

The *purpose* of expository writing is to convey information to the reader, but the *challenge* is to keep the reader interested. Reread "Lessons From a Walk in a Rain Forest" and note the techniques Suzuki uses to hold the reader's attention. Provide specific examples of each technique. Did Suzuki meet the challenge of engaging your interest? Why or why not?

3. Writing Fact Sheet

In activity 1. d above, you selected one environmental issue of interest to you. Your task is to draft a **fact sheet** covering that issue. Do some research to gather background information. Your fact sheet might provide some or all of the following: statistics, definitions, answers to frequently-asked questions, predictions, graphs, maps, resource lists, and so on. When you present your fact sheet, explain what was most difficult about preparing it

A **fact sheet** presents key information about a particular topic, issue, or organization. It provides concise answers to basic questions. Some fact sheets are written in point form, others in full sentences.

4. Critical Thinking

A critical thinker seeks out information from a variety of sources before coming to a conclusion. In a group, make a plan for obtaining additional perspectives about rain forest management and preservation; then carry out that plan. What difficulties did you face in locating and analysing the information? Based on your experience, develop five guidelines or principles for obtaining and evaluating multiple points of view on an issue.

"W.O. Mitchell was larger than life, even in life."

In Memory of W.O. Mitchell

By Fred Stenson

n 1974, when I published my first book, a book which aspired to be funny, a reviewer wrote, "Stenson is trying to be Western Canada's next W.O. Mitchell." It was a strange statement, not least of all because the job was taken and remained so for twenty-four years. But that was what the reviewer wrote and, having established what my goal was, he went on to demonstrate, illustrate and prove that I wasn't apt to attain it. It was a negative review, no doubt about it, but I was thrilled. One way or another I had been mentioned in the same sentence as W.O. Mitchell, and I was honoured.

Asked to speak at this tribute, to speak about W.O. Mitchell's humour, I am honoured again. Part of how I will pay tribute to W.O. will be to illustrate, once again, that, when it comes to being funny, I can't hold a candle to him. Few people could.

Twenty-two years ago, in a large gathering of Canadian writers, W.O. Mitchell came up to me and gave me a powerful hug. Lifted me right off the floor. He had mistaken me for Andreas Schroeder. He expressed his delight at seeing me.

I expressed my delight at seeing him. After a time, we moved on. I remember that, by then, he was looking somewhat perplexed. I tell that story now because of how much I wished at the time that the exuberance of that greeting had been meant for me. I was about 23 years old and I admired W.O. Mitchell greatly. He was a writer and he was funny—and those were the two things in life that I most hoped to be.

I actually did meet W.O. Mitchell not long after, when he was teaching at the Banff Centre and I was working there too. I was working in the farthest corner of the Cameron Hall basement in a room with blacked out windows. I called out numbers—sort of like a bingo announcer—16, 29—to two fellows who spun wheels and pushed buttons on a giant animation camera called "The Oxberry."

The people in the writing program at Banff were kind enough to invite me to some of their parties and, if I could escape the Oxberry, I went. A mushroom-coloured, half-starved gnome who scoffed as much Camembert and red wine as possible. And the great attraction of those evenings was the opportunity to watch and listen to W.O. Mitchell in action.

I hope my writer friends will forgive me for saying so, but writers are usually a little smaller in life than in print. And why not? In print you get as many runs at a thing as you care to take. In life, you get one chance and often you blow it. But, in the case of W.O. Mitchell, this was not true. W.O. Mitchell was larger than life, even in life.

Whatever his mood, sunny or furious, he dependably poured forth a stream of verbiage that was original, irreverent, unexpected—and funny. I was just one of the admiring many and I didn't get to know him well. I expect he wondered why the hell, in the full-blown glory of both youth and summer, I didn't go out and get myself some sun. As for me, I listened and laughed until my face was sore.

Though I was never an official student of W.O. Mitchell's, I learned a lot from him, by watching and listening. I learned about pacing, at which he was a master, and pausing, and turning abruptly against the flow of your own story, and writing dialogue between people who aren't listening to a damn thing the other is saying. I learned about mixing high and low diction, and repeating a joke so that people will laugh more each time they hear it—and when to stop at the peak of that arc, before it starts going the other way.

Biography lends to death a new terror.

Oscar Wilde

I learned what happens to a bull's ass in fly time, and about the nervousness of cats in rooms full of rocking chairs, and about the speed achieved by manure in its passage through a goose. I learned that the correct words for expressing the song of the meadowlark are: *"Tar Tar Diddly Boo."*

I learned that humour is a serious craft and that one of its fundaments is the breaking of taboo. I remember W.O. explaining one time, very seriously, that if you want a child to laugh, what you must say is PEE PEE. POO POO. If you want to make an adult laugh, what you should say is PEE PEE. POO POO. And if they're still not laughing, say "FART." He had discovered that people don't change much from when they're children, and that often the job of the humorist is to say the taboo things on behalf of others, especially those who can't themselves.

I remember another time when W.O. Mitchell was giving a reading in a small town in eastern Alberta, one renowned as the heart of the bible belt, or at very least a valve in that heart. It was a full house as usual and W.O. Mitchell out and performed one of his more scatological stories. (There's a five dollar word for you. Scatological.) And that audience, which looked very like a rural church audience, all dressed up and permed, laughed until they cried. No one looked offended, or even vaguely uncomfortable. W.O. Mitchell was calling a bull's ass a bull's ass, on all our behalfs, and we were grateful.

On that same occasion, W.O. invited me to have dinner with him and Andy Russell—and I couldn't go, or I thought I couldn't. I have kicked myself ever since. I decided solemnly that when your life is so complicated that you can't sit down to dinner with two of the people you most admire, it's time to get a new life.

Anyway, the invitation came as W.O. was sitting in the lobby taking snuff and a small boy had come up to ask what he was doing. A lot of adults would not have bothered to explain but W.O. did. He explained in great detail, in great seriousness. He demonstrated frequently. He explained snuff-taking to that small boy as if it were something we must all do eventually and that it was his duty to make sure that the boy grew up knowing how to do it right. The teaching was done the way Jake would have taught the Kid, or like Daddy Sherry would have taught young Keith. Small boys, whose fathers are dead or otherwise not of much use, was always a big theme in the writing and humour of W.O. Mitchell. The job of the men who taught the boys was mostly to counteract the forces of society that aspire to regulate and restrict fun. W.O. Mitchell's message, expressed in this way, was that it was okay to have fun, that most of what you are told is bad might be good at least once in a while, and that it's best to find out for yourself in any case.

One of the great things about being young is that you simply *are*. Only as a grown-up do you find out *what* you are. In my case, I found out that I was a rural Western Canadian, which made me different than what most other folks were. I discovered the uniqueness of the culture I had grown up in.

In my opinion, rural Western Canadians are some of the funniest people on this earth. When I go home to Twin Butte, Alberta, I don't tell many stories or jokes. Mainly, I listen. And I laugh. And I marvel at how these people seem to effortlessly contain within them the art of humour. I think W.O. Mitchell must have discovered that too—in places like Weyburn and Castor and High River—how, in the cigar smoke around the potbelly stove at the curling rink on a night in the dead of winter, some of the funniest stories anywhere were told by people who would never stand on a stage or write much more than their names on a cheque, or an IOU. I believe W.O. Mitchell heard those stories, and ingested the secrets of their manufacture, and made a brilliant career out of never forgetting where he came from.

Sometimes I worry that my parents' generation—almost to the birth year, the W.O. Mitchell generation—will be forgotten; swept aside by the current, and I think deeply foolish and empty, fad of globalization. Nobody lives globally. W.O. Mitchell knew that. I expect he also knew that the thing closest to global is a good, "regional" story, well told. In that sense, in the sense that his books will always exist like a rosetta stone for the rediscovery of Western Canadian rural life, W.O. Mitchell has done more for the West than any of the powers of righteousness and wrath he used to counsel small boys to guard against.

It makes me very proud to have been asked to come here and speak about the humour of W.O. Mitchell. He was a profoundly, and seriously, funny man.

Fred Stenson has written the novels *Last One Home*, and *Lonesome Hero*, and the short story collections *Working Without a Laugh Track* and *Teeth*. He has also written for series on *History TV* and *Discovery*.

W.O. Mitchell. Photo by Charles Clarke

Do you think this photo portrait of W.O. Mitchell is a good representation of the qualities Stenson describes in his essay? Explain.

1. Response

    a. What purposes do you think Fred Stenson had in mind when he wrote this tribute? How well does he achieve those purposes? Explain.

    b. Do some research to obtain background information about W.O. Mitchell, then create a time line that traces his achievements as a writer.

    c. Paraphrase what Stenson means by the last line of his tribute. What examples does Stenson provide to help him make this point?

    d. In the second-last paragraph, Stenson calls Mitchell's writing a *rosetta stone*. Define this term, and explain what Stenson is suggesting with this comparison. Do you think any writer's work can be a rosetta stone for a whole community or nation? Provide reasons, and evidence if possible, for your view.

    e. If someone were writing a tribute in your honour, what personal achievements and qualities would you want them to mention?

2. *Language Focus* *Colloquial Language* In his tribute, Stenson chooses to quote several examples of W.O. Mitchell's use of *colloquial language* (everyday, informal language). What explanation does Stenson offer in defence of colloquialism? How does he demonstrate that he has considered the appropriateness of using this language? Do you agree with its use? Why or why not?

3. *Oral Language* *Reading Aloud* "A Tribute to W.O. Mitchell" was meant to be delivered as a speech. Select a passage (about four or five paragraphs) and practise reading it aloud. Before you present your reading, experiment with pacing, volume, and tone of voice. Do you enjoy public speaking? Give your view on the rewards and/or challenges of addressing an audience.

4. *Writing* *Tribute* Discuss the features of a tribute, referring to this selection as a model. Write your own tribute to someone you know and admire.

5. *Making Connections* Read an example of W.O. Mitchell's work, and write a brief review of it. Describe your critical assessment of the work, as well as your personal response to it. Include quotations that support your conclusions.

Mann and Machine

from *Contemporary Canadian Biographies*

Few people know exactly what to make of Steve Mann, a pioneer in the field of wearable computers. "A physicist once said he felt that I had the intelligence of a dozen experts in his discipline," Mann told Steve Ditlea of MIT's *Technology Review*. "A few minutes later, someone else said they thought I was mentally handicapped." Despite the mixed reactions, Mann's faith in wearable computers has never faltered. "Some things look crazy now," he told *Business Day*, "but will make sense in about 20 years."

Mann's interest in wearable electronic devices seems to run in the family. His father was a hobbyist who built what may have been the first wearable radio in the 1950s. As a high-school student in Hamilton, Ontario, Mann was known as Computer Steve. He would do strange things, like show up at school dances wearing a sound-controlled device with a light-emitting diode that changed colour in time with the music. He also built a Walkman and a boombox before the commercial versions were on the market. In the 1970s, he came up with portable battery-powered light sources he called photographer's assistants; he used them to create altered perceptions of visual reality that he dubbed light paintings.

In 1981, Mann built his first true wearable computer, using an Apple II placed in a knapsack. It transmitted and received information through antennae mounted in a helmet. These early proto-types, made from scavenged computer parts, electronic camera flashes and toy walkie-talkies, weighed as much as 45 kilograms and made him look like an alien creature. "People would cross the street to avoid me," he told Ditlea.

Mann's wearable computers have been in a continuous process of evolution ever since. In 1982, he began to experiment with building components directly into his clothing. In his first year at McMaster University, he built a rig that allowed him to connect—through a serial data cable—with a friend. He added sensors that monitored his heart rate and other physiological signals and later created something he called a vibravest, which remains part of his technological repertoire today. The vest used radar to trigger vibrations that showed the size of objects in his path, as well as how far away they were.

By the mid-1990s, Mann's rig consisted of a computer clipped to his belt, a one-handed keyboard called a Twiddler, a helmet-mounted video camera with antennae, and a visor with a built-in monitor that enabled him to watch computerized video images as they were being

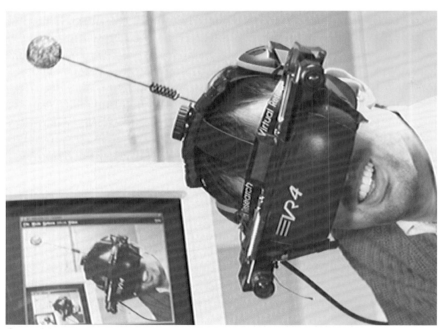

Steve Mann

What elements of this photo suggest that it was carefully thought out and composed? In a sentence or two, state what this image tells the viewer about Steve Mann.

recorded. WearComp7, the name of the current version of his creation, includes a hard drive, miniature keyboard and radio equipment that are strapped across his back and chest. His sweater conceals sensors that monitor body temperature, breathing and heart rate. Sensors in his shoes monitor each step and chunky black sunglasses called WearCam conceal a tiny camera and laser beam that write patterns directly onto his eye, so that images and text seem to hover on objects that exist in the real world. Mann calls the resulting combination of human and computer a cyborg—short for "cybernetic organism," a term coined by author Manfred Clynes in 1960 to describe a technologically aug-mented human being.

The effect of this equipment can be disconcerting, to say the least. In conversation, wrote Jan Cienski of Associated Press: "(Mann's) eyes often shift between the person he is talking with and his computer screen, depending on which is more interesting." Mann defends the effect of the technology on others. "There are times when you want to be isolated. You still want to be aware of your surroundings but scale them out. I often turn the outside world gray while I do my work. All those things can be better done with a curtain between me and the out-side world."

In 1991, Mann enrolled at the Massachusetts Institute of Technol-ogy in Cambridge, Massachusetts. His aim was to earn his Ph.D. at the school's Media Lab, which had been founded in 1985 by Nicholas Negroponte. At first, Negroponte told Judith Gaines of the Fort Worth *Star-Telegram*, Mann's ideas were "very much on the lunatic fringe." In fact, for several years, he was the only person working on the concept. Eventually, however, the faculty and students became intrigued, and Mann established what would become the Media Lab's Wearable Computer Project. It wasn't until 1995, Mann told Ditlea, that his work began to attract serious attention from his peers. By 1997, the "lunatic fringe" was becoming almost mainstream; that year, a conference Mann had proposed to the Institute of Electrical and Electronic Engineers' Computer Society attracted more than 700 researchers, and the accom-panying fashion show drew an audience of more than 3,000. After grad-uating from MIT in 1997, Mann joined the department of electrical and computer engineering at the University of Toronto.

In fact, Mann's ideas had been attracting the attention of a curious public and the media long before they became professionally accept-able. In the 1980s, he found himself becoming a kind of cyborg per-formance artist as he began receiving invitations to demonstrate his wearable computer at galleries and other events. In 1994, his Wearable Wireless Webcam, a helmet-mounted camera that transmitted images of whatever he was looking at through antennae to his Web page, drew a great deal of media comment. As a result, Mann began receiving as many as 30,000 e-mail messages every day from visitors to his Web site. When he invited the public to experience a virtual reality version of Boston's First Night New Year's Eve festivities in 1995, so many people tried to connect that his system crashed under the load. Mann even made the pages of the *National Enquirer* when he replaced the broken thermostat in his apartment with a radio receiver that used signals from sensors in his underwear to control the heat by measuring his body temperature. The headline read, "Web Man Walking."

Though he welcomes the attention, Mann and others are convinced that his technology is much more than a freaky media fad. They believe that his work will enable people to create new forms of communication; for example, Mann's wife is able to help him pick out the ripest fruits and vegetables at the grocery store even when she isn't physically present. "If everyone has this sort of connection, then we all become more productive," Mann told Dylan Jones of *People Weekly*.

A variety of uses have been suggested for the rig. It could function as a personal safety device, both as a sort of personal black box that records information and as part of a virtual community of individuals watching out for one another. The device could assist victims of Alzheimer's by helping them remember where they put things. For the visually impaired, it could connect a camera to a computer that would recognize faces or compress visual images into a smaller area for people with limited peripheral vision. At the 1997 Beauty and the Bits wearable computer show in Cambridge, Massachusetts, a design called Accessor-eyes featured a navigational system that would guide the blind by using audible directional clicks. "This way, you don't have to reconfigure the world, you just have to reconfigure the individuals," Mann told Robert Everett-Green of *The Globe and Mail*.

Mann has also suggested that the machine could have a more political purpose. He objects to the video cameras that have become almost omnipresent in urban environments and used his wearable computer to produce a short film titled *Shooting Back*. It explored the issue of what he calls "unreciprocated video surveillance." He also uses his wearable computer as part of a personal crusade against advertising. "I see it as personal empowerment," he told J. L. O'Brien of *Computer Dealer News*. "If the eye is the window to the soul, shouldn't it have some locks on it? Right now, we walk around with things unlocked and our minds are open for anybody to shove anything they want in there, and that is theft of my solitude. Billboards are theft. Nobody asked my permission to put that image of Calvin Klein underwear into my head."

Mann uses his computer to replace advertisements with something he would rather look at—images of his own choosing, for example, or e-mail messages. He calls this mixture of real and electronic worlds "mediated reality." It's something very different from virtual reality, he insists. "Virtual reality is flawed because you are shutting out the real world. It's like putting on a blindfold," he told Mark Nusca of *The National Post*. "Mediated reality connects you to the real world." In effect, his wearable computer enables Mann to place a thin electronic membrane between himself and the world.

There is a sense that Mann's real interest in wearable computers stems from his earliest experiments with photography. He sometimes calls the system his visual memory prosthetic. His most recent versions constantly record visual information in a memory buffer. If something unusual happens, sensors pick up the sudden change in Mann's heart rate, and the video record of the event can be pulled from the buffer into permanent storage. For Mann, this represents a step forward in the relationship between human and machine. "Your brain is using the machine as a second brain, and it's using your brain as a second CPU," he told Everett-Green. "It's a two-way street. My machine modifies me and I modify it." This is a prime example of what Mann calls "human-istic intelligence," a collaboration between human and computer, which he views as different from artificial intelligence. "My point is that computers are really good at some things and humans are really good at others," he told Nusca. He believes that the wearable computer will bring out the best in both human and machine.

Others, too, have ideas about the potential of wearable computers. At a 1996 conference on wearable computers, many possible applications were discussed and, since then, some of these have become reality. For example, Xybernaut Corp., based in Fairfax, Virginia, recently released the fourth generation of its Mobile Assistant, a wearable computer used in manufacturing situations where workers not only need to use computers but must also be able to move around the factory or have both hands free for their work. The United States Army is testing prototypes that map a soldier's location, show where the enemy is hiding, and enable him or her to aim and fire a weapon without being exposed to the enemy. The Army is also testing a T-shirt made of cotton woven with fibre optics that can relay medical information from wounded soldiers.

All this means that the wearable computer could be big business. Research in the field is sponsored not just by Microsoft and IBM, but by Nike, Levi-Strauss and Swatch. Sony owns the rights to the name WebMan, and is planning a consumer version of the wearable computer. Companies like Nokia, Motorola, Hewlett-Packard and Samsung are also interested in the concept.

In September 1998, Mann introduced University of Toronto students to what he calls the world's first course on how to be a cyborg. Flyers advertising the course were posted around the campus. They read: "You will be assimilated. Become the world's first 'cyborgs.' " The course attracted 20 electrical engineering students who explored the theory, philosophy and practice of wearable computers and used the machines to produce collaborative digital visual art. Though Xybernaut donated 20 Mobile Assistants to the class, students quickly became aware of the shortcomings of the technology. There were complaints about its weight and short battery life, as well as its reliance on voice-recognition software. "I despise the whole idea (of operating the equipment by voice recognition)," Mann told Everett-Green. "If I'm on the subway talking to myself, people will think I'm crazy." Despite these technical limitations, however, the course was a success, and most of the students are planning to pursue further studies in the field.

For Mann, the next step is to make the equipment less obtrusive. In the beginning, he told Everett-Green, "There was a freakish, outlandish essence to it that I'm trying to shake now. The early stuff used to look a little dorky. I got a lot of gee-whiz reactions." He is certain that as the machines continue to develop, they will become smaller, lighter and less noticeable.

Mann and machine have become inseparable. He removes the devices only to sleep, shower, or swim. "I wouldn't live any other way," he wrote in MIT's *Technology Review*. "I have melded technology with my person and achieved a higher state of awareness than would otherwise be possible ... Every morning I decide how I will see the world that day. Sometimes I give myself eyes in the back of my head. Other days I add a sixth sense, such as the ability to feel objects at a distance." He can use visual effects—a stroboscope, for example—to see things he would otherwise be unable to see.

Despite his enthusiasm for the devices, Mann acknowledges that there is a downside to wearable computers. On his Web site, he warns those who would build their own machines of the potential dangers of faulty wiring, long-term exposure to radio waves, eye damage, reduced attention span and flashbacks. There is another problem associated with the technology, too. Speaking at a 1996 conference, Mann wryly confessed: "I do find myself in a somewhat confused and bewildered state when my system goes down."

I. *Response*

a. Reread the profile and list the words and phrases used to describe Steve Mann, including descriptions appearing in statements by Mann himself and others. Sort the expressions into categories. How do you account for the wide variation? Write a description that expresses your own view of Mann.

b. In your own words, explain how *mediated reality* differs from *virtual reality*, and how *humanistic intelligence* differs from *artificial intelligence*.

c. Reread the description of WearComp7 that appears in the fifth paragraph. Look as well at the capabilities of the technology as described in the second-last paragraph. Would you want to try WearComp7 yourself, becoming what Mann calls a "cyborg"? Give reasons for your answer.

d. Mann says, "Nobody asked my permission to put that image of Calvin Klein underwear into my head." Do you think Mann's solution to omnipresent advertising makes sense? Explain your point of view and suggest alternative ways of coping.

2. *Media* Ad

Mann seems to have high expectations for the technology he is developing, as do many prominent businesses. Develop an ad that conveys the value and potential of one of Mann's computer innovations. Create your ad for a medium of your choice.

3. *Writing* Science Fiction

Is it true that "the wearable computer will bring out the best in both human and machine"? Write a short science fiction story that provides your perspective on that proposition.

4. *Language Conventions* Comma Use

Commas have more functions than any other punctuation mark. Their uses include separating items in a series, separating the different parts of a place name, dividing a subordinate clause from a main clause, marking the beginning and end of an appositive or a non-restrictive clause, and inserting a pause before a quotation. Reread "Mann and Machine" to find examples of each of these uses of the comma. If necessary, use a reference book to clarify the rules for using commas.

In 1962, Nelson Mandela went to Algeria for military training and was arrested for leaving South Africa illegally and for incitement to strike. Mandela was jailed for five years and, while in prision, was charged with sabotage and sentenced to life imprisonment.

from Long Walk to Freedom

The Autobiography of Nelson Mandela

By Nelson Mandela

We were awakened at 5:30 each morning by the night warder, who clanged a brass bell at the head of our corridor and yelled, *"Word wakker! Staan op!"* (Wake up! Get up!) I have always been an early riser and this hour was not a burden to me. Although we were roused at 5:30, we were not let out of our cells until 6:45, by which time we were meant to have cleaned our cells and rolled up our mats and blankets. We had no running water in our cells and instead of toilets had iron sanitary buckets known as "ballies." The ballies had a diameter of ten inches and a concave porcelain lid on the top that could contain water. The water in this lid was meant to be used for shaving and to clean our hands and faces.

At 6:45, when we were let out of our cells, the first thing we did was to empty our ballies. The ballies had to be thoroughly cleansed in the sinks at the end of the hallway or they created a stench. The only pleasant thing about cleaning one's ballie was that this was the one moment in those early days when we could have a whispered word with our colleagues. The warders did not like to linger when we cleaned them, so it was a chance to talk softly.

During those first few months, breakfast was delivered to us in our cells by prisoners from the general section. Breakfast consisted of mealie pap porridge, cereal made from maize or corn, which the general prisoners would slop in a bowl and then spin through the bars of our cells. It was a clever trick and required a deft hand so as not to spill any of the porridge.

After a few months, breakfast was delivered to us in the courtyard in old metal oil drums. We would help ourselves to pap using simple metal bowls. We each received a mug of what was described as coffee, but which was in fact ground-up maize, baked until it was black, and then brewed with hot water. Later, when we were able to go into the courtyard to serve ourselves, I would go out into the courtyard and jog around the perimeter until breakfast arrived.

Like everything else in prison, diet is discriminatory.

In general, Coloureds and Indians received a slightly better diet than Africans, but it was not much of a distinction. The authorities liked to say that we received a balanced diet; it was indeed balanced—between the unpalatable and the inedible. Food was the source of many of our protests, but in those early days, the warders would say, "Ag, you kaffirs[1] are eating better in prison than you ever ate at home!"

In the midst of breakfast, the guards would yell, *"Val in! Val in!"* (Fall in! Fall in!), and we would stand outside our cells for inspection. Each prisoner was required to have the three buttons of his khaki jacket properly buttoned. We were required to doff our hats as the warder walked by. If our buttons were undone, our hats unremoved, or our cells untidy, we were charged with a violation of the prison code and punished with either solitary confinement or the loss of meals.

After inspection we would work in the courtyard hammering stones until noon. There were no breaks; if we slowed down, the warders would yell at us to speed up. At noon, the bell would clang for lunch and another metal drum of food would be wheeled into the courtyard. For Africans, lunch consisted of boiled mealies, that is, coarse kernels of corn. The Indian and Coloured prisoners received samp, or mealie rice, which consisted of ground mealies in a souplike mixture. The samp was sometimes served with vegetables whereas our mealies were served straight.

For lunch we often received *phuzamandla*, which means "drink of strength," a powder made from mealies and a bit of yeast. It is meant

---

[1]**kaffir:** a derogatory term for a black person, used mainly in South Africa, especially during the apartheid era

to be stirred into water or milk and when it is thick, it can be tasty, but the prison authorities gave us so little of the powder that it barely colored the water. I would usually try to save my powder for several days until I had enough to make a proper drink, but if the authorities discovered that you were hoarding food, the powder was confiscated and you were punished.

After lunch we worked until four, when the guards blew shrill whistles and we once again lined up to be counted and inspected. We were then permitted half an hour to clean up. The bathroom at the end of our corridor had two seawater showers, a saltwater tap, and three large galvanized metal buckets, which were used as bathtubs. There was no hot water. We would stand or squat in these buckets, soaping ourselves with the brackish water, rinsing off the dust from the day. To wash yourself with cold water when it is cold outside is not pleasant, but we made the best of it. We would sometimes sing while washing, which made the water seem less icy. In those early days, this was one of the only times that we could converse.

Precisely at 4:30, there would be a loud knock on the wooden door at the end of our corridor, which meant that supper had been delivered. Common-law prisoners were used to dish out the food to us and we would return to our cells to eat it. We again received mealie pap porridge, sometimes with the odd carrot or piece of cabbage or beetroot thrown in—but one usually had to search for it. If we did get a vegetable, we would usually have the same one for weeks on end, until the carrots or cabbage were old and moldy and we were thoroughly sick of them. Every other day, we received a small piece of meat with our porridge. The meat was usually mostly gristle.

For supper, Coloured and Indian prisoners received a quarter loaf of bread (known as a *katkop*, that is, a cat's head, after the shape of the bread) and a slab of margarine. Africans, it was presumed, did not care for bread as it was a "European" type of food.

Typically, we received even less than the meager amounts stipulated in the regulations. This was because the kitchen was rife with smuggling. The cooks—all of whom were common-law prisoners—kept the best food for themselves or their friends. Often they would lay aside the tastiest morsels for the warders in exchange for favors or preferential treatment.

At 8 P.M., the night warder would lock himself in the corridor with us, passing the key through a small hole in the door to another warder outside. The warder would then walk up and down the corridor, ordering us to go to sleep. No cry of "lights out" was ever given on Robben Island because the single mesh-covered bulb in our cell burned day and night. Later, those studying for higher degrees were permitted to read until ten or eleven.

The acoustics along the corridor were quite good, and we would try to chat a bit to each other before going to sleep. But if we could hear a whisper quite clearly, so could the warder, who would yell, *"Stilte in die gang!"* (Quiet in the passage!) The warder would walk up and down a few times to make sure we were not reading or writing. After a few months, we would sprinkle a handful of sand along the corridor so that we could hear the warder's footsteps and have time to stop talking or hide any contraband. Only when we were quiet did he take a seat in the small office at the end of the passage where he dozed until morning.

One morning ... we were taken to the head office. The head office was only about a quarter of a mile away and was a simple stone structure that resembled our own section. Once there, we were lined up to have our fingerprints taken, which was routine prison service business. But while waiting, I noticed a warder with a camera. After our fingerprints had been taken, the chief warder ordered us to line up for photographs. I motioned to my colleagues not to move, and I addressed the warder: "I would like you to produce the document from the commissioner of prisons authorizing our pictures to be taken." Photographs of prisoners required such authorization.

It was always valuable to be familiar with regulations, because the warders themselves were often ignorant of them and could be intimidated by one's superior knowledge. The warder was taken aback by my request and was unable to offer any explanation or produce anything in writing from the commissioner of prisons. He threatened to charge us if we did not consent to have our photographs taken, but I said that if there was no authorization, there would be no pictures, and that is where the matter remained.

As a rule, we objected to having our pictures taken in prison on the grounds that it is generally demeaning to be seen as a prisoner. But there was one photograph I did consent to, the only one I ever agreed to while on Robben Island.

A word is not a crystal, transparent and unchanged; it is the skin of a living thought, and may vary greatly in color and content according to the circumstances and the time in which it is used.

Oliver Wendell Holmes

One morning, a few weeks later, the chief warder, instead of handing us hammers for our work in the courtyard, gave us each needles and thread and a pile of worn prison jerseys. We were instructed to repair the garments, but we discovered that most of these jerseys were frayed beyond repair. This struck us as a curious task, and we wondered what had provoked the change. Later that morning, at about eleven o'clock, the front gate swung open, revealing the commanding officer with two men in suits. The commanding officer announced that the two visitors were a reporter and photographer from the *Daily Telegraph* in London. He related this as if visiting members of the international press were a regular diversion for us.

Although these men were our first official visitors, we regarded them skeptically. Firstly, they were brought in under the auspices of the government, and second, we were aware that the *Telegraph* was a conservative newspaper unlikely to be sympathetic to our cause. We well knew that there was great concern in the outside world about our situation and that it was in the government's interest to show that we were not being mistreated.

The two journalists walked slowly around the courtyard, surveying us. We kept our heads down concentrating on our work. After they had made one circuit, one of the guards plucked me by the shoulder and said, "Mandela, come, you will talk now." In those early days, I often spoke on behalf of my fellow prisoners. The prison service regulations were explicit that each prisoner was permitted to speak only for himself. This was done to negate the power of organization and to neutralize our collective strength. We objected to this rule, but made little headway. We were not even permitted to use the word *we* when we made complaints. But during the first few years, when the authorities needed one prisoner to speak on behalf of others, that individual would be me.

I talked to the reporter, whose name was Mr. Newman, for about twenty minutes, and was candid about both prison and the Rivonia Trial. He was an agreeable fellow, and at the end of our talk, he said he would like the photographer to take my picture. I was reluctant, but in this case relented because I knew the photograph would only be published overseas, and might serve to help our cause if the article was even the least bit friendly. I told him I would agree provided Mr. Sisulu could join me. The image shows the two of us talking in the courtyard about some matter that I can no longer remember. I never saw the article or heard anything about it. The reporters were barely out of sight when the warders removed the jerseys and gave us back our hammers....

In jail, all prisoners are classified by the authorities as one of four categories: A, B, C, or D. A is the highest classification and confers the most privileges; D is the lowest and confers the least. All political prisoners, or what the authorities called "security prisoners," were automatically classified as D on admission. The privileges affected by these classifications included visits and letters, studies, the opportunity to buy groceries and incidentals—all of which are the lifeblood of any prisoner. It normally took years for a political prisoner to raise his status from D to C.

We disdained the classification system. It was corrupt and demeaning, another way of repressing prisoners in general and political prisoners in particular. We demanded that all political prisoners be in one category. Although we criticized it, we could not ignore it: the classification system was an inflexible feature of prison life. If you protested that, as a D Group prisoner, you could receive only one letter every six months, the authorities would say, Improve your behavior, become a C Group prisoner, and you will be able to receive two letters every six months. If you complained that you did not receive enough food, the authorities would remind you that if you were in A Group, you would be able to receive money orders from the outside and purchase extra food at the prison canteen. Even a freedom fighter benefits from the ability to buy groceries and books.

The classifications generally ran parallel to the length of one's sentence. If you were sentenced to eight years, you would generally be classified as D for the first two years, C for the next two, B for the following two, and A for the last two. But the prison authorities wielded the classification system as a weapon against political prisoners, threatening to lower our hard-won classifications in order to control our behavior.

Though I had been in prison for nearly two years before I was taken to Robben Island, I was still in D Group when I arrived. While I desired the privileges that came with the higher classifications, I refused to compromise my conduct. The fastest way to raise one's classification was to be docile and not complain. "Ag, Mandela, you are a troublemaker," the warders would say. "You will be in D Group for the rest of your life."

Every six months, prisoners were called before the prison board to have their classifications evaluated. The board was meant to assess our behavior in terms of prison regulations, but we found that it preferred to act as a political tribunal rather than a mere evaluator of behavior. During my first meeting with the board, the officials asked me questions about the ANC and my beliefs. Although this had nothing to do with the classification system, I was vain enough to answer and think that I might convert them to my beliefs. It was one of the few times we were treated as human beings, and I for one responded. Later I realized that this was simply a technique on the part of the authorities to glean information from us, and I had fallen for it. Shortly afterward, we agreed among ourselves not to discuss politics with the prison board.

As a D Group prisoner, I was entitled to have only one visitor, and to write and receive only one letter every six months. I found this one of the most inhumane restrictions of the prison system. Communication with one's family is a human right; it should not be restricted by the artificial gradations of a prison system. But it was one of the facts of prison life.

Visits and letters were restricted to "first degree" relatives. This was a restriction we not only found irksome but racist. The African sense of immediate family is far different from that of the European or Westerner. Our family structures are larger and more inclusive; anyone who claims descent from a common ancestor is deemed part of the same family.

In prison, the only thing worse than bad news about one's family is no news at all. It is always harder to cope with the disasters and tragedies one imagines than with the reality, however grim or disagreeable. A letter with ill tidings was always preferable to no letter at all.

But even this miserable restriction was abused by the authorities. The anticipation of mail was overwhelming. Mail call took place once a month, and sometimes six months would go by without a letter. To be allowed one letter in six months and then not to receive it is a great blow. One wonders: What has happened to my wife and children, to my mother and my sisters? When I did not receive a letter I felt as dry and barren as the Great Karroo desert. Often the authorities would withhold mail out of spite. I can remember warders saying, "Mandela, we have received a letter for you, but we cannot give it to you." No explanation of why, or whom the letter was from. It required all my self-discipline not to explode at such times. Afterward, I would protest through the proper channels, and sometimes get it.

When letters did arrive, they were cherished. A letter was like the summer rain that could make even the desert bloom. When I was handed a letter by the authorities, I would not rush forward and grab it as I felt like doing, but take it in a leisurely manner. Though I yearned to tear it open and read it on the spot, I would not give the authorities the satisfaction of seeing my eagerness, and I would return slowly to my cell as though I had many things to occupy me before opening a letter from my family.

During the first few months, I received one letter from Winnie, but it was so heavily censored that not much more than the salutation was left. The island's censors would black out the offending passages in ink, but they later changed this when they realized we could wash away the ink and see what was underneath. They began to use razors to slice out whole paragraphs. Since most letters were written on both sides of a single piece of paper, the material on the other side would also be excised. They seemed to relish delivering letters in tatters. The censorship delayed the delivery of mail because warders, some of whom were not proficient in English, might take as long as a month to censor a letter. The letters we wrote were censored as well; they were often as cut up as the letters we received.

At the end of August, after I had been on the island less than three months, I was informed by the authorities that I would have a visitor the following day. They would not tell me who it was. Walter [Sisulu] was informed that he, too, would have a visitor, and I suspected, I hoped, I wished—I believed—that it would be a visit from Winnie and Albertina.

From the moment Winnie learned we had been brought to the island, she had been trying to arrange a visit. As a banned person, Winnie had to receive a special dispensation from the minister of justice, for she was technically not permitted to communicate with me.

Even with the help of the authorities, visiting Robben Island was not an easy proposition. Visits were a maximum of thirty minutes long, and political prisoners were not permitted contact visits, in which the visitor and prisoner were in the same room.

Visits did not seem to be planned in advance by the authorities. One day, they would contact your wife and say, "You have permission to visit your husband tomorrow." This was enormously inconvenient, and often had the effect of making visits impossible. If a family member was able to plan a visit in advance, the authorities would sometimes deliberately delay issuing a permit until after the plane had departed. Since most of the men's families lived far from the Cape and had very little money, visits by family members were often far beyond their means. Some men who came from poor families did not see their wives for many years at a time, if at all. I knew of men who spent a decade or more on Robben Island without a single visit.

The visiting room for noncontact visits was cramped and windowless. On the prisoner's side, there was a row of five cubicles with small square pieces of glass that looked out on identical cubicles on the other side. One sat in a chair and looked through the thick, smudged glass that had a few small holes drilled into it to permit conversation. One had to talk very loudly to be heard. Later the authorities installed microphones and speakers in front of the glass, a marginal improvement.

Walter and I were called to the visitors' office in the later morning and took seats at the far end of the room. I waited with some anxiety, and suddenly, filling out the glass on the other side of the window was Winnie's lovely face. Winnie always dressed up for prison visits, and tried to wear something new and elegant. It was tremendously frustrating not to be able to touch my wife, to speak tenderly to her, to have a private moment together. We had to conduct our relationship at a distance under the eyes of people we despised.

I could see immediately that Winnie was under tremendous strain. Seeing me in such circumstances must have been trying. Just getting to the island itself was difficult, and added to that were the harsh rituals of the prison, the undoubted indignities of the warders, and the impersonality of the contact.

Winnie, I later discovered, had recently received a second banning order and had been terminated from her job at the Child Welfare Office as a result. Her office was searched by the police shortly before she was fired. The authorities were convinced that Winnie was in secret communication with me. Winnie loved her job as a social worker. It was the hands-on end of the struggle: placing babies with adoptive parents, finding work for the unemployed and medical help for the uninsured. The banning and harassment of my wife greatly troubled me: I could not look after her and the children, and the state was making it difficult for her to look after herself. My powerlessness gnawed at me.

Our conversation was awkward at first, and was not made easier by the presence of two warders standing directly behind her and three behind me. Their role was not only to monitor but to intimidate. Regulations dictated that conversation had to be in either English or Afrikaans—African languages were forbidden—and could involve family matters only. Any line of talk that departed from the family and verged on the political might mean the abrupt termination of the visit. If one mentioned a name unfamiliar to the warders, they would interrupt the conversation, and ask who the person was and the nature of the relationship. This happened often, as the warders were generally unfamiliar with the variety and nature of African names. It was frustrating to spend precious minutes of one's visit explaining to the warder the different branches of one's family tree. But their ignorance also worked in our favor: it allowed us to invent code names for people we wanted to talk about and pretend that we were referring to family members.

That first visit was important, for I knew that Winnie was anxious about my health: she had heard stories that we were being physically abused. I quickly informed her that I was fine and she could see that I was fit, though a bit thinner than before. She, too, was thinner, something I always attributed to stress. After a visit in which Winnie's face looked drawn or tense, I would urge her to put on a bit of weight. She was always dieting, and I was always telling her not to. I inquired one by one about all the children, about my mother and sisters, and Winnie's own family.

Suddenly, I heard the warder behind me say, "Time up! Time up!" I turned and looked at him with incredulity. It was impossible that half an hour had passed. But, in fact, he was right; visits always seemed to go by in the blink of an eye. For all the years that I was in prison, I never failed to be surprised when the warder called, "Time up!" Winnie and I were both hustled from our chairs and we waved a quick farewell. I always felt like lingering after Winnie left, just to retain the sense of her presence, but I would not let the warders see such emotion. As I walked back to the cell, I reviewed in my head what we had talked about. Over the next days, weeks, and months, I would return to that one visit again and again. I knew I would not be able to see my wife again for at least six months. As it turned out, Winnie was not able to visit me for another two years.

Nelson Rolihlahla Mandela was born near Umtata in the Transkei, South Africa, on 18 July, 1918. At the University College of Fort Hare, he participated in a protest boycott and was expelled. In 1944, he helped found the African National Congress (ANC) Youth League and organized resistance to discriminatory legislation, countrywide. He was one of the accused in the Treason Trial and, when the ANC was banned after the Sharpeville massacre in 1960, he was detained until 1961, when he went underground to lead a campaign for a new national convention. The military wing of the ANC, Umkhonto we Sizwe (MK) was established in the same year. Mandela was finally released from prison in 1990 and, shortly afterwards, he and his delegation agreed to the suspension of armed struggle. He was inaugurated as the first democratically elected State President of South Africa on 10 May 1994. He retired in 1999 and currently resides in his birthplace.

1. *Response*
   a. In a group, discuss what you know about South Africa, apartheid, and Nelson Mandela. Make point-form notes of the key information you cover in your discussion.
   b. How does the information you learn in this excerpt fit in with what you already know about life in South Africa before the end of apartheid?
   c. What was done to the prisoners to intimidate them and break their spirit? How did Mandela react?
   d. Mandela writes, "My powerlessness gnawed at me." Was he entirely without power during these years in prison? Explain, using references to the selection.
   e. What was your personal response to Mandela's account?
   f. Make a list of five questions you would like to ask Mandela after reading this excerpt from his autobiography.

2. *Language Focus* Diction Find examples of words and phrases that help to create the formal tone that characterizes Mandela's writing. How do you think the warders and officials would have responded to Mandela's formality? What inferences might you draw about Nelson Mandela's character from the way he writes?

3. *Literature Studies* Biography and Autobiography Though biographies and autobiographies both focus on an individual's life story, they have different strengths and weaknesses. What do you think you could learn from Mandela's autobiography that no biography could offer? What might a biography of Mandela offer instead? Make some suggestions about what a reader should keep in mind when reading both formats.

4. *Visual Communication* Create a Presentation Research Mandela's life after he was released from prison. Prepare a visual presentation (a collage, time line, or PowerPoint slide show, for example) of the major events in Mandela's life. Include a commentary that tells the impact Mandela had on his country.

Media

The hand that rules the press, the radio,
the screen and the far-spread magazine,
rules the country.

Learned Hand

Looking at the Media

Essay by CAM MACPHERSON

A *medium* of communication is any method by which we spread information. The human voice was the first medium; our voices enabled us to develop spoken language and become a race of speechmakers and storytellers. Thousands of years later, various societies developed written language which allowed much more complex civilizations to emerge. With written language, we could record information accurately and send it long distances. No longer was the human memory our only storage device. Using tablets, scrolls, and finally printed books, we could store knowledge and accumulate it over generations. As increasing numbers of people learned to read and write, there was an increasing demand for printed material. Through the medium of the printed page, information became accessible to ordinary people, not just the wealthy and privileged.

> **mass media:** any method by which a message is communicated to a large audience at the same time—movies, radio, TV, books, magazines, the Internet
>
> **media text:** any media product —movie, radio show, CD, TV program, et cetera—that is selected for critical examination
>
> **deconstruction:** With any media text that is created from many components, *deconstruction* is the process of taking it apart to analyse its component parts.

Over the past few centuries, science and technology have provided us with different and more powerful ways of recording, storing, and transmitting words, sounds, and images. Today, in our information-rich society, we spend more time using the media than performing any other activity except, perhaps, sleep.

Consider the amount of time you spend watching movies and TV; reading books, magazines, and newspapers; surfing the Internet; listening to music on the radio, computer, or compact disc player; and looking at advertisements. In addition to the mass media that transmit the same information to everyone, there are also a growing number of personal media devices that keep individuals in touch with each other, such as pagers, the telephone, and e-mail.

Why Understanding the Media Is Important

Here are five good reasons to increase your understanding of the media:

1. The media are our major source of entertainment. Think about the time and the money that you, and your family, spend every year to enjoy movies, watch TV, and listen to music. In addition to buying tickets at the local multiplex cinema, many families invest thousands of dollars in TV, stereo, and computer equipment, and probably pay hundreds of dollars a year to a TV cable, or Internet provider. To get the best return for the money you're spending, you need to understand the steadily evolving technology you use, as well as the program and product choices that are available.

2. The media are a major area of employment. One of the fastest growing sectors of our economy is involved with making the shows we watch, the music we listen to, and the computer software that manages our information at school and at work. There are hundreds of career choices available in the media for students who take the time to examine the possibilities and obtain the right training.

3. The media control much of our knowledge and understanding of the world. Most of what we know does not come from direct, personal experience, but through TV, radio, the Internet, and other media sources. How truthful and accurate is this information? Who controls what we see and hear? We need to ask questions about the information the media gives us, and not accept it uncritically.

4. Advertising and public relations messages pay for much of the media content we enjoy, but the purpose of these messages is to persuade us to buy products, accept ideas, and support governments and corporations. We need to examine the persuasive techniques that lie behind these messages so that we can make informed decisions and avoid being easily manipulated.

5. As they entertain us and inform us, the media shape our attitudes and values in a number of ways. The actors and models that are featured in programs and ads influence our ideas of how we should look, dress, and speak. These performers present us with images against which we measure ourselves and those around us. The lifestyles and occupations of people in the media influence our own ideas of how we should live our lives. Unlike our own multicultural society, the societies we see in many of our favourite media programs lack diversity.

ANALYSING MEDIA TEXTS

When we analyse or "deconstruct" media texts we need to remember that every product of the media has three main components. We can understand each component better when we ask some basic questions:

About the text—the product itself—the movie, CD, et cetera
What category does this text fall into? (for example, romance, comedy)
Does the text tell a story or connect to a larger story?
Does the text follow a formula or familiar pattern?
What are the characters in the text like—are they like me?
What do I need to know to understand this text?

About production—the manufacture and distribution process
Where does this text come from? Who created it?
How is this text made? What techniques were used?
How is this text distributed or sold to the public?
What rules or laws affect this text?
Who owns it?
How could I produce a similar text?

About the audience—the reactions of consumers
How does this text appeal to me? What do I like/dislike?
Who is the intended target audience? How do I know?
How does this text appeal to its intended audience?
In what different ways do people use or consume this text?
How would I change this text to make it more enjoyable?

KEY CONCEPTS OF MEDIA STUDIES

Another way to organize our understanding and analysis of media texts is to apply what are called the "key concepts"—fundamental principles that apply to all media texts.

1. All media are constructions:
Media stories, characters, and settings may look natural and completely realistic, but they are artificial, and are only made to look real. Just as performers are carefully made up, dressed, and photographed to create a certain image for the part they are playing, so is the entire text a construction. Everything we see and hear is the product of the skills and decisions of the people who have created and produced the text.

2. The media construct reality:
Much of what we know and believe about the world we have learned through the media. Therefore, our understanding of reality is a

"construct" put together by others. Our impression of a city or country, for example, as shaped by the media, may be quite different from the impression we get when we actually visit the place.

3. Audiences negotiate meaning:
What we get out of a media text—how we respond to it—depends on who we are and what we bring to the text. Our age, gender, education, ethnic background, religion, and other factors influence our response. If one person enjoys a certain kind of music, another person may hate the same music. Whose response is the "right" one? They're both right.

4. Media have commercial implications:
While some individuals may produce a media text just to satisfy their artistic impulses, media products are almost always manufactured to make money. As a result, most media products are designed to have maximum audience appeal, and to increase this appeal the appearance and content of the text may be greatly affected.

5. Media contain ideological and value messages:
The media reflect the values of their creators and sponsors, and often stress the values of consumerism, and a middle-class, western way of looking at the world. Most TV shows, for example, deal with the lives of successful, attractive, middle-class people. Similarly, while some movies may glamorize criminals, they almost always get caught in the end.

6. Media have social implications:
Media products are powerful and persuasive. As a result, they can influence how we think, shop, dress, behave, judge other people, and feel about ourselves. Media celebrities are good symbols of this power. Their personal and professional lives are the subject of constant media chatter. As well, they can exert great influence on fashion trends and body image for their audiences, simply by changing their own appearance.

Today, we recognize the media as an essential component of our daily lives. Those who control our TV networks, radio stations, and other sources of information, shape what we know about the world and the people in it. At the same time, the media sells us products to buy, celebrities to admire, and lifestyles to envy. Much of our education, outside of school, is provided by the media, and we must not accept what we are taught uncritically. The better we understand how media products are created and sold to us, the better we are able to make informed choices. ❯

What did media guru, Marshall McLuhan, envision as a
"classroom without walls"? This article was written in 1957.
How has our view of media changed?

Classroom Without Walls

Essay by Marshall McLuhan

It's natural today to speak of "audio and visual aids" to teaching, for
we still think of the book as norm, of other media as incidental. We
also think of the new media—press, radio, movies, TV—as MASS
MEDIA & think of the book as an individualistic form.

*Individualistic because it isolated the reader in silence & helped create
the Western "I." Yet it was the first product of mass production.*

With it everybody could have the same books. It was impossible in medieval times for different students, different institutions,
to have copies of the same book. Manuscripts, commentaries, were
dictated. Students memorized.

Instruction was almost entirely oral, done in groups. Solitary
study was reserved for the advanced scholar. The first printed
books were "visual aids" to oral instruction.

Before the printing press, the young learned by listening,
watching, doing. So, until recently, our own rural children learned
the language & skills of their elders. Learning took place outside
the classrooms. Only those aiming at professional careers went to
school at all.

Today in our cities, most learning occurs outside the classroom.
The sheer quantity of information conveyed by press-mags-
film-TV-radio *far exceeds* the quantity of information conveyed by
school instruction & texts. This challenge has destroyed the
monopoly of the book as a teaching aid & cracked the very walls
of the classroom, so suddenly, we're confused, baffled.

In this violently upsetting social situation, many teachers naturally view the offerings of the new media as entertainment, rather
than education. *But this view carries no conviction to the student.*

Find a classic which wasn't first regarded as light entertainment. Nearly all vernacular works were so regarded until the 19th
century.

Many movies are obviously handled with a degree of insight &

maturity at least equal to the level permitted in today's textbooks. Olivier's *Henry V* & *Richard III* assemble a wealth of scholarly & artistic skill which reveal Shakespeare at a very high level, yet in a way easy for the young to enjoy.

The movie is to dramatic representation what the book was to the manuscript. It makes available to many & at many times & places what otherwise would be restricted to a few at few times & places. The movie, like the book, is a ditto device. TV shows to 50,000,000 simultaneously. Some feel that the value of experiencing a book is diminished by being extended to many minds. This notion is always implicit in the phrases "mass media," "mass entertainment"—useless phrases obscuring the fact THAT *English itself is a mass medium.* Today we're beginning to realize that the new media aren't just mechanical gimmicks for creating worlds of illusion, *but new languages with new & unique powers of expression.* Historically, the resources of English have been shaped & expressed in constantly new & changing ways. The printing press changed, not only the quantity of writing, but the character of language & the relations between author & public. Radio, film, TV pushed written English towards the spontaneous shifts & freedom of the spoken idiom. They aided us in the recovery of intense awareness of facial language & bodily gesture. If these "mass media" should serve only to weaken or corrupt previously achieved levels of verbal & pictorial culture, it won't be because there's anything inherently wrong with them. *It will be because we've failed to master them as new languages in time to assimilate them to our total cultural heritage.*

These new developments, under quiet analytic survey, point to a basic strategy of culture for the classroom. When the printed book first appeared, it threatened the oral procedures of teaching, and created the classroom as we now know it. Instead of making his own text, his own dictionary, his own grammar, the student started out with these tools. He could study, not one, but several languages. Today these new media threaten, instead of merely reinforce, the procedures of this traditional classroom. It's customary to answer this threat with denunciations of the unfortunate character & effect of movies & TV, just as the comic book was feared & scorned & rejected from the classroom. Its good & bad features in form & content, when carefully set beside other kinds of art & narrative, could have become a major asset to the teacher.

Popular magazines multiply while the library shelves remain undisturbed.

Elisabeth Marbury

Where student interest is already intensely focused is the natural point at which to be in the elucidation of other problems & interests. *The educational task is not only to provide basic tools of perception, but to develop judgement & discrimination with ordinary social experience.*

Few students ever acquire skill in analysis of newspapers. Fewer have any ability to discuss a movie intelligently. *To be articulate & discriminating about ordinary affairs & information is the mark of an educated man.*

It's misleading to suppose there's any basic difference between education & entertainment. *This distinction merely relieves people* of the responsibility of looking into the matter. *It's like setting up a distinction between* didactic & lyric poetry on the ground that one teaches, the other pleases. *However, it's always been true* that whatever pleases teaches more effectively.

(Herbert) Marshall McLuhan was born in 1911 in Edmonton, Alberta. He taught in schools and at St. Michael's College of the University of Toronto, where he became director of the Centre for Culture and Technology. McLuhan is well known for his theories about the role of the electronic media in mass popular culture. He prophesied that printed books would become obsolete, killed off by TV and other electronic information technology.

I. *Response*

a. What is the thesis of this essay? What points in McLuhan's essay prove his thesis?

b. Is there any statement in this essay that you agree or disagree with strongly? What is it? What is your viewpoint?

c. This article was written in 1957, before the introduction of the Internet. How do you think McLuhan would have responded to the Internet? How would his essay change if it were written today?

d. Examine the use of italics, capital letters, and symbols within this essay. How does the typography the author has chosen to use affect the reader? The essay's meaning?

e. Who do you think McLuhan's target audience is? What is his purpose in addressing this audience? What makes you think so? How has he created a voice appropriate to his audience and purpose?

2. ***Research and Inquiry*** Consider how media have been used in the past to help educate the masses—whether students or the general public. For example, in the late nineteenth/early twentieth centuries in England, suffragettes handed out pamphlets and carried signs to help persuade the general populace that women deserved the right to vote. And in Germany in the 1930s, film documentaries and radio were used to spread propaganda and build support for the Nazi party.

    Choose a time period and region and research how media were used to persuade the masses. Speculate on the effectiveness of the media for causing change or educating people.

    Alternatively, you could research the impact of one medium—such as radio—on education, or on people in general.

3. ***Media*** *Choose a Format* Produce a media work that will convince your board of education to use media more widely in the classroom. You could choose to design a Web page, a print ad, a TV show, or a poster, for example. Your use of language, visuals, and design should reflect your audience and purpose.

4. ***Literature Studies*** *Diction* Examine the author's choice of words and explain which of the following most aptly describes McLuhan's diction: formal, colloquial, abstract, concrete, literal, figurative.

Identify the thesis statement in "The Psychological Power of Radio." As you read the rest of the essay, list the arguments the author uses to support his thesis.

The Psychological Power of Radio

Essay by Tim Crook

When you consider the history of the twentieth century, broadcasting skits or hoaxes are more associated with radio than with television. This is because radio was the first electronic medium of mass entertainment, and radio is a more psychological medium. Its relationship with its audience is based on an emotional and imaginative bond. Today radio has not lost its importance as a huge and significant source for news and entertainment and the opportunity to hoodwink the audience is as strong as it has ever been.

There are few people who are unaware of the panic created by the Mercury Theatre on Halloween night, 1938. The radio adaptation of H. G. Wells' novel *The War of the Worlds* had been transformed into a close representation of an American entertainment programme interrupted by urgent news bulletins. Orson Welles is credited with the idea, Howard Koch is credited with writing the script and the outstanding acting of the cast is credited with convincing hundreds of thousands of people that the Martians really were invading New Jersey.

Professor Hadley Cantril at Princeton University researched and published the only study into the relationship between the power and effectiveness of a broadcast of this kind and the reaction of the audience. "The Invasion From Mars: A Study in the Psychology of Panic" remains one of the most significant sociological and psychological studies of radio.

We can now say that the panic was the result of a mischievous determination to shock and confuse by Orson Welles, as well as the unusual circumstances of the period. The evidence available to us indicates quite strongly that Welles deliberately sought to create alarm, although he did not anticipate the scale of the panic.

CBS was aware of the risks of listeners being taken in by the realism of the writing and performance. Documentary evidence shows that producers insisted on changing real place names to fictitious ones, but the place names still had a ring of authenticity. Welles was conscious of the psychological impact of Herbert Morrison's emotional ad-libbed radio description of the destruction of the *Hindenburg*[1] just over a year before. In fact the actor playing the reporter in the production was directed to listen to and study the broadcast in a CBS booth during the rehearsals. An attempt was made to mimic the voice of President Roosevelt, and the production imitated the texture of contemporary networks which were continually interrupting music and soap opera broadcasts to bring the latest news developments from European crises.[2]

The rest, as they say, is interesting history. The power of radio was established, Orson Welles' name reverberated around the world, Campbell's Soups decided to sponsor the programme, and Welles later readily acknowledged that his plan to "make a radio splash" got him to Hollywood to make *Citizen Kane*. In fact his entrée to Hollywood was exceptional in the degree of artistic freedom given him.

The hysteria and controversy surrounding the *War of the Worlds* broadcast was also intensified by the hostility of the newspaper media which had seen the infant, and now adolescent, radio medium aggressively competing for advertising revenue. Here was an opportunity to exaggerate the degree of the panic. It does not appear that anyone died as a result, but listeners were treated for shock, hysteria and even heart attacks. Somewhat suspiciously there were more newspaper offices than police stations swamped with frantic queries: "What is happening? Where's the nearest bomb shelter? What must we do?"

The author of the original novel, H. G. Wells, was not particularly impressed. On the following day he is reported as saying "the dramatisation was made with a liberty that amounts to a complete rewriting and made the novel an entirely different story. It's a total unwarranted liberty." By 1940 his attitude had somewhat mellowed and he was happy to meet and be interviewed by Welles on live American radio. Why had

---

[1] *the* **Hindenburg:** a Zeppelin, an early type of airship, which exploded and crashed May 6, 1934, killing 35 people
[2] ***European crises:*** political unrest in Europe before the outbreak of World War II

his early objections evaporated? It might have something to do with the fact that the broadcast and publicity had boosted sales of one of his more obscure novels.

Attempts have been made to imitate the *War of the Worlds* scam within regulatory controls. Not surprisingly the US Federal Communications Commission launched an urgent enquiry and produced a raft of laws for US broadcasters to guard against deception of this kind again. Regulators in other countries followed suit.

The 1996, BBC Radio One FM's production of *Independence Day* on Nicky Campbell's show is an example of imitation. The invasion of British locations by aliens had powerful parallels. The Phoenix, Arizona radio station KTAR 620AM lovingly produced a 1995 version placing the *War of the Worlds* story in contemporary Arizona and engaging their entire on-air and production talent in the project. Producer Doren Fronterhouse went to St. Mary's Basilica in downtown Phoenix to record the bells as they chimed on Halloween night 1995. The station also warned its audience for many weeks that this programme was going to be aired as their special Halloween "trick or treat."

Television has never been able to match up to radio for the force and terror of "broadcast panics." A British ghost-hunting programme created a murmur of alarm one Halloween night in the 1990s and BBC Television's early *Panorama* April Fool's joke about the spaghetti harvests in Switzerland had a fair number of people fooled in 1957. Television was a relatively new medium of mass communication and the authoritative introduction and endorsement by Richard Dimbleby[3] helped emboss the item with credibility.

Orson Welles' 1938 portrayal of the expert astronomer, Professor Pierson, who is lost for words and has nothing to say in *War of the Worlds*, underlines how the audience's reliance on experts and information icons can be used to deceive and panic.

It is also worth bearing in mind that the year 1957 belonged to an era when recreational travelling abroad was still the preserve of only the few. So faked pictures of growing spaghetti combined effectively with the voice over:

> "Spaghetti cultivation in Switzerland is not on anything like the scale of the Italian spaghetti farms . . . Many of you will have seen the huge spaghetti plantations in the Po Valley."

---

[3] ***Richard Dimbleby:*** a British actor

Richard Dimbleby's sign off cue "And that is all from *Panorama* on this first day of April" was too subtle a remark for those who had been easily deceived. Viewers wrote in to ask where they could buy spaghetti plants and one viewer asserted that the programme had got it wrong; spaghetti grew horizontally, not vertically.

In recent decades, radio has been effective in developing a "skit genre" which engages the listeners in ironic entertainment rather than fooling them. This is the realm of the spoof broadcaster who uses mimicry to deceive ordinary people, politicians and public figures into making fools of themselves. *Candid Camera* is the television equivalent. It is copied across the world and provides huge entertainment. It also has the capacity to satirise and play a subversive role. In Britain, Chris Morris has developed the technique on Radio One FM and has transferred these skills to his Channel Four *Brass Eye* television series. He has achieved a sophisticated level of entertainment as well as exposing the cynicism of the media's relationship with politicians and pressure groups.

America's legendary shock jock Howard Stern has used "spoofing" as just one of the many subversive mechanisms to lampoon the world around him. But the radio spoofer of the century award should probably go to Montréal's Pierre Brassard whose *Blue Powder Drive Home Show* on station CKOI has successfully duped His Holiness the Pope and Her Majesty the Queen.

In October 1995, Brassard convinced the Queen that he was Canadian Prime Minister Jean Chrétien. He was able to persuade her in a 17-minute telephone conversation that it would be a good idea if she could broadcast an appeal to the French-speaking province of Québec not to break away from Canada in yet another nail-biting referendum. Part of the extraordinary conversation was in French with Brassard asking "Are you wearing a costume for Halloween?" She replied: "No, no. It's for the children." This scam was achieved through the skill of Brassard's cheek and mimicry and the Queen's misfortune that her officials could not confirm the authenticity of the call beforehand because Chrétien had been out campaigning.

The development of phone-in and talkback programming in the last 25 years has provided the opportunity for audience interactivity so that listeners can now turn the tables against the broadcasters themselves. The limited amount of time and resources available to check phone-in contributors provides an environment "ripe for the picking." US "over the edge" sound artists have already succeeded in disrupting licensed programmes through phone-in participation as well as using illegal transmitters to "crash" on established frequencies. It would not be impossible for a group of subversive broadcasters to "swamp" an existing news phone-in programme with realistic reports of a catastrophic event tinged with political embarrassment. Back-up calls from apparent emergency services could easily convince the station's newsroom of the authenticity of the event. More highly staffed and experienced national newspapers have been duped by lone hoaxers such as "Rocky Ryan"[4] whose efforts have created front page embarrassment, and the newspapers had the advantage of hours to make a proper evaluation. In radio, presenters and producers have minutes and seconds.

So the spoof potential of radio lies in the willing desire to suspend disbelief. If this can be described as a human weakness then it is present in all of us. In radio, both listener and broadcaster can now find ways of exposing the medium's vulnerability.

[4]***Rocky Ryan:*** a hoaxer who made up believable stories and sold them to the British tabloids in the 1970s and 1980s

Tim Crook has written textbooks on radio journalism and radio drama. He is head of Radio in the department of Media and Communications at Goldsmiths' College, University of London, England, and presents *Through the Night* and *Newsfile* on the British radio station, LBC.

1. Response
a. Who is Orson Welles? Who is H. G. Wells?
b. Describe what happened on October 31, 1938.
c. How did Orson Welles and the producers of the radio program, *War of the Worlds*, convince the audience that New Jersey had been invaded by aliens from Mars? Would an audience today be fooled by such a broadcast? Explain.
d. Do you think Tim Crook proved his thesis? Explain.

2. Media *Radio Productions* Locate a recording of the radio program *War of the Worlds* at your local library, or on the Internet. As you listen to it, make notes about how the show was produced and introduced. Discuss the effectiveness of the production.

In this radio script by humorist Paul Moth, no cultural icons or popular ideas are spared his cutting humour. As you are reading, keep a list of all the things that Paul and Kath spoof as they discuss the books anxious gift-givers can choose from.

Christmas Consumer Frenzy

Script by Paul Moth

from The Great Eastern: Newfoundland's Cultural Magazine

PAUL: The Xmas consumer frenzy is upon us, and that means the last hope for many bookstores. Here to discuss the Yuletide crop of bound scribbles, doodles and snaps is Ms. Wordworks herself, Kathleen Hanrahan.

KATH: Hello, Paul.

PAUL: Now, the gift book is truly the life blood of retailers isn't it?

KATH: Yes it is. People don't read so much anymore, but a book is … well it's readily available, usually in the price range for a Christmas book and hey, it's easy to wrap.

PAUL: Backing up a bit, why aren't people reading?

KATH: First I think there's a lifestyle question—more onerous work, greater demands at home—people can't find the time or are simply too tired to read. And secondly they've grown stupid.

PAUL: You know I'd thought that but I'm glad you said it. On to the Christmas goodies. You promised us only books 100% guaranteed to satisfy. Whaddaya got, whaddaya got?

KATH: First, *Places You Will Never Go*, a sumptuous marriage of glossy photographs and fluffy text, by Harriet Burton.

PAUL: Owww very sumptuous. The paper is … I don't know how to put it … so soft.

KATH: It's infused with hand lotion.

PAUL: Nice. This book is about?

KATH: The homes and extravagant lifestyles of our filthy rich.

PAUL: Ouch! Look at this bathroom! I'd dine there any day.

KATH: If you were ever invited.

PAUL: I don't have a hope, do I?

KATH: No.

PAUL: Not all fluff, Kathleen. The photographs are accompanied by handy and informative discussions about the architectural and design principles of the grand estates.

KATH: And some of the history of these great old families.

PAUL: I see the Woolrights made their money through child labour.

KATH: Several generations ago. They now keep the industrial engine running with a canny mix of banking and offshore athletic footwear manufacturing.

PAUL: Maintaining that tradition of child labour through the ages, that's great. Oh, and here's a photo essay about the local debutante ball.

KATH: Young, beautiful and so incredibly wealthy.

PAUL: A winning combination.

KATH: Still this photographic essay shows the well-heeled lifestyle, warts and all.

PAUL: Ah yes … here's a debutante being sick … all that *Veuve Cliquot.*[1]

KATH: There's one humiliating a busboy.

PAUL: Those wacky super rich. We just can't get enough of them, can we.

KATH: Prestige Press, and just about affordable at 47.50.

PAUL: Next?

KATH: *The Absolution Vodka Book.*

PAUL: The booze people who do those fabulous ads?

KATH: The same. This is a book of those advertisements.

PAUL: What? I pay to look at their ads!

KATH: They're quite exceptional and creative.

PAUL: Where is this going to end? You can't buy clothes that don't have company logos plastered all over them; you try to phase out in front of the tube and you're subjected to infomercials; you … ahhhhh look at this one, the little mouse, he's trapped in the vodka bottle, I think he's drunk. That's adorable. My Mom might like this, what's the asking price?

KATH: Thirty-two dollars.

PAUL: Oh no, that's too much. Next.

KATH: For the kids there is yet another *Goofoids* book.

PAUL: I hate those cartoons, the noise, the graphic violence, the supply-side economics—but you know my brother's kids can't get enough of them.

KATH: And I'll bet they love the *Goofoids* breakfast cereal.

PAUL: My brother is afraid not to give it to them; claims they get ill without it, nauseous, sweaty, irritable . . .

---

[1] *Veuve Cliquot:* a type of champagne

KATH: That's because it's addictive.

PAUL: Wow.

KATH: Still it's a complete breakfast.

PAUL: I have a bad feeling about this stuff; again I can't see the line between entertainment and advertising.

KATH: That's standard fare though these days isn't it, and look the RCMP have a contract with Disney so I mean … in a way, this kind of predatory children's entertainment has the state's sanction.

PAUL: But the *Goofoids* characters smoke!

KATH: Cigars though, Paul, they're just hip to the scene.

PAUL: Next?

KATH: *Edna Greeley's Christmas Homemakers Extravaganza.*

PAUL: Get-a-load of the centrepiece. So woodsy, it's a virtual pine forest!

KATH: It's all carved from cheese. There … pretzel skiers, little caper toques.

PAUL: The skis are anchovy I'd guess.

KATH: It's so pretty I don't think I could eat it.

PAUL: With the anchovies I'd attempt it, what kind of cheese is it?

KATH: That's a dip pond by the walnut grove. The ducks are …

PAUL: I love a good Muenster, a ripe non-pasteurized Muenster. Sorry Kathleen, this looks like a lot of work.

KATH: Today's homemaker has to really put out lest they be accused of being a bad parent or spouse.

PAUL: Things are so different for kids these days hey? When I was growing up Catholics fasted through Advent so they would really appreciate their Christmas porridge.

KATH: Paul!

PAUL: Just kidding Kathleen. We always got a big feed of utility road-kill every Christmas.

KATH: That's comforting.

PAUL: At least you knew they weren't fed steroids. Thanks Kathleen and buy, buy, buy!

KATH: You too.

PAUL: God Bless.

KATH: Let's keep God out of it!

> To perceive Christmas through its wrappings becomes more difficult every year.
>
> E. B. White

Paulitorial by Paul Moth

Let's peel back the veil of personality that covers the media. Underneath that, what do you find?

You find me, Paul Moth. I am two people, I am Paul Moth, public radio host, and I am Paul Moth, the private individual. And you know nothing about the private individual. And I really mean nothing. That's the way I want it. Believe me, that's the way you want it, too.

Then there's the public Paul Moth, the radio presence.

It seems every time I become this public person, every time I pick up a microphone, the universe changes. The reality-modifying capabilities of the microphone have not been fully investigated.

Whatever, whenever the radio waves start rolling, weird things happen to me.

What is it about the emanation of radio pulses that disturbs the brains of some addled listeners?

And if those people are tuned in now, I have one message from both the public and private Paul Moth.

Who are you? And what are you doing in my head?

Paul Moth was born in 1949 in St. John's, Newfoundland and Labrador. He first worked in radio as a sports reporter with the Broadcasting Corporation of Newfoundland (BCN) in 1970, eventually hosting *In the Corners*, a weekly roundup of sport. Moth then entered the film industry and became well known in Mexican cinema, writing and directing 13 episodes of *Pepito el Grande* (Pepito the Great). After living in Los Angeles for a while he returned to Canada where he became host of the BCN's legendary *The Great Eastern*.

1. Response

a. Discuss the items on your list of all that Paul Moth pokes fun at or spoofs in this radio script. Do you think he was being fair? Do you appreciate Moth's sense of humour? Why or why not?

b. From the two examples here, describe the type of radio show that Moth hosts. Who do you think is his target audience? What is his purpose in producing this show? Would you enjoy listening to it? Explain your answer.
c. What explicit and implicit messages does "Christmas Consumer Frenzy" deliver?
d. Reread Moth's "Paulitorial." Discuss what he is saying about celebrity and media personalities. Do you agree or disagree? Explain.

2. ***Media*** *Radio Habits* List the reasons you have for listening to radio. What is it you expect to hear when you tune in to a radio station? What types of stations do you listen to? Question other students and family members about their radio listening habits. What conclusions can you draw about people's reasons for listening to radio?

   Listen to at least five different radio stations over the next five days. Make sure you listen at different times during the day, for at least half an hour each time. Keep a list of everything you hear. Compare your lists to the lists of other students in the class. What types of programs do radio stations air? What is the most common type of programming? What do you think is the purpose of most radio programs? What different audiences are each of the stations you listened to trying to reach? What role does advertising play on each of these stations?

3. ***Writing*** *Various Formats* Choose a format to convey your response to one of Paul Moth's selections—an essay or editorial about your view of what it means to be a celebrity, a letter or anecdote about your experiences with Christmas shopping—or another format of your choice. Ask a peer editor to read your first and second drafts and suggest ways to improve your writing.

4. ***Oral Language*** *Group Discussion* Discuss your personal experiences and knowledge about the "Xmas consumer frenzy." What do you know about the practices of the media during the Christmas season? What happens to TV stations' broadcasting and advertising? What happens in stores? How does the Christmas season affect movie theatres? What relationship do entertainment media, advertising, and stores have with the consumer? How does all of this affect those who do not celebrate Christmas? Do you think the media are now showing more tolerance for those who do not celebrate it? Explain.

One Ocean

One-act radio play

by Betty Quan

*Using the Chinese myth of the Jingwei bird,
a daughter tries to bridge the physical and
emotional gulf with her father in this memory play
about the ideas of immigration and subsequent
separation of families.*

SCENE 1: *Narration. Inside memory.*
MUSIC: *Establish theme, continue under:*

DAUGHTER: *(older)* A long time ago. It was my favourite. A story. No, our story. Just a Chinese folktale. Yes. About the Jingwei bird and why she is always dropping sticks and stones in the ocean. When I was small, I used to pretend I was that little bird. I would soar through our communal courtyard with arms for wings. That was when we were still allowed to enjoy our stories, to tell our stories, before, before ... *Bah-bah.* Father. Do you remember like I do? Tell me about the Jingwei. Yes, like you used to do when I was small. You told me that story when I left Hong Kong for Canada. Do you remember? I was sad. We were both sad. Like a bird in your hand I was until you set me free across the sky, across the ocean. Such a long time ago, yet so close I can still see it unfolding before me. Father? Tell me a story. Like you used to do. *(as if repeating what she hears in memory)* "A long time ago." It seems like yesterday. A long time ago. But that is how we begin our stories, isn't it? We begin with "a long time ago."

Scene 2: *Folktale remembered.*

Father: A long time ago there was an emperor who had a young daughter. They loved each other very much. But although his powers could touch all corners of the land, the emperor could see only as far as the shoreline that divided his kingdom with the sea.

Daughter: Beyond that shoreline, his vision was limited, like a kite held high in a strong breeze—he could see the shape, but not the colours.

Music ends. Sound effects: birds, breeze, ocean, continue under:

Daughter: Father, look at the waves, so tall they must be hiding something behind them. I will take my boat for a ride.

Father: *(as Emperor)* Not so far, not so far.

Daughter: *(as Jingwei)* Don't worry, father. I'll be careful.

Father: *(as Emperor)* Why don't you wait a while? I'll join you. We can journey to the horizon together, where the sea meets the sun.

Daughter: *(as Jingwei)* When? When can we do this? *(laughing)* You're always promising such things, father! You're too busy as Emperor. I'll go out on my own first. On my own adventure. Then, I'll show you what I've seen.

Father: *(as Emperor, laughing)* When?

Daughter: *(as Jingwei)* What does that matter? We have all the time in the world.

Daughter: *(older)* The sun was warm upon the little girl's face—

Father: —and the salty breeze off the water tempted her to travel farther and farther. To see what hid behind the tall waves of the sea.

Daughter: *(older)* Far far far away she went, when suddenly—

Sound effects: thunder and rainstorm.

Father: *(as Sea God)* Who dares come this far upon the ocean of my reign?

Daughter: *(older)* The Sea God's bad temper came upon the little girl.

Sound effects: Jingwei screams as the waves engulf her.

Father: The water became a blanket that covered her. And the little girl died.

Sound effects: all suddenly end.

DAUGHTER: *(older)* Died? I don't remember her dying. Is that right? I thought the water changed her into a bird. Like magic.

FATHER: I would tell you that when you were small. When you didn't understand death.

DAUGHTER: *(older)* Like I do now.

FATHER: It is only a story. *(continues)* The little girl's soul became a small bird called Jingwei.

Music begins.

DAUGHTER: *(older)* Father, I died that day you sent me away.

FATHER: No, child, you were reborn. Now, continue the story.

DAUGHTER: Angry was the spirit in that bird, angry at the sea it was for taking her away from her beloved father. And every day the Jingwei would carry in her beak stones and twigs from the mountains of the east and flying west ahead drop her small stones and twigs into the sea. And the Sea God finally noticed what Jingwei was trying to do.

Music ends. Sound effects: ocean. Close: the wings of a bird in motion.

FATHER: *(as Sea God, laughing)* Silly creature, my sea is wider and deeper than your limited imagination. You can never fill me up in a million years.

DAUGHTER: *(as Jingwei)* But I can. Every day for a million years I will do this. Every day until one day. Until one day ... *(begin fade down)* Until one day ... Until one day ...

FATHER: And the small bird flew back to land—

FATHER & DAUGHTER: *(older)* —only to return with another small stone or twig to drop into the sea.

DAUGHTER: *(older)* And Jingwei said: "One day, there will be a bridge-between me and my father. One day, even if it takes a million years to build it." *(she no longer speaks as the Jingwei)* Soon, father. I will see you again. Soon.

Sound effects: fade down.

> Acting is just a way of making a living,
> the family is life.
>
> Denzel Washington

SCENE 3: *Airport.*

Sound effects: airplane's acceleration and ascent. Fades into airport interior: Chinese public address system, etc. Close: a swallow singing.

FATHER: Yes, yes, sing a goodbye song to my daughter. Here's a sunflower seed.

DAUGHTER: I don't think pets are allowed here.

FATHER: This is not just a pet, eh my little friend? Now keep your bag in full sight. Many pickpockets. There is more freedom here in Hong Kong but that doesn't mean there is less danger. Here's your ticket. Show it to that man over there. Where's your passport?

DAUGHTER: I don't want to go to Vancouver, father. Why me?

FATHER: Your big brother has a family now. You will go first, then settle down. Then we can join you.

DAUGHTER: When?

FATHER: Soon. Soon. Look at us now. We used to have a fine house and good food to eat. First the Japanese and the war, now Mao. Remember, just a few years ago, Mao decided China must have its Great Leap Forward? And the country went two steps forward and five steps back?

SCENE 4: *Narration. Inside memory. Music fades under:*

DAUGHTER: *(older)* Mosquitos, flies, rats, and sparrows: Mao called these the "four pests." 1958: It was the year I turned sixteen. *(bitter laugh)* Do you remember? Mao believed grain production was down because the sparrows were feeding on the backs of the people. Families were armed with pots and pans. We were to scare the sparrows out of the trees so they would eventually drop dead from exhaustion. 600 million of us, running under trees, in the countryside, in the cities, making enough noise to waken the dead. Yes, the sparrows ate the grain, but they also ate the insects. Without the sparrows, no one could control the insects. The sky would rain the corpses of little birds to join the corpses of 300 million people, dead of starvation.

SCENE 5: *Airport.*

Sound effects: airport interior. Close: the swallow singing.

FATHER: You know how lucky we were to get out of China?

DAUGHTER: I know.

FATHER: How can we Chinese have luck when we are killing birds!? This is why it is good we are here now. No more death. No more hunger. No more sacrificing our own symbols of fortune and happiness. Maybe my good luck has returned right here in this cage. Maybe now we will all have good luck.

DAUGHTER: Maybe's, nothing but maybe's.

FATHER: You have a chance now, can't you see? To start a new life in a new place.

DAUGHTER: Let me finish school first.

FATHER: *(joking)* Maybe you'll find a rich Canadian and marry him.

DAUGHTER: I'm 18 years old; I don't need a husband. I can try to find a job here, in Hong Kong.

FATHER: Just a temporary thing, you'll see. Your mother, your brother, me. We'll be a family again. We're relying on you. Work hard. Stay out of trouble. Be a citizen your new country can be proud of. When you're settled, you'll sponsor us to come. We'll join you later.

DAUGHTER: Please don't make me go, father.

FATHER: Who is the parent here? Who makes the decision?

DAUGHTER: Please, father, don't make me go all alone.

FATHER: Look, my Jingwei. Yes, you have always been like a little bird to me. If I could, I would always try to protect you, away from bad things. But this—this—is a good thing.

DAUGHTER: I don't want to go!

FATHER: Believe me, it's for the best. You'll like it in Canada.

DAUGHTER: Don't you want me to stay here, with you?

FATHER: It doesn't matter what I want. It's what I want for you.

FEMALE: *(over sound system, filtered)* Last boarding call for Flight 973 departing for Vancouver, Canada.

The announcer repeats this in Cantonese.

DAUGHTER: I've never been in a plane before, father. Have you?

FATHER: No. Not yet. But in time, no?

DAUGHTER: Yes, in time.

SCENE 6: *Airfield.*

Sound effects: airport exterior. Plane accelerating and ascending. Closer: the swallow's song.

FATHER: Goodbye! *(to himself)* Goodbye.

Sound effects: swallow singing.

FATHER: What's that? What are you singing about?

Sound effects: swallow singing. Metal clink of the cage being opened.

FATHER: Come on, there. No, it's not a trick. Out. Yes. Fly, go on, fly. Fly.

Sound effects: Close: the acceleration of a bird's wings, heard under:

FATHER: Build a bridge between me and my daughter. Make our ocean one.

SCENE 7: *Narration. Inside memory.*

Music: begins and continues under:

DAUGHTER: *(older)* You broke your promise. You never came. You let me leave you behind. I waited for you, father. For the family. A long time ago. Where are you? Are you here, with me? Did you follow on the shadow of the airplane's wings? *(voice begins to break)* Did I fly away like a kite in the breeze? So high up you can see the shape, but not the colours? Can you see me? I'm so far away but all you have to do is pull me home. Father. Father. When I finish building a bridge, will you cross it? Even if the stones are loose, and the twigs are breaking. Will you cross it? Father? *(beat)* Bah-bah? How big is the ocean?

Music ends. Sound effects: exterior: airfield. Plane's acceleration and ascent crosses into that of birds in flight, their wings in motion. Fade into ocean, water lapping on a beach. Up and out.

Betty Quan writes for radio, TV, and stage. She graduated from the University of British Columbia, and has served residences at The Canadian Film Centre Television Drama program and the Tarragon Theatre. In 1996 her play, *Mother Tongue*, was a finalist in the Governor General's Literary Award for Drama. She has written three plays, and her other work has appeared in the anthologies *Beyond the Pale* and *Taking the Stage*. This play aired on CBC's *Morningside* radio drama program.

I. Response

    a. What is the message, spoken or unspoken, in this radio play? What makes you think so?

    b. How does Betty Quan use a folktale to tell her story?

    c. Use a graph or chart to show the changing emotion of the daughter. What clues to her emotions are there in the language she uses?

2. Making Connections Compare this play with "Christmas Consumer Frenzy" by Paul Moth. What is the purpose of each? Who is the audience? How are mood, theme, and message the same or different?

3. Drama *Perform a Radio Play* In a small group, prepare a presentation of this radio play, or one of Paul Moth's pieces. Consider how you will use your voice—volume, tone, pace, expression—to portray the emotion or humour of the piece you choose. Since no one sees the actors on radio, you don't have to memorize your lines, but can read them aloud. But you should be able to speak the lines smoothly and expressively. When you are ready, record your presentation on audio tape, using music and sound effects, as appropriate. Share your presentation with your class or a younger audience. Ask your audience for feedback on your performance and the production of the play.

4. Literature Studies *Mood* Discuss the mood of this piece, and how Quan achieves this mood. Compare her use of mood to other plays you have read or seen.

What is the most important aspect of mass media? What is their primary purpose? Read on to find out what one media critic thinks.

People as Products

Essay by Jean Kilbourne

MAKE NO MISTAKE: The primary purpose of the mass media is to sell audiences to advertisers. We are the product. Although people are much more sophisticated about advertising now than even a few years ago, most are still shocked to learn this.

Magazines, newspapers, and radio and television programs round us up, rather like cattle, and producers and publishers then sell us to advertisers, usually through ads placed in advertising and industry publications. "The people you want, we've got all wrapped up for you," declares the *Chicago Tribune* in an ad placed in *Advertising Age*, which pictures several people, all neatly boxed according to income level.

Although we like to think of advertising as unimportant, it is in fact the most important aspect of the mass media. It *is* the point. Advertising supports more than 60 percent of magazine and newspaper production and almost 100 percent of the electronic media. Over $40 billion a year in ad revenue is generated for television and radio, and over $30 billion for magazines and newspapers. As one *ABC* executive said, "The network is paying affiliates to carry network commercials, not programs. What we are is a distribution system for Procter & Gamble." And the CEO of *CBS* said, "We're here to serve advertisers. That's our *raison d'être*."

The media know that television and radio programs are simply fillers for the space between commercials. They know that the programs that succeed are the ones that deliver the highest number of people to the advertisers. But not just any people. Advertisers are interested in white people aged 18 to 49 who live in or near a city. *Dr. Quinn, Medicine Woman*, a program that was No. 1 in its time slot and immensely popular with older, more rural viewers, was canceled in 1998 because it couldn't command the higher advertising rates paid for younger, richer audiences.

This is not new: *The Daily Herald*, a British newspaper with 47 million readers, double the combined readership of the *Times*, *Financial Times*, *Guardian* and *Telegraph*, folded in the 1960s because its readers were mostly elderly and working class and had little appeal to advertisers.

The target audience that appeals to advertisers is becoming more narrow all the time. According to Dean Valentine, the head of Viacom's *UPN*, most networks have abandoned the middle class and want "very chic shows that talk to affluent, urban, unmarried, huge-disposable-income 18-to-34-year-olds because the theory is, from advertisers, that the earlier you get them, the sooner you imprint the brand name."

"Tripod Delivers Gen-X," proclaims a website/magazine's sinister ad, featuring a delivery man carrying a corpselike consumer wrapped from neck to toe in brown paper. Several other such "deliveries" are propped up in the truck. An ad for the newspaper *USA Today* offers the consumer's eye between a knife and a fork and says, "12 Million Served Daily." The ad explains, "Nearly six million influential readers with both eyes ingesting your message. Every day." There is no humanity, no individuality in this ad or others like it—people are simply products sold to advertisers, of value only as potential consumers.

Newspapers are more in the business of selling audiences than in the business of giving people news, especially as more and more news-papers are owned by fewer and fewer chains. They exist primarily to support local advertisers, such as car dealers, realtors and department store owners.

Once we begin to count, we see that magazines are essentially cat-alogs of goods, with less than half of their pages devoted to editorial content (and much of that in the service of the advertisers). An ad for a custom publishing company in *Advertising Age* promises, "The next hot magazine could be the one we create exclusively for your product."

> Millions of dollars' worth of advertising shows
> such little respect for the reader's intelligence
> that it amounts almost to outright insult.
>
> James Adams

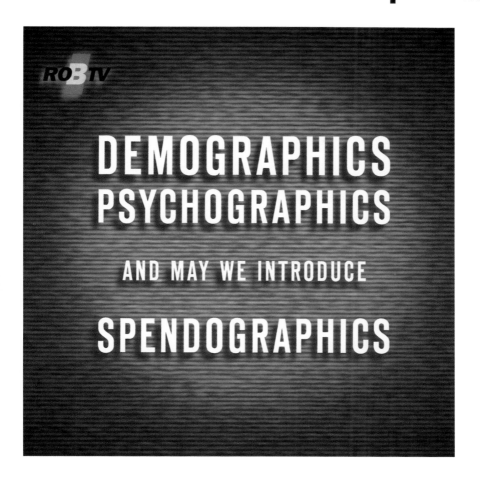

Tap into Canada's most affluent television audience | If you're looking for Canadians with potential to spend, turn to ROBTv. 95% of our core audience viewers have household incomes in excess of $75,000*.

REPORT ON BUSINESS **TELEVISION**

* Tandemar Media Research, May 2000.   *robtv.com 416-960-3700*

Examine this advertisement that appeared in an issue of *Marketing Magazine*, a magazine aimed at advertisers and marketers. Discuss the target market, purpose, and features of this ad, as well as its effectiveness.

And, in fact, there are magazines for everyone from dirt-bike riders to knitters to mercenary soldiers, from *Beer Connoisseur* to *Cigar Aficionado*. There are plenty of magazines for the wealthy, such as *Coastal Living*, "for people who live or vacation on the coast." *Barron's* advertises itself as a way to "reach faster cars, bigger houses and longer prenuptial agreements" and promises a readership with an average household net worth of over a million.

The Internet advertisers target the wealthy too, of course. Not surprisingly, there are no magazines or Internet sites or television programs for the poor. They might not be able to afford the magazines or computers, but, more importantly, they are of little use to advertisers.

Jean Kilbourne is a media critic, writer, lecturer, and expert on addictions, gender issues, and the media. She is internationally recognized for her pioneering work on the effects of alcohol and tobacco advertising, and for raising public awareness of how advertising encourages addictive behaviour. Kilbourne has made several documentaries based on her lectures, including *Killing Us Softly: Advertising's Image of Women*, and its sequel, *Still Killing Us Softly*. This selection is taken from her book *Deadly Persuasion: Why Women and Girls Must Fight the Addictive Power of Advertising*.

I. *Response*

a. Revisit the questions in the introductory paragraph of this article. How does Jean Kilbourne answer these questions? Do you agree with her? Why or why not?

b. Reread the second paragraph and identify the simile Kilbourne uses. Do you think it is an appropriate or effective comparison? Explain your answer.

c. What is the target audience for most advertisers identified in the article? Would you agree with the author that most advertisers are not interested in the poor or elderly? Explain.

d. Explain, in your own words, how the mass media "sell" us—the people who watch and listen to the media—to advertisers.

e. According to Kilbourne, advertisers only support TV and radio programs that attract a young, middle-class or upper middle-class audience. Do you think that this attitude affects the content of programs? Can you think of a TV show that depicts the lives of the poor or elderly?

f. How do you think someone in the advertising business would respond to the following assertion: "People are simply products sold to advertisers, of value only as potential consumers."

2. **Media** *Analysing Audiences* Choose one of the media mentioned in the article and examine several examples of it. Can you identify the audience that is targeted in the ads in each example? Do these examples support Kilbourne's argument? Explain.

    Kilbourne says that magazines are "essentially catalogs of goods" increasingly aimed at narrow audiences with highly specialized interests. Is this a bad thing? Visit a large magazine stand and note which interests and hobbies seem to have the most magazines. Note how many general interest magazines that would appeal to a very wide audience are still on the market.

3. **Language Conventions** *Comparatives and Superlatives* Advertising copy often uses comparatives or superlatives to make a product appear better than others. A cereal is not just good, it is great. A car is not just fast, it is the fastest. Look through a number of newspapers and magazines and consider the use of comparatives and superlatives in ads. What effect does this use have on the reader? Discuss how words sometimes seem to lose their meaning when you see them too often in ads or other media.

Advertise, or go under.
> —*Dorothy L Sayers*

Consider the following statement from a magazine in the 1950s: "In very few instances do people really know what they want, even when they say they do."

—Advertising Age

Have things changed?

The *Trouble* With People

Essay by Vance Packard

Marketers always encountered difficulties in trying to persuade people to buy all the products their companies could fabricate.

One particularly disturbing difficulty was the apparent perversity and unpredictability of the prospective customers. Marketers repeatedly suffered grievous losses in campaigns that by all the rules of logic should have succeeded. The marketers felt increasing dissatisfaction with their conventional methods for sizing up a market. These methods were known in the trade most commonly as "nose-counting." Under nose-counting, statistic-minded interviewers would determine the percentage of married women, ages twenty-one to thirty-five, in Omaha, Nebraska, who said they wanted, and would buy a three-legged stove if it cost no more than $249.

The trouble with this approach, they found, was that what people might tell interviewers had only a remote bearing on how the people would actually behave in a buying situation when confronted with a three-legged stove or almost anything else.

Gradually, many perceptive marketers began becoming suspicious of three basic assumptions they had made, in their efforts to be logical, concerning the predictable behavior of human beings, especially customers.

First, they decided, you can't assume that people know what they want.

A major ketchup maker kept getting complaints about its bottle, so it made a survey. Most of the people interviewed said they would prefer another type the company was considering. When the company went to the expense of bringing out this other bottle in test markets, it was overwhelmingly rejected in favor of the old bottle, even by people who had favored it in interviews.

Second, some marketers concluded, you can't assume people will tell you the truth about their wants and dislikes even if they know them. What you are more likely to get, they decided, are answers that will protect the informants in their steadfast endeavor to appear to the world as really sensible, intelligent, rational beings. One management consulting firm has concluded that accepting the word of a customer as to what he wants is "the least reliable index the manufacturer can have on what he ought to do to win customers."

The Advertising Research Foundation took magazines to task for asking people what magazines they read frequently, and naïvely accepting the answers given as valid. The people, it contended, are likely to admit reading only magazines of high prestige value. One investigator suggests that if you seriously accepted people's answers you might assume that *Atlantic Monthly* is America's most-read magazine and some of the confession magazines the least read; whereas actually the confession magazines in question may have twenty times the readership of *Atlantic Monthly*.

A brewery making two kinds of beer made a survey to find what kind of people drank each beer, as a guide to its merchandisers. It asked people known to favor its general brand name: "Do you drink the light or the regular?" To its astonishment it found people reporting they drank light over the regular by better than three to one. The truth of the matter was that for years the company, to meet consumer demand, had been brewing nine times as much regular beer as light beer. It decided that in asking people that question it was in effect asking: Do you drink the kind preferred by people of refinement and discriminating taste, or do you just drink the regular stuff?

In another case the Color Research Institute asked a group of people if they borrowed money from personal-loan companies. Every person said no. Some of them virtually shouted their answer. The truth was that all those selected for interviewing were people who were listed in the records of a local loan company as borrowers.

Finally, the marketers decided it is dangerous to assume that people can be trusted to behave in a rational way.

A department store that had become skeptical of the rationality of its customers tried an experiment. One of its slowest-moving items was priced at fourteen cents. It changed the price to two for twenty-nine cents. Sales promptly increased 30 per cent when the item was offered at this "bargain" price.

Our toothbrushing habits offer a prime example of behavior that is at least seemingly irrational. If you ask people why they brush their teeth, most of them will tell you that their main purpose in doing so is to get particles of food out of the crevices of their teeth and thus combat decay germs. Toothpaste producers accepted this explanation for many years and based their sales campaigns on it. Advertising men who made a study of our toothbrushing habits, however, came upon a puzzle. They found that most people brushed their teeth once a day, and at the most pointless moment possible in the entire twenty-four-hour day, from the dental hygiene standpoint. That was in the morning just before breakfast, after decay germs had had a whole night to work on their teeth from particles left from supper—and just before the consumption of breakfast would bring in a new host of bacteria.

One advertising agency puzzling over this seemingly irrational behavior made a more thorough study of the reasons why we brush our teeth. It concluded that we are motivated by differing reasons, based on our personality. Some people, particularly hypochondriacs, are really concerned about those germs and are swayed by a "decay" appeal. (The hammering in recent years on all the wondrous anti-decay pastes has swollen the size of this group.) Another group, mostly extroverts, brush their teeth in the hope they will be bright and shiny. The majority of people, however, brush their teeth primarily for a reason that has little to do with dental hygiene or even their teeth. They put the brush and paste into their mouth in order to give their mouth a thorough purging, to get rid of the bad taste that has accumulated overnight. In short, they are looking for a taste sensation, as a part of their ritual of starting the day afresh. At least two of the major paste merchandisers began hitting hard at this appeal in 1955 and 1956. One promised a "clean mouth taste" and the other proclaimed that its paste "cleans your breath while it guards your teeth." (More recently one of these products got itself a new ad agency, as often happens, and the new mentor began appealing to the extrovert in us through the slogan, "You'll wonder where the yellow went—." Good results are reported, which simply proves there is always more than one way to catch a customer.)

Business Week, in commenting on the often seemingly irrational behavior of consumers, said: "People don't seem to be reasonable." However, it made this further point: "But people do act with purpose. Their behavior makes sense if you think about it in terms of its goals, of people's needs and their motives. That seems to be the secret of understanding or manipulating people."

Another aspect of people's behavior that has troubled marketers is that they are too easily satisfied with what they already have. Most of the marketers' factories have ever-larger warehouses full of goods to move.

By the mid-fifties American goods producers were achieving a fabulous output, and the output with automation promised to keep getting more fabulous. Since 1940, gross national product had soared more than 400 per cent; and man-hour productivity was doubling about every quarter century.

One way of viewing this rich, full life the people were achieving was the glowing one that everyone could enjoy an ever-higher standard of living. That view was thoroughly publicized. But there was another way of viewing it: that we must consume more and more, whether we want to or not, for the good of our economy.

In late 1955 the church publication *Christianity and Crisis* commented grimly on America's "ever-expanding economy." It observed that the pressure was on Americans to "consume, consume and consume, whether we need or even desire the products almost forced upon us." It added that the dynamics of an ever-expanding system require that we be "persuaded to consume to meet the needs of the productive process."

With growing productivity and prosperity the average American had five times as many discretionary dollars as he had in 1940. (These are dollars we have after we take care of our basic, immediate needs.) But discretionary dollars are also deferrable dollars—we can defer spending them if we are satisfied with what we already have. This hazard posed by so many optional dollars in our pockets was summed up quite eloquently in the October 24, 1955, issue of *Advertising Age* by an executive of the publishing firm of McGraw-Hill. He stated:

> As a nation we are already so rich that consumers are under no pressure of immediate necessity to buy a very large share—perhaps as much as 40%—of what is produced, and the pressure will get progressively less in the years ahead. But if consumers exercise their option not to buy a large share of what is produced, a great depression is not far behind.

In the early fifties, with overproduction threatening on many fronts, a fundamental shift occurred in the preoccupation of people in executive suites. Production now became a relatively secondary concern.

Executive planners changed from being maker-minded to market-minded. The president of the National Sales Executives in fact exclaimed: "Capitalism is dead—consumerism is king!"

There was talk at management conventions of "the marketing revolution" and considerable pondering on how best to "stimulate" consumer buying, by creating wants in people that they still didn't realize existed. An auto maker talked of increasing his car sales by selling to "those who do not yet know what they need."

This urgently felt need to "stimulate" people brought new power, glory, and prosperity to the professional stimulators or persuaders of American industry, particularly the skilled gray-flanneled suiters of New York's Madison Avenue, known as "ad alley." In 1955, $9,000,000,000 was poured into United States advertising, up a billion from 1954 and up three billion from 1950. For each man, woman, and child in America in 1955 roughly $53 was spent to persuade him or her to buy products of industry. Some cosmetics firms began spending a fourth of all their income from sales on advertising and promotion. A cosmetics tycoon, probably mythical, was quoted as saying: "We don't sell lipstick, we buy customers."

One big and intimidating obstacle confronting the stimulators was the fact that most Americans already possessed perfectly usable stoves, cars, TV sets, clothes, etc. Waiting for those products to wear out or become physically obsolete before urging replacements upon the owner was intolerable. More and more, ad men began talking of the desirability of creating "psychological obsolescence."

At a conference of gas-range people the conferees were exhorted to emulate the more up-to-date car makers in this business of creating psychological obsolescence. They were reminded that auto merchandisers strive to make everyone ashamed to drive a car more than two or three years. The gas-range people were told bluntly by the director of American Color Trends: "Ladies and gentlemen, you know and I know that too many housekeepers have the attitude that 'any old piece of equipment will do so long as it works at all.'" He described the recent trend to change the color of many products and explained: "All of these trends have a definite bearing on what you can do to step up the obsolescence of gas appliances."

By the mid-fifties merchandisers of many different products were being urged by psychological counselors to become "merchants of discontent." One ad executive exclaimed with fervor: "What makes this country great is the creation of wants and desires, the creation of dissatisfaction with the old and outmoded."

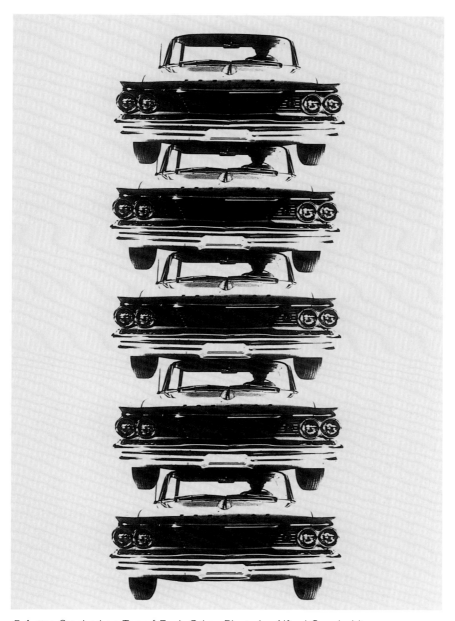

5 Autos Stacked on Top of Each Other. Photo by Alfred Gescheidt.

Write a short essay explaining how the above photo represents the society or marketing attitudes described in this essay. Alternatively, search for another photo that you think represents this society, or your own society.

Vance Oakley Packard was born in Granville Summit,
Pennsylvania, in 1914. He was a U.S. non-fiction writer of
popular sociological tracts, including *The Hidden Persuaders*
and *The Status Seekers.* He died in 1996.

1. *Response*
   a. List the three basic assumptions marketers were making
   about people, according to this essay. For each assumption,
   list one piece of evidence that proved to marketers that
   these assumptions were false.
   b. Explain the phrases *merchants of discontent* and *psychological
   obsolescence.* List any other marketing or media terms found
   in the essay. Include a definition for each term.
   c. This essay was first published in 1957. Discuss how it
   represents that era. Is this essay still relevant? Do you
   think media literacy courses in school have created wiser
   consumers? Explain your answer.
   d. Discuss some of the techniques that advertisers used, or
   still use, to reach their customers.
   e. What effect does the gender-biassed language in this essay
   have on the reader? Why are words like *ad men* no longer
   appropriate?

2. *Making Connections* Discuss the argument that both
   Kilbourne and Packard present in their essays. What stance
   does each writer take toward the advertising media? What
   would they have to say to one another about consumers
   or consumerism?

3. *Media Reaching Consumers* Find examples of ads—in print, or
   on TV, radio, or the Internet—that use any of the methods for
   reaching consumers discussed in this essay. Choose one ad to
   present to your class, commenting on the techniques it uses,
   the messages it sends, and its effectiveness.
   Is there a product that you think consumers are eagerly
   awaiting? Develop an ad for this new product. Choose one
   of the techniques mentioned in any of the advertising or
   marketing articles you have read so far.

Advertising is the key to world prosperity;
without it today modern business would be paralysed.
   —*Julius Klein*

In the following selection, two young boys discuss the difference in their lives now that they are Canadian; it is 1949, and their province, Newfoundland and Labrador, has just joined Confederation.

All Part of Becoming Canadian

Autobiographical anecdote by Al Pittman
from the essay "The Day I Became a Canadian"

"Listen Johnny," I said as soon as I got the chance, "you know what this means, now that we're living in Canada?"

"Of course I do," replied Johnny. But he didn't so I told him.

"It means all kinds of things. It means maybe now we'll be able to wear those U.S. Keds sneakers that they wear in the comics, instead of these old gum boots."

"How come?"

"Because Canada is a big place, my son. Bigger than the States even. My father said so."

"So?"

"So, if Canada is as big as the States, then it must have all that stuff in it."

"What stuff?"

"You know. The stuff in comics. Like where you can join a club and get all kinds of free prizes like spy glasses and roller skates and model airplanes and Double Bubble Gum."

"So what? My mother won't let me chew bubblegum. She says it's rude to blow bubbles, and it causes germs."

"Still, I bet you'd sneak a chew if it could make you fly."

"What do you mean, fly?"

"You know, like the kid in the comics. The one who blows big bubbles and flies all over the place. If you could blow a bubble big enough you could go right over your house, over the school even. If it was Double Bubble Gum you could."

"Go on! That's just comic book stuff."

"No. It's real. Cross my heart and hope to die. They really have things like that in places like the States and Canada. And now that we live in Canada, we'll have them too. Just imagine, being able to fly!"

Johnny was a real skeptic and refused to believe a word of it. But back then, when it all began, when I was nine, I, for one, firmly believed in Double Bubble Gum ads. The comic books had convinced me that if we could get Double Bubble Gum, then I could fly like the boy in the advertisements and float, borne up by the biggest bubble imaginable, over buildings and hills. And I could catch bank robbers if there were any around to catch, and I'd be a hero then to everyone who knew me. As far as I was concerned, it was all part of becoming Canadian.

Al Pittman was born in Placentia Bay, Newfoundland and Labrador, in 1940. He is a publisher, teacher, and editor and has written short stories, essays, plays, poetry, and children's stories. Some of his books include *Once When I Was Drowning* and *One Wonderful Fine Day for a Sculpin Named Sam.*

1. Response
a. How would you describe the tone of this article? Explain your reasoning.
b. In your opinion, is the narrator unusually naïve for a boy his age? Explain.
c. Have you, or anyone you know, ever had a similar experience to young Al Pittman's? Describe what happened and how you (or the other person) felt.

2. Media *Selling to Children* Investigate the rules that control various media and advertisements that are directed toward children. Do you think the existing rules are sufficient to protect children from being fooled by advertisers? Explain.

Watch a children's program on TV, or examine a magazine designed for children, and analyse any ads you see. What conclusions can you draw about these ads?

3. Making Connections Choose one of the following activities:
With a small group, improvise a discussion between the two boys in this selection, and the two adults in "The Sea-Monkey Lady" interview, which follows.

Write another paragraph for the Vance Packard essay, "The Trouble with People," that uses this selection as an example to expand on, support, or disprove one of his points.

Be careful what you order from the back of comic books—your whole life could be affected, as Susan Barclay reveals in this radio interview with Arthur Black. Barclay is the author of the book The Ultimate Guide to Sea-Monkeys.

The Sea-Monkey Lady: Susan Barclay

Radio interview
by Arthur Black

ARTHUR: Susan Barclay of Chilliwack, British Columbia, is known as the Sea-Monkey Lady. She happens to be with me right now. Hi Susan.

SUSAN: Hi.

ARTHUR: Sea-monkeys, now these are the things that were on the back of the comic books, along with the X-ray spectacles and the Charles Atlas body-building programs.

SUSAN: Yep. Those are the same ones.

ARTHUR: I didn't know they were still even around.

SUSAN: They've been around for forty years now. Most people don't know they're still around.

ARTHUR: How did they start out? Do you know?

SUSAN: Back in the fifties, Harold Von Braunhut, who created these little guys, decided to tinker around with the genetics of different crustaceans, and came up with these ones.

ARTHUR: So, these are kind of a manipulated breed. You don't find these out in the ocean, right?

SUSAN: No. The actual name is *Artemia Salina*. That's the name for a regular brine shrimp.

ARTHUR: Brine shrimp. OK …

SUSAN: … Yes. And these are called, because they're a genetically modified hybrid, they call these *Artemia Nyos*, N-Y-O-S, for New York Oceanic, I can't remember the S … *(laughs)*

ARTHUR: That's OK. *(laughs)* You could have faked it. I wouldn't know.

SUSAN: I *should* have made something up.

ARTHUR: So, uh, how do they go with pasta? No that's not funny, that's not funny, eh?

SUSAN: Oh, that's mean. *(laughs)*

ARTHUR: No, they're tiny. But you know, there's something missing here, Susan. 'Cause the ones that I saw on the back of the comic books, they all had little tiaras, and they carried a sceptre. These guys seem to be quite naked.

SUSAN: Well, if you look *real* close. No, I'm kidding. Unfortunately, if you look at the box it does say, "illustration is fanciful." Because I'm sure, I remember when I was six, I was convinced I was going to have a kingdom of my own. *(Arthur's voice over hers: Yeah, Yeah!)* But unfortunately, no, they look like … brine shrimp.

ARTHUR: Are these guys full grown? 'Cause these aren't even as big as the tip of my finger.

SUSAN: Um. Most of them are. Most of them in this tank are full grown. They get to about three quarters of an inch at the very most. And that's partially to do with the genetic modification, and that's also because they're brine shrimp and they're small.

ARTHUR: Yeah, they're small all right. Space is not a problem here. *(Susan laughs)* I've got, I guess you could call it a tank, and there's at least thirty of the guys in there. And the tank isn't much bigger than a … sort of like half a beer stein.

SUSAN: *(laughs)* It's twelve ounces, about the same as a Coke can. *(Arthur speaking over Susan: Yeah?)* It's not a lot. But if you look *very, very* closely you can see some of the *little* babies around there. It looks like, as you said, about thirty, but if you look *very* closely there's probably another twenty babies, and there's a few pregnant in there, so we're looking at …

ARTHUR: You can tell they're pregnant?

SUSAN: Yeah …

ARTHUR: … Wow! …

SUSAN: … You can actually tell male from female, you can tell when they're pregnant, and when they're not. They're … *(Arthur, over Susan:*

Holy smokes) … they're actually quite complicated little creatures for being such a … a small crustacean …

ARTHUR: *(speaking over Susan's last words)* A tiny thing. Yeah. They just look like a little eyelash. There's not much to them. Do you consider yourself the Jane Goodall of sea-monkeys?

SUSAN: *(Susan laughs)* That's an excellent question. Actually, I do know a man who's an expert who's called Jacques Goodall. So, I would have to say I'm more of the … the woman who used to … *Gorillas in the Mist,* Diane Fossey. *(Arthur over Susan: Yeah. Yeah, OK.)* Whereas Jane Goodall kept a hands-off approach, I prefer to get right in the sea-monkey …

ARTHUR: … You're real folksy with it. *(Susan over Arthur: Yeah. Yeah.)* I can see that. In fact, you have carrying arrangements I seem to see here. *(Susan over Arthur: Yes!)* In fact, you've got sea-monkeys on your wrist! What's that about?

SUSAN: I do! It's the sea-monkey watch! And it's an aquarium that not only tells the time, which is useful for getting to appointments, but you can pop the top off and pop a few of your favourite sea-monkeys in and take them around with you.

ARTHUR: Well, don't they get shaken up a lot?

SUSAN: They do, but sea-monkeys can handle it. Same concept as, they say you could drop an *ant* from the Empire State Building, *(Arthur over Susan: Uhn-hunh.)* and it wouldn't get hurt. Same thing with sea-monkeys, with their exoskeleton they're very strong, they haven't got, you know, the flesh to get hurt.

ARTHUR: So maybe it's like a roller coaster for them, I guess.

SUSAN: They really like the ride. *(Arthur over Susan: Yeah.)* So when I'm bringing the sea-monkeys down for a hundred kilometre drive today they quite enjoyed … I actually heard them going "Wheeee!" at one point. *(Susan laughs)*

ARTHUR: I was going to say … I thought I heard a little singing …

SUSAN: Well, they do sing. You know one of the things …

ARTHUR: They don't really, do they?

SUSAN: *(Susan laughs)* No! *(Arthur laughs)* One of the things I warn people … I have a list of do's and don't's with sea-monkeys, and sometimes people write to me and say "Is this true?" 'cause one of them is don't let them mow your lawn as they're allergic to freshly cut grass. *(Arthur over Susan: Oh?)* And people are always saying "Is this true?" They're three quarters of an inch long. I don't think they should be cutting grass in the first place; that's just animal cruelty. *(Arthur laughs)* And I say, don't lie to them, because they don't like being lied to any more than people do.

ARTHUR: Susan, do you spend a lot of time alone?

SUSAN: Yeah. A little too much. *(Both laugh)* With tanks and tanks of sea-monkeys around the room.

ARTHUR: I've been looking at these guys closely, trying to figure out how they *breathe*.

SUSAN: They breathe through their legs.

ARTHUR: Ah. I should have guessed.

SUSAN: I told you they were *fascinating*. They have little tubes that go through their legs.

ARTHUR: Yeah.

SUSAN: And they breathe in that fashion. Which is why they don't wear shoes. So, it's …

ARTHUR: Well, I can't even see legs, never mind … shoes.

SUSAN: They're *little* tiny legs. If you look very closely …

ARTHUR: Now how the heck would you know that?

SUSAN: That they breathe through their legs?

ARTHUR: Yeah.

SUSAN: 'Cause someone told me.

ARTHUR: *(laughs)* That's the best way to learn.

SUSAN: I'm not a marine biologist, although I do play one on TV.

An ad circa 1957

Compare these images with current packages or ads for similar products.

A package circa 1962

ARTHUR: *(laughs)* I've always regretted that I never—I guess I didn't believe that there were kings and queens brine shrimp—but if I was going to get into this, what, I get a starter sea-monkey kit? What happens then?

Susan: Yeah. There's a number of different kits. But the basic sea-monkey kit is about $10. It's not a lot of money, I mean, in it you get three packages, you get the water purifier, where, just like goldfish, you have to prepare the water, you get the package of eggs, and you get yourself a package of food. And the tank. And that's all you need to start with. And then there are accessories that go with it, but …

Arthur: Yeah.

Susan: And you put the water in, put the water purifier in, and 24 to 36 hours, put the eggs in, and you have instant life.

Arthur: This is beginning to sound like the shopping channel.

Susan: *(laughs)* You know … well I have to admit, having explained this before, I've learned to make it quick for people.

Arthur: So. Can I use dog kibble? What do you feed them?

Susan: *(laughs)* Please don't. People have asked if they can put bananas in too. Don't put … anything you wouldn't stick in your ear, don't put in the tank. Basically, they live on algae and diatoms …

Arthur: Those are the little tiny tiny things …

Susan: Yes. You get the sea-monkey package food, which, everyone says, "Well, what if I run out?" It's so little the amount you use, I mean they're just little tiny creatures.

Arthur: Yeah.

Susan: You put a little scoop in and they'll feed themselves for weeks with it.

Arthur: Can you teach them to do tricks?

Susan: You can!

Arthur: No?!

Susan: You can, honestly. One of the things that sea-monkeys have is they're photo-reactive. So, just in the same way that a plant will turn to the light, sea-monkeys will react to light as well. So, if you turn the lights off, in your room, or wherever you have them, get your flashlight out, say you take the flashlight from one side of the tank to the other, they'll follow it.

Arthur: Really?

Susan: So if you do it in spirals, they look like they're spiralling …

Arthur: … No kidding?

Susan: And one of the tanks I've brought with me has a lighted cover on the top and what you can do is put that on. And if you leave that light on you'll see them all … gravitate to it … if it's in a dark room, they'll all gravitate eventually. And the ghostly galleon, which is another one of the tanks, comes with a glow-in-the-dark little ship. And if you put that in, eventually you'll see just that they're spending a little bit more time around this glow-in-the-dark …

ARTHUR: This already sounds like way more fun than the Internet.

SUSAN: Yeah. *(laughs)* I *enjoy* them. It's funny, 'cause people can't understand how brine shrimp could be so much fun, but in the same way that having goldfish is fun, these are great, *and* they have a lot of *kitsch* value to them, because everyone remembers them from when we were kids. So …

ARTHUR: *(speaking over Susan's last word)* Yeah, yeah, of course. Now listen, Susan, if I get attached to these guys, how long is it going to be before they leave me?

SUSAN: They say two years now. *(Arthur speaking over Susan: Yeah?)* And the only reason I haven't been able to prove that is because this new formulation has only been out for a little over a year. But this tank that's before you right now was started last February. And they're all doing great, they're doing fine, and they keep having … there's eggs and babies.

ARTHUR: Well, that's a problem. I can see an overpopulation, if I didn't want a whole bunch could I get them neutered?

SUSAN: OH! Please no! But you could in *theory*, you know, just take all the females out, and you wouldn't have any more babies. But that would be boring. And they tend to … once you see a couple of sea-monkeys mating, odds are they will stay like that … for … the rest of their natural lifetimes. They like to mate.

ARTHUR: They'll stay mating?

SUSAN: Yes. Well, they'll at least stay attached. The male has whiskers that come out of his chin, *(Arthur: AH!)* and what he does is he clings on to the woman, the female, and doesn't let go. And so they will stay …

ARTHUR: Is this like a really bad date?

SUSAN: *(laughs)* Yes. I always say, you know that's the one thing with sea-monkeys: you should set up a singles tank for them, and serve banana daiquiris, and keep them away, because they will mate like *silly!*

ARTHUR: Listen, there's something else unusual on the table here. This looks like one of those snow globes. What's that? There's a *castle* in the middle of it.

SUSAN: It's the sea-monkey magic castle and it's brand new. They've decided to soup some of the things up, instead of having the boring old little tank. And this thing rocks. It's the magic castle …

ARTHUR: The globe itself is maybe four or five inches high, and the castle is maybe two and a half inches high in the middle and it's got little crenellations around the top and spires and towers.

SUSAN: And there's little sea life on it. That has got to be the coolest tank they have. It's like a snow globe, and you can shake it up, not obviously too vigorously, but you can shake it up. And I actually had a friend at work, Wanda, who has the tank in her office. And she can't count how many times people have come in and said "Cool!" and started shaking … and you know there's water everywhere. So you have to be careful with them. But this is one of the new tanks that they've come up with. They're just fantastic.

ARTHUR: The other problem that occurs to me, is what if these accidentally get flushed down the toilet? Are we going to have killer brine shrimp …

SUSAN: Mutant sea-monkeys? *(laughing)*

ARTHUR: Yeah, running around in the sewers?

SUSAN: You must have read the weekly World News report from a few years ago. *(Arthur laughs)* There was an article in the weekly *World News* and it said "Killer Mutant Sea-monkeys Attack Swimmers off Florida Coast."

ARTHUR: I knew it. I knew it. You know, Susan, I don't think we have to interview anyone else. *(Susan laughs)* We'll just call you in once a week. You are like every *Basic Black* guest I've ever had, all in one.

SUSAN: I'm in here. Just tell me when to come and I'll be here. And the sea-monkeys love the ride so they enjoyed themselves. Although it seems like a very *strange* hobby to have—sea-monkeys—people get such a laugh out of it …

ARTHUR: Well, they're totally unthreatening. You couldn't possibly find anything sinister about them, could you?

SUSAN: But you'd be surprised, some people, I mean I get people asking me all the time, horrible, horrible ways to eat them. "My Granpa drank them. Are they poisonous?" And …

ARTHUR: … Somebody drank them?

SUSAN: Yeah. You know, I was asking my mom about this. "How would you accidentally drink sea-monkeys?" Mom said, "Well, if they put them in a cup." I said, "But don't you look at what you're about to drink? If you saw something moving …"

ARTHUR: So you never drank a sea-monkey?

SUSAN: No, well … OK, I have to confess.

ARTHUR: *(laughs)* You had a guilty look about you.

SUSAN: This is such an embarrassing story, because I'm encouraging people not to drink them. When I was in England, I had them in a Coke-type bottle with a cap on it so I could carry them around. 'Cause the tank does have two holes in the side for air, so I was scared they would tip out. And on the second-to-last day, I'd been doing so much travelling and having so much fun I wasn't sleeping much. And I woke up to take a swig of water, popped the top open and took this giant swig of sea-monkey water and I was about to drink it and I went "Whooooh" and I spat it everywhere. And then I just felt, after washing my mouth out, oh my … And I drank probably a good inch of the water before I'd realised it.

ARTHUR: So Susan, how were they?

SUSAN: Horrible! *(both laugh)* You know, it's not just the sea-monkeys, it's the *algae*. It's a lot of things people should *not* be eating.

ARTHUR: Do not put this in your mouth.

SUSAN: No, no!

ARTHUR: Good advice. Thanks for coming in, Susan, with your friends. Your dozens and dozens of friends.

SUSAN: Thank you very much.

ARTHUR: OK.

SUSAN: It's been a real pleasure.

ARTHUR: For me too. Susan Barclay of Chilliwack, B.C. She is the Sea-Monkey Lady. If anybody could possibly doubt that.

Music: "Under the Sea" instrumental music.

Arthur Black was born in Toronto in 1943. He has hosted the weekly national radio show, *Basic Black*, since 1983, and has written a series of books including *Black in the Saddle Again* and *Black by Popular Demand*. He has won many awards, including a 1977 George Cadogan Award for best weekly columnist; the 1986 National Radio Award for Best Opinion/ Commentary; and the Stephen Leacock Medal for Humour in both 1997 and 1999.

I. *Response*

a. Have you ever ordered anything from the back of a comic book or magazine? If so, describe your experience, and how you felt.

b. List the idioms and slang used in this interview, for example, *soup* or *rocks*. Define each item on your list, according to the context in which it is used. Why is this usage appropriate or effective in this context?

2. *Oral Language* *Discussion* Arthur Black and Susan Barclay raise several interesting media topics or issues—for example, the "souping" up of the tank as a snow globe or the false advertising of sea-monkeys with accessories like the tiaras or sceptre. Discuss these issues.

3. *Media* *Promotions* Susan Barclay appeared on *Basic Black* partly to promote her book *The Ultimate Guide to Sea-Monkeys*. Discuss what you know about the process of gener-ating publicity for a book or other product or service. What else will authors or publishers do to raise public interest in a book? Who might be involved in a publicity campaign?

4. *Language Conventions* *Revising* As you read this script you probably noticed a lot of dashes, commas, and ellipses were used throughout. These often indicated a faltering or pause in the speech as the speakers responded spontaneously to each other in a live broadcast. Compare this to the two previous radio scripts in this unit—which were scripted and delivered smoothly—"Christmas Consumer Frenzy" and "One Ocean." Which of these scripts is the most realistic, representing everyday speech? How does the dialogue in "Sea-Monkey Lady" compare to dialogue you hear on other media—for example, TV shows, TV news, or movies?

Choose one of the following tasks:

Revise one of the scripts, removing any faltering speech, to make it read smoothly.

Revise one of the scripts to make it seem more natural, like a conversation you might have at school or home.

The marketing department of any company needs to know how to use the media to generate publicity. The following article is a practical guide to publicity.

NO NEWS IS BAD NEWS

Using Publicity to Your Advantage

How-to article by Alexander Hiam
from *Marketing for Dummies*®

Publicity is coverage of your product or business in the editorial portion of any news medium. If, for example, *Consumer Reports* runs an article praising your product as best in a category, that's publicity. Good publicity. If, in contrast, the evening television news programs run a story saying that your product is suspected of causing numerous accidents, that's publicity, too. Bad publicity.

These two examples illustrate common reasons for journalists to cover a product as a story—either because the product is better or worse than expected. In both cases, *product quality is the key to publicity*. Keep this fact in mind.

The best way to initiate positive publicity is to design and make a truly superior product. The best way to generate negative publicity is to make something bad. So the quality of your product development and production/delivery processes is an important factor in your use of publicity. Good publicity starts with a pursuit of quality throughout your firm's management processes!

Here's a simple rule: When your organization and products are not getting covered at all, that's your fault as a marketer.

Marketers need to be proactive and generate some positive publicity. But when your product is getting bad coverage in the press, that's generally management's fault. Of course, you still have to take the rap and cope with the negative exposure, but because the problem most likely originates with management errors, you should involve senior management right away.

Public relations (PR) is the active pursuit of publicity for marketing purposes. PR is what you do to generate good publicity and try to minimize bad publicity. Generally, marketers are responsible for generating good publicity. If they create good stories and communicate them to the media effectively, the stories will be picked up and turned into news or entertainment content. Good publicity.

Marketers or general managers also wear the PR hat in smaller organizations, but large companies generally have a PR person or department whose sole job is to generate positive publicity. Also, many businesses hire *publicists* or *PR firms*—experts who do PR on a freelance or consulting basis.

There is also such a thing as *bad publicity*. Any negative news needs to be countered and the root causes eliminated if at all possible. Handling bad publicity is also an important marketing issue.

Marketers don't go looking for bad publicity. Bad publicity is usually the result of poor overall management (which produces bad financial results or poor quality products), or it is the result of specific management errors (like approving an unsafe design in order to get a product out quickly). And sometimes bad publicity is the result of plain bad luck—in which case, you'll need to present an honest, concerned face to the media until the storm blows over.

When something goes really wrong and the media are having a field day reporting it, then you have a *PR crisis*. The first step in solving a PR crisis is to get a top executive alone in a room and force him or her to tell you what really happened; once the media starts digging, the truth will eventually come out anyway. The next step is to try to get the executive to agree to come clean with the media by making a truthful statement about what went wrong and how the company plans to try and fix the problem. If you can't get management to do so, forget it. You won't be able to stem the tide of negative PR. The crisis will keep growing. In that case, your best fallback is to polish your resume and find a better job. (Only kidding!)

Crisis management is a gloomy topic, and hopefully you won't ever have to do it. In contrast, generating positive PR should be a daily or at least weekly marketing activity. The following sections show you how to do so.

How do I sniff out good stories?

To a journalist, a *good story* is anything that has enough public interest to attract readers, viewers, or listeners and hold their attention. More specifically, a good story for a journalist covering the plastics industry must be sufficient to hold the interest of people in that industry. And I'm sorry to say that most of what you want to communicate to your market is pretty far from a good story.

Journalists and editors do *not* want stories about

- Your new product or service and how it differs from competitors or your previous models (unless that's their coverage specialty)
- Why you or your company's senior executive think your products are really great
- Your version of an *old story*—one that they've covered in the same way before
- Anything that seems boring or self-serving to anyone who doesn't work for your firm

Yet those are the kinds of stories reporters often get, because the people handling PR generally aren't skilled journalists, and aren't even trying to *think like* skilled journalists. That's what you must do. You have to sniff out a story, put together sufficient information to back up the story, and script a version that is virtually ready to be run in your target media. To be good at generating positive publicity, all you have to do is …

… think like a journalist!

What's the hook?

If you don't know how to think like a journalist, here's a simple exercise to help you get the idea. Scan today's newspaper (whichever one you like to read) and rank the top five stories based on their interest to you. Now analyze each one in turn to identify the one thing that made that story interesting enough to hold your attention. The *hooks*, the things that made each story interesting to you, will differ. But each story will have hooks. And even though they differ, these hooks have certain elements in common:

> A good ad should be like a good sermon: It must not only comfort the afflicted—it must also afflict the comfortable.
>
> Bernice Fitz-Gibbon

- Hooks are often based on new information (information you didn't know or weren't sure of).
- Hooks make that new information relevant to your activities or interests.
- Hooks catch your attention, often by surprising you with some thing you hadn't expected.
- Hooks promise some benefit to you—although the benefit may be indirect—by helping you understand your world better, avoid something undesirable, or simply enjoy yourself as you read the paper.

If you performed the preceding exercise, I think you could write the next paragraph as well as I can:

The logical conclusion is that you need to design hooks to make your marketing message into appealing stories for journalists to use. And your hooks need to be just like the ones that attracted your attention to those newspaper stories, with one exception: They must, somehow, be tied to your marketing information. At least a thin line has to exist from the hook to your brand identity, the news that you've just introduced a new product, or whatever else you want the public to know. That way, when journalists use your hook in their own work, they will end up including some of your marketing information in their stories as an almost accidental side effect.

Journalists don't want to help you communicate with your target market. They couldn't care less about your target market. But journalists are happy to use any good stories that you're willing to write for them, and if your product gets mentioned or your marketing manager gets quoted as a result, that's not a problem. So the secret, the key, the essence, of good publicity is to develop stories with effective hooks and give them away to overworked journalists who are eager for a little help from volunteers like you.

How do I communicate a story to the media?

When teaching PR most people start here—with the form, not the content. In my experience, content is 90 percent of the battle, form 10 percent, so I've reversed the traditional emphasis. But form does matter, too. You need to put your story into an appropriate and professional format so that journalists know what the story is and find it easy to work with.

The most important and basic format for communicating a story is the *press release* or *news release*, a short, written document with a clear headline at the top, sufficient facts and quotes to support a short news story, brief supporting background on the company/product involved, a date, and contact information for journalists who want to follow up with a phone call to get more information or to arrange an interview.

Yes, I know that's a lengthy definition, much longer than the ones in the textbooks on public relations. But when I define press release that way, I don't have to tell you much more about it for you to be able to write one yourself. Just make sure that you include all the elements that are in the definition—and that you have good content, a hook, to start with—and you will write an effective press release.

Figure 1 includes all the essential elements of format and style. You can use the release shown in the figure as a template for your own press releases.

March 31, 1997

FOR IMMEDIATE RELEASE

For more information, contact:
Alexander Hiam (413) 253-3658

CRAZY AUTHOR WRITES BOOK FOR DUMMIES

FIRST MARKETING TITLE TO ADDRESS REAL-WORLD NEEDS

AMHERST, Mass. — He's nearly done now. Just a section on public relations. Then the manuscript is off to production and — perhaps — history will be made. This title isn't just another book about business. This book is a redefinition of the marketing field that finally brings it up to speed with the harsh realities of business. And the book is, appropriately, by an author who straddles the boundaries between the ivory tower of business schools and the trenches of marketing management.

"What we teach about marketing on campus is pure fiction," complains Alexander Hiam, author of *Marketing For Dummies* (IDG Books Worldwide, Inc., 1997). "It's based on academic research, not on real-world practices and problems." Hiam threw out all his textbooks and visited past clients and other marketing practitioners before designing his new book. As a result, it …

Figure 1:
Writing a
killer press
release

The odds of your release getting picked up by the media and receiving any coverage at all are terribly low. Sorry to disappoint you. Journalists and editors throw away more than 90 percent of the releases they receive. So your goal is to beat the odds by writing a release that stands out from the junk in a journalist's in-box.

To beat the odds, pay attention to content (to make sure you have a good story—see preceding). And avoid these errors that journalists complain about in press releases:

Don't send inappropriate or late releases. Target the right media and contacts. The food critic doesn't need a release about a new robotics manufacturing facility. And the business correspondent doesn't either, if the facility opened two months ago.

You need to build up an accurate database of media contacts, and to mail your press release first class on occasion to validate it (with first class mail, you get envelopes back if addresses don't work). Faxing or e-mailing your release is often sensible because journalists work on tight deadlines, so include fields for fax and e-mail numbers in your database. But I recommend developing a list by identifying authors of stories you like and think are similar to your own stories. That way you get a smaller list, but one that is a much tighter match with your content and target audience. Commercial lists and directories of journalists are readily available from mailing list vendors.

Don't make any errors. At all. Typos throw the facts into question. And don't include any inaccurate facts. You want the journalist to trust you to do his or her research, which is a big leap of faith. Prove that you are worthy.

Don't give incomplete contact information. Be sure that you include names, addresses, and phone numbers that work. Brief the contacts as to when to be available and what to say so they will be cooperative. Also, brief the switchboard or give journalists instructions for how to navigate through the computerized voice mail system. You don't want gatekeeping to prevent a reporter from making that interview!

Don't ignore the journalists' research needs. The more support you give them, the easier they can cover your story. You can include photos of the expert you've quoted in a mailed release (date, name of person, and information about the supplier of the photo to be included on the back or in the margin). Also consider offering plant tours, interview times, sample products, or whatever else may help journalists cover your story.

Don't bug the reporters. Journalists don't want to send you clippings of the articles they write, so don't bother asking. Nor do they care to discuss with you why they didn't run a story, or why they cut off part of that quote when they did run a story. They are busy with the next story. Forget about it. You should focus on the next story, too.

Don't forget that journalists work on a faster clock than you do. When a journalist calls about your release, return the call (or make sure that somebody returns it) in hours, not days. If you handle their requests slowly, they will have found another source or written another story by the time you get back to them.

SHOULD I CONSIDER VIDEO AND ELECTRONIC RELEASES?

You can get a story out to the media in other ways, too. You can generate a video release, with useful footage that a television producer may decide to run as is or as part of a news story. You can also put a written press release on the PR newswire or other such services that distribute hard copy or electronic releases to their media clients—for a fee to the source of the release, of course. You can also pitch your stories to the Associated Press and other newswires. I'm not going to cover these options, because they are not that important to many marketers, and because if you want to pursue them you will most likely need to hire a publicist or PR firm anyway. Just know that the options exist, and ask your publicist for details if these options seem appropriate to your story.

Alexander Hiam has worked in marketing for many years. He obtained degrees from Harvard, and from U.C. Berkeley, where he obtained an MBA in marketing and strategy. He taught marketing and advertising at the School of Management of the University of Massachusetts at Amherst, and has written many marketing books including *The Portable MBA in Marketing* and *The Entrepreneur's Complete Sourcebook.*

I. *Response*

a. List the steps a marketing manager will take to develop a good publicity campaign.

b. In your own words define the following: *good publicity, bad publicity, hook,* and *news release.*

c. This selection was picked up from the reference book, *Marketing for Dummies: A Reference for the Rest of Us!*® This book is intended to help instruct people just learning about marketing, or those who are in the business. How would you describe the style and tone of this selection? Do you think it is suitable to the author's purpose and intended audience? Explain.

d. How does publicity differ from advertising?

2. *Media* Relationships Discuss the relationship between the news media, publicity and marketing departments, and the audience of the news media. Why is it important for consumers to know about this relationship?

3. *Drama* Role Play Choose one of the following scenarios and role-play the possible conversation with a partner or small group:

• The marketing manager of a large fast-food chain is called by a newspaper that wants to speak to him/her about mistreatment of union representatives.

• The marketing department of a movie studio tries to generate media interest in the studio's remake of a 1950s classic.

• The president of a large company that manufactures wheelchairs inadvertently reveals a major malfunction of the company's biggest seller while appearing on a hard-hitting news show.

• The president of a toy company announces a new scholarship program at a press conference attended by local and national press.

Take turns playing a variety of roles within your chosen scenario. Add as many details as you like to make your role play more realistic and interesting.

4. *Language Conventions* Relative Pronouns A *relative pronoun* is a pronoun that can introduce a subordinate clause. The relative pronouns are *who, whom, whose, which,* and *that.* When a subordinate clause is introduced by a relative pronoun, that clause serves as an adjective, modifying a word or antecedent in the main clause. For example:

> Margaret Atwood, who recently won the Booker, has written over twenty books.

Find one example in this article of a relative pronoun. How do relative pronouns increase clarity? How can you use relative pronouns in your writing?

"I cheered with each stinging tag and swinging blow delivered by this bunch of big-bat-swinging bullies."

SPORTS LOGOS
an Insult

Opinion piece by Noah Augustine

Last Thursday evening, I watched rather helplessly as nine Indians were thrashed and battered about by just as many men in blue and white uniforms. Normally, I would have done something about it—called for backup, at least. Instead, I cheered with each stinging tag and swinging blow delivered by this bunch of big-bat-swinging bullies.

They were the Toronto Blue Jays, of course, beating up on the celebrated Cleveland Indians. And, although I am an Indian (Mi'kmaq, I prefer) hailing from the Maritimes, I remain a big fan of the Indian-swatting Jays. One might assume that because Cleveland proudly displays an image of some misshapen Indian that all people of Indian descent must be Cleveland fans. Not true. In fact, the use of this imagery is insulting to most aboriginal people.

> A **logo** is an identifying symbol used as a trademark, in advertising, et cetera.

The issue of professional sports teams using Indian symbols is one that may not concern most Canadians, although it can be argued that Canadians have less tolerance for racism—and are less blatant in its exercise—than our neighbours in the U.S. We are, as they say, politically correct, at most times.

Nonetheless, for me, as an aboriginal person, the use of these religious symbols and caricatures of Indian chiefs or spiritual leaders as sports logos is as offensive to my cultural heritage as it would be for an African Canadian to observe the "Boston Blacks"—or for religious people to see the image of a rabbi, an archbishop or the Dalai Lama stitched into the shoulder patches of professional sports teams.

If a television image of thousands of baseball fans screaming "war chants" and waving fake tomahawks in support of the Atlanta

Braves is baffling me and my understanding of society, I can only wonder how such acceptance of less-than-subtle racism is affecting our younger generations. Who said it was okay for professional sports teams—and their millions of adoring fans—to adopt our cultural icons and images for mass ridicule?

One American youth, in a 1997 Grade 8 writing assignment on his school's use of an Indian symbol, explained it this way: "We simply chose an Indian as the emblem. We could have just as easily chosen any uncivilized animal." Is the education system the most effective tool we have in our fight against racism? I sometimes wonder.

With baseball's Atlanta Braves and Cleveland Indians, football's Kansas City Chiefs and Washington Redskins, and hockey's Chicago Blackhawks, professional sports organizations are turning a blind eye to racism in professional sports.

Professional athletes within these organizations serve as role models for all youth, including aboriginal youth. With this comes a certain responsibility.

Like so many Canadian kids, it is the dream of many aboriginal youth to someday lace up a pair of skates and face off against hockey's best. When Everett Sanipass, a Mi'kmaq from Big Cove First Nation, was drafted by the Chicago Blackhawks in the 1986 NHL draft, almost every aboriginal youth in Atlantic Canada proudly displayed the team logo—an Indian face with war paint—on everything from jerseys to lunch pails. Sanipass was the Wayne Gretzky of aboriginal hockey. It didn't matter which team he played for; what mattered was that he played in the big league. And if Sanipass said it was good, then it was great. The logo he wore could have just as easily been any "uncivilized animal." Kids do not recognize such symbols of racism but do become victims of the assault.

With dreams and aspirations comes sacrifice. It is admirable for sacrifice to be recognized as hard work and dedication, but let it not be admirable to accept tolerance of racism as just one more sacrifice.

Many feel that aboriginal people should be honoured that Indian imagery is the logo of some sports communities. But what honour lies in ridicule and mockery? Take, for example, a 1998 *Washington Post* sports headline, referring to a Dallas football victory over Washington, which read: "Cowboys finish off Redskins."

At the root of this issue is the trademark business. It's a multi-million-dollar industry. However, change is in the air. Last year, the Washington Redskins had seven trademarks, including their logo, cancelled for federal registration based on a complaint from several tribes. The Trademark Trial and Appeal Board found "Redskins" to be "disparaging" to native Americans. The ruling is under appeal.

Even though, as it is said, money makes the world go 'round, court actions can change that. Perhaps, someday, respect will have a greater value than the almighty dollar.

Noah Augustine is a newspaper columnist who has written articles for *The Toronto Star.*

1. *Response*
   a. Do you agree with Noah Augustine? Give reasons for your opinion.
   b. How does Noah Augustine feel about the statement "We could have just as easily chosen any uncivilized animal"?
   c. What do you think would be a fair solution to the problem of Aboriginal sports logos?
   d. What do you think players could or should do if they found their team's logo offensive?

2. *Media* Logos Discuss other logos, how they developed, and what they represent. Consider other sports teams' logos, the logos used for TV stations, and those used for large corporations. What purpose do logos serve? What makes a logo good? Compare at least five logos, their meaning, their effectiveness, and their appropriateness.
   Obtain copies of team logos that use representations of Native people, such as the ones mentioned in the article. Design new logos for these teams that are non-offensive, yet are still interesting and eye-catching.

3. *Writing* Letter Assume you work in the public relations department of one of the sports teams that has an offensive logo. Write a reply to Augustine acknowledging his position, presenting your own, and suggesting a solution or compromise.

4. *Critical Thinking* With a small group, discuss the phrase *big-bat-swinging-bullies.* Is violence in sports a problem, in your opinion? Explain.

**When you watch TV, is your brain
or your body responding to
the stimulus?**

TELEVISION
The Collective Imagination

ARTICLE BY DERRICK DE KERCKHOVE

The New Media Context

Stephen Kline is the Director of the Media Analysis Lab at Simon
Fraser University in Vancouver. He and his brother Rob have invented
a sophisticated system to analyze people's physiological responses to
anything they are being shown. Anything, everything and, especially,
television. Kline's work on the impact of television advertising and programming is well-known. Recently, Stephen and his brother invited
me to be one of their guinea pigs. They wired me to a computer with
various skin-response devices. They attached one to my left middle
finger for skin conductivity, another to my forehead—presumably to
probe my brain activity—a third to my left wrist to take my pulse and
the last over my heart area to monitor circulation. Another device, a
rather crude joystick, was placed in my right hand. By pushing it for-
wards or backwards, I could indicate whether I liked or disliked what I
was watching. Then Rob and Stephen left the lab and the show began.

I watched a fast paced jumble of typical viewing fare: sex, advertising, news, talk shows, sentimentality and tedium. The cuts seemed to
average around fifteen seconds each. By normal TV standards, that
speed does not appear to be excessive, though in my new role as
a knee-jerk critic, I found it very difficult to keep up the pace with
the joystick. By the end of the twenty-minute experiment, I was
thoroughly frustrated, having failed to express much more than limp-
wristed approvals or disapprovals. For many cuts, I hadn't had enough
time to express anything at all.

When Rob and Stephen came back to rewind the tape and check
the graphs on the computer, I told them my feeling of helplessness.
They laughed and invited me to watch the screen while they replayed

the tape in sync with the data. To my absolute amazement, I saw that every cut, every jolt, every change of image had been recorded by one sensor or another and fed into the computer. I could see the busy outlines of the graphs corresponding to my skin conductivity, pulse, heartbeat and to whatever mysterious response my forehead had been giving. I was flabbergasted. As I was labouring to express an opinion, my whole body had been listening and watching and reacting instantaneously.

TV Talks to the Body, Not the Mind

I drew two important conclusions from that experience. The first is that television talks primarily to the body, not to the mind. This is something I'd suspected for several years. The second conclusion was that, if the video screen has such a direct impact on my nervous system and my emotions, and so little effect on my mind, then most of the information-processing was actually being performed by the screen. These are hypotheses I want to explore in this study of our ubiquitous, intimate and yet so little-known relationships to our screens: our videominds.

Why is it so difficult, if not impossible, to concentrate when the TV is on? Because television is hypnotically involving: any movement on the screen attracts our attention as automatically as if someone had just touched us. Our eyes are dragged towards the screen like iron to a magnet.

Orienting and Defensive Responses

Understanding our television culture depends upon understanding how and why television fascinates us beyond our conscious control. As I've proved to myself with the Kline brothers' experiment, my neuromuscular system constantly follows images on video, even if my mind occasionally wanders. This is involuntary because of our antediluvian biological programming: the autonomic nervous systems of higher

> [TV] is our latest medium—we call it a medium because nothing's well done ... It has already revolutionized social grace by cutting down parlour conversation to two sentences: 'What's on television?' and 'Good night.'
>
> Goodman Ace

mammals are trained to respond to any perceptible change in the environment that might be relevant to survival. We are conditioned to respond involuntarily to any kind of stimulation, internal or external, with what in clinical psychophysiology is called the Orienting Response (OR). This will either draw our attention towards the stimulus or alert the Defensive Response, which makes us recoil from it.

Now, you may well ask, in what way is TV relevant to our survival? In terms of content, not much. But television's principal action, as McLuhan never tired of repeating, happens not at the level of content but at the level of the medium itself, with the flickering light of the electron beam scanner. The changes and cuts in the shows provoke continuous OR's, drawing attention without necessarily satisfying it. In life, we accommodate stimuli as we get to know them: either we recognize them immediately or we quickly develop a strategy to deal with them. A completed response to a stimulus is called a closure. So in life, most stimuli awake an OR, call for a closure and receive it. With television, though, we are never done with the initial stimulus: TV provokes rapid successions of OR's without allowing time for closure.

The "Collapse of the Interval" Between Stimulus and Response

In a paper on cognitive responses to television, German media theorist Hertha Sturm made an important observation. When we watch television, we are denied enough time to integrate the information on a fully conscious basis.

> Rapidly changing presentations impair verbalization. Among these are uninterpreted changes in viewing angle, unpredictable flip-flops from picture to text or from text to picture. When confronted with rapidly changing presentations and speeded-up action, the viewer is literally driven from image to image. This demands constantly new and unexpected adaptation to perceptual stimulation. As a result the viewer is no longer able to keep up and ceases to internally label. When this occurs, we found, the individual acts and reacts with heightened physiological arousal which in turn results in a reduction of comprehension. The viewer becomes, so to speak, a victim of an external force, of rapid audio-visual sequencing.[1]

Picking up on this theme, Edward Renouf Slopek, a McGill University communications researcher and McLuhan Program Associate, coined the expression "collapsing the interval" to indicate that TV eliminates the distancing effect—the interval between stimulus and response—and the time to process the information in our conscious mind.[2] The suggestion is that television leaves us little if any time to reflect on what we are watching.

Jolts-Per-Minute (JPM's) and the "Missing Half-Second"

Orienting responses elicited by television are quite different from those elicited by the cinema. The light from the video screen does not bounce back into our eyes, it comes right at us through the screen, challenging us to respond, like the spotlight of the police interrogator in a movie. Hertha Sturm claims that it takes the mind at least half a second to provide proper closure to complex stimuli. She claims that TV denies this to the viewer, in what she terms "the missing half-second syndrome." It certainly took my mind several seconds to deal, albeit inadequately, with the material compiled by Stephen Kline. Sturm is probably correct in implying that television programming is deliberately geared to preventing verbalized responses, so as to make us easy victims of advertising messages.

Recently, Toronto media critic Morris Wolfe created the concept of "jolts-per-minute"—or JPM's—to describe how TV shows hit us.[3] The notion behind JPM's is that it takes a critical number of cuts to prevent the viewer from falling asleep or switching channels. TV must zap the zapper before he or she zaps the channel. JPM's that keep the attention alive may also prevent cognitive closure.

Sub-Muscularization and "Felt-Meaning"

However much people moralize, this is not necessarily a bad thing. One effect of the collapse of the interval is that in order to make sense of the rapid images we must somehow emulate the action with our bodies. Just as children faced with a new concept often find it helpful to act it out, we follow TV action with our bodies and even imitate the odd expression to better interpret it. This is what I call the "sub-muscularization effect"—analogous to the "sub-vocalization" strategy adopted by slow readers. Sub-muscularization is the interpretation of motion and action by a sort of sensorimotor mimicry involving the whole body. I suggest that we interpret gestures, postures and expressions on TV with a kind of sub-muscular response, expressed in muscle tone and stress factors. (The need for this kind of patterning can be observed in people's behaviour on the telephone where we usually accompany our sentences with many gestures and movements that we use in face-to-face conversation; perhaps this is because such physical involvement helps us to make sense of what we are saying.) Thus, "television sense" is not the same as "book sense." It is closer to what the American psychologist and philosopher, Eugene T. Gendlin, calls "felt-meaning."

Gendlin defines felt-meaning as "the equivalent of hundreds of thousands of cognitive operations" done in a split second by the body in response to stimuli.[4] Felt-meaning could be said to be a product of sub-muscularization. Indeed, as we experience events in our immediate surroundings, we store their relevant effects in various ways within our neuromuscular system. That is precisely what Hans Selye called stress. The Montreal-based clinical psychologist developed the theory of General Adaptive Syndrome (GAS) to account for the way we absorb the pressures of daily life, and how our body helps us to manage stress by sorting and storing stress's energy.

Although we know that we stop breathing when we are anxious or that we blush when we are put to shame, we are not usually aware of physical events happening within our bodies when we respond to people and situations. Felt-meaning is rarely conscious. But, in the background, it regulates and conditions our overall response to everyday matters. Felt-meaning precedes logic and may be more comprehensive than thought. Thus, the deeper effect of television might occur at the level of felt-meaning, offering little chance of response. Television evokes Orienting Responses that are woven into the fabric of our neuromuscular system.

"Grazing and Zapping Is the Way We Attend to Everything"

With this comment, social critic Michael Ignatieff condemned television. It probably reflects the opinion of many Canadians when he claims that "TV is turning us into a clever but shallow culture." It is easy to heap blame upon television. Often, without more than a hunch to go on, people attribute to television the instigation of social evils, everything from rape and murder to cynical apathy. Recently, a group of committed citizens in Vancouver felt so strongly about the dangers of television that they commissioned a series of TV ads to discourage people from watching. ("This sight is bad for you: stop looking right now.")

> I'm always amazed that people will actually choose to sit in front of the television and just be savaged by stuff that belittles their intelligence.
>
> Alice Walker

There are arguments about programming, ethics, aesthetics and invasions of privacy. But only a handful of critics, people like Jerry Mander, George Gerbner, Joshua Meyrowitz, Neil Postman and, certainly, McLuhan, have begun to understand the deeper message of the medium. TV is challenging our previously dominant, literate mindset by substituting its own tactile, collective orality. It threatens the sacrosanct autonomy we have acquired through reading and writing.

You Don't Watch TV, TV Watches You

There is not much that is "innocent" about the way we use our eyes. The following observation is by Jean-Marie Pradier, a professor of drama at the University of Paris and founder of an international association on Organized Human Performing Behaviours (OHPB).

> Social life, sexuality, and aggression are mainly ruled by visual components. This is perhaps why gazing is so severely controlled by precise codes and display rules. It is also why most of the human cultures have created freely viewed objects (paintings, sculptures, photographs, films) and freely viewed individuals (sportsmen and women, dancers, actors, and actresses, but also priests and public figures) along with free viewing spaces and events (theatre, carnival, hot urban districts) where it is possible to be a voyeur.[5]

Is television a free-viewing area? The relevance of this question was brought home to me at a clever video art installation by Mit Mitropoulos, a Greek communication artist from MIT. In *Face to Face*, two live participants sit back to back and converse with each other's images in real time on closed-circuit TV. Deceptively simple, the experience was unforgettable when I participated as one of the conversational partners. Irrespective of whether I did or didn't know my partner beforehand, I felt as if there were none of the usual barriers to staring someone right in the face. You could almost pick your nose in the context of this new electronic intimacy. True, I measured for the first time the extent to which we are terrified of faces in live contact, but what struck me more was that for the last thirty years we have unwittingly been watching our TV personalities without a trace of shyness. TV voyeurism is the "uncensored gaze." Perhaps television does provide a free-viewing area.

Or so it seems. The deep involvement required by viewing and the fact that most of our responses are involuntary bear witness to the changing power relationship between consumer and producer. When we read, we scan the books, we are in control. But when we watch TV, it is the TV scanner that "reads" us. Our retinas are the direct object of the electron beam. When scanning meets glancing, and makes eye contact between human and machine, the machine's glance is the more powerful. In front of the television set, our defences are down; we are vulnerable and susceptible to multi-sensory seduction. Thus, the real meaning of Prime Time could be "priming time," that is, the best time to prime the mind of the television viewer. As Tony Schwartz, New York advertising executive and TV critic, suggested, "TV is not a window on the world, it's a window on the consumer."[6]

Notes

1. Hertha Sturm, *"Perception and Television: The Missing Half Second," The Work of Hertha Sturm*, edited and translated from German by Gertrude J. Robinson (Montréal: McGill University, Working Papers in Communications, 1988), 39.

2. Edward R. Slopek, "Collapsing the Interval," *Impulse* (n.d.): 29–34.

3. Morris Wolfe, *Jolts: The TV Wasteland and the Canadian Oasis* (Toronto: James Lorimer and Co., 1985).

4. Eugene T. Gendlin, *Experience and the Creation of Meaning* (New York: Free Press, 1964), 27.

5. Jean-Marie Pradier, "Toward a Biological Theory of the Body in Performance," *New Theatre Quarterly* (February 1990): 89.

6. Tony Schwartz, *Media: The Second God* (Garden City, NY: Anchor Books, 1983).

Derrick de Kerckhove is Professor in the Department of French and Director of the McLuhan Program in Culture and Technology at the University of Toronto. He worked with Marshall McLuhan in the seventies, acting as translator, assistant, and co-author. *The Skin of Culture* is his first major Canadian publication.

1. *Response*

   a. Is Derrick de Kerckhove's attitude toward TV positive or negative in this article? How did you reach that conclusion?
   b. Are you "in control" when you watch TV, or is the TV in control, as de Kerckhove suggests? Explain.
   c. What is the most interesting point this article makes, in your opinion? Why is this point interesting?

2. *Vocabulary*
   Reread the selection and list any words you are unfamiliar with. Can you figure these words out from their context? Can you use clues in how the words are constructed—their prefixes, roots, suffixes, et cetera? List a definition for each word and then check a dictionary. How does working out the meaning of unfamiliar words in context help you understand the selection?

3. *Making Connections*
   Note the people and studies de Kerckhove quotes or refers to in this article. Choose one of these to investigate further. Read the original article, or at least part of the book, or read other works by that person. Are the author's arguments sound? Explain. What stance does that person take toward media? Did de Kerckhove faithfully represent that stance in his use of the work?

4. *Media* *Anti-TV Ads*
   In this selection, de Kerckhove describes a TV ad that tries to persuade viewers to shut off the TV. Why is this advertising campaign ironic? Why might a TV network refuse to run such ads? How effective do you think these ads would be? What might make these ads more effective? What might be a better medium for this campaign?

The quiz show has been around for a very long time, and the quiz show format described in this article will seem strangely familiar.

The Quiz Show Format

Article by David Halberstam

THE RADIO QUIZ SHOWS WERE, IN RETROSPECT, SMALL POTATOES, with prizes to match. On *Take It Or Leave It*, the ultimate challenge was the "$64 question"—a phrase that even worked itself into the American vernacular by 1945. In the new age of television, though, everything had to be bigger and better. Americans were not going to sit home, glued to their television sets, wondering whether some electronic stranger, who had briefly entered their living rooms, was going to be able to double his winnings from $32 to $64. In the postwar era that was pocket money.

Such was the dilemma facing Lou Cowan in early 1955. Cowan, one of the most inventive figures in the early days of television, needed a gimmick for a game show worthy of television, one so compelling that millions of Americans would faithfully tune in. He needed high drama, and what better way to achieve that than a *very* large prize? Six hundred and forty dollars? Not so terribly exciting. Nor, for that matter, was $6,400. "But $64,000 gets into the realm of the almost impossible," he thought. Cowan liked the double-or-nothing format—so he envisioned a contestant who had answered a series of questions correctly and won the dizzying sum of $32,000. At that point it would be time to play double or nothing, for $64,000. With one answer to one question, an ordinary American could be wealthy beyond his or her wildest dreams.

The concept depended on the belief that seemingly unexceptional Americans did indeed have secret talents and secret knowledge. That appealed greatly to Cowan, who, with his Eastern European Jewish background, had a highly idealized view of his fellow citizens' potential to reach beyond the apparent limits life had dealt them. His was an idealistic, almost innocent belief in the ordinary people of the country. Cowan's wife, Polly, daughter of a successful Chicago businessman and a graduate of Sarah Lawrence College, most decidedly did not like the idea for the show. She thought it essentially a corruption of the real uses of learning—glorifying trivial memorization rather than true thought and analysis. She believed that the rewards for knowledge should not be huge amounts of cash, doled out in front of millions of cheering strangers, ultimately to benefit commercial hucksters; instead, it should be the joy of knowledge itself. She did not hesitate to make her feelings known to her husband and in a way the debate in the Cowan household reflected the schizophrenic nature of the program itself—a compelling mix of achievement, purity and, of course, avarice.

Polly's doubts did not deter her husband. With his generous and optimistic nature, he saw the show as emblematic of the American dream; it offered everyone not only a chance to become rich overnight but to win the esteem of his fellow citizens. It proved every American had the potential to be extraordinary. It reflected, one of his sons said years later, a "White Christmas" vision of America, in which the immediate descendants of the immigrants, caught up in their optimism about the new world and the nobility of the American experiment, romanticized America and saw it as they wanted it to be.

Cowan was an independent television packager, a familiar figure in the early days of television; he and others like him came up with ideas, found sponsors, and then sold the entire package to the then rather passive networks. He sold this idea to Revlon, which was so enthusiastic that Walter Craig, an executive of the advertising agency that worked for Revlon, locked the door at Cowan's initial presentation and said, "Nobody leaves this room until we have a signed contract."

The name of the program was *The $64,000 Question*. It aired for the first time from 10:00 to 10:30 P.M. in June 1955, on CBS. It was an immediate hit. Millions of people identified with the contestants—who were very much like neighbors. The program showed a CBS psychologist named Gerhart Wiebe who said, "We're all pretty much alike, and we're all smart." The show contained all kinds of dramatic touches attesting to its integrity. The questions sat all week in a locked vault at a bank, and when they finally arrived on the set, they were transported by an executive from Manufacturers Trust, who was accompanied by two armed guards. An IBM machine shuffled the questions on the set.

Eight thousand dollars was the maximum a contestant could win on one show; then he or she had to come back next week. Suspense would start building. At the eight thousand-dollar level, the contestant had to enter an isolation booth; presumably so no one in the studio audience could whisper an answer. The speed with which the program enthralled the entire country was breathtaking. Its success surprised even Lou Cowan. The show offered hope of an overnight fortune, and it proved that ordinary people were not in fact necessarily ordinary. As such there was a powerful chord of populism to it. But more than anything else, it appealed to the viewers' sense of greed. Five weeks after its premiere, *The $64,000 Question* was the top-rated show on television. Studies showed that approximately 47.5 million people were watching. The sales of Revlon ("the greatest name in cosmetics") skyrocketed. Some Revlon products sold out overnight, and the show's master of ceremonies had to beg the public to be more patient until more Revlon Living Lipstick was available. The head of Hazel Bishop, a rival cosmetics company, subsequently blamed his company's disappointing year on the fact that "a new television program sponsored by your company's principal competitor captured the imagination of the public." It was the most primal lesson yet on the commercial power of television.

The contestants became the forerunners of Andy Warhol's idea of instant fame: people plucked out of total anonymity and beamed into the homes of millions of their fellow Americans. Between ten and twenty thousand people a week wrote letters, volunteering themselves or their friends to be contestants. After only a few appearances on the show, audiences began to regard the contestants as old and familiar friends. Perhaps, in retrospect, the most important thing illuminated by the show was how easily television conferred fame and established an image. Virtual strangers could become familiar to millions of their fellow citizens.

One of the first contestants, Redmond O'Hanlon, a New York City policeman, whose category was Shakespeare, reached the $16,000 plateau. At that point he decided to stop and, in his words, put "the conservatism of a father of five children" over "the egotism of the scholar." Soon Catherine Kreitzer, a fifty-four-year-old grandmother whose category was the Bible, reached $32,000. She was confident, Mrs. Kreitzer said, that she could win the full amount, but she stopped, quoting from the Bible: "Let your moderation be known unto all men." Perhaps the most engaging of all the early contestants was Gino Prato, a New York shoe repairman, whose category was opera. He easily reached the $32,000 plateau, whereupon his ninety-two-year-old father in Italy cabled him to stop at once. Prato, in time, became roving ambassador for a rubber-heel company, was given season tickets to the Metropolitan Opera, and went on to other television shows as well.

If the producers faced a dilemma in the beginning, it was the hesitance of the top contestants to go for the ultimate question. Some of it was the fear of losing everything and some was the nation's then extremely harsh income tax schedules. As Kent Anderson pointed out in his book *Television Fraud*, a contestant who went for the whole thing was risking almost $20,000 in order to win only $12,000 more.

A Marine captain named Richard McCutcheon became the first contestant to go all the way. Bookies kept odds on whether or not he could get the right answer. His field was cooking, not military history. With an audience estimated at 55 million watching, on September 13, 1955, he became the first contestant to climb the television Mt. Everest. For $64,000 he was asked to name the five dishes and two wines from the menu served by King George VI of England for French president Albert Lebrun in 1939. He did: consommé quenelles, filet de truite saumonée, petits pois à la françaises, sauce maltaise, and corbeille. The wines were Château d'Yquem and Madeira Sercial. The nation was ecstatic—it had a winner. "If you're symbolic of the Marine Corps, Dick," said Hal March, the emcee, "I don't see how we'll ever lose any battles."

Everyone involved seemed to profit from the show: Lou Cowan soon became president of CBS; the bank official who was in charge of the questions became a vice-president at Manufacturers Trust. But no one profited more than Revlon. The impact of the show upon its revenues was a startling reflection of changes that were taking place every day in more subtle ways because of the ferocious commercial drive of television and its effect upon both consumers and industry.

Revlon, at the time, was the leading cosmetics company in the nation, but Coty, Max Factor, and Helena Rubinstein were relatively close behind in net sales. In 1953, for example, Revlon had net sales of $28.4 million; Helena Rubinstein had $20.4 million; Coty had $19.6; Max Factor, $19 million; and Hazel Bishop, $9.9. All in all, it was a fairly evenly divided pie, and Revlon's sales increased on average about 15 percent annually in the years just before 1955. But sponsoring the quiz show changed all that. In the first six-month season, Revlon increased its sales from $33.6 million to $51.6—a stunning 54 percent increase. The stock jumped from 12 to 20. The following year saw sales increase to $85.7 million. By 1958 Revlon completely dominated its field. (Asked later by a staff member of a House subcommittee whether sponsoring *The $64,000 Question* had anything to do with Revlon's amazing surge to the top, a somewhat disingenuous Martin Revson answered, "It helped. It helped.")

Not surprisingly, *The $64,000 Question* produced a Pavlovian response to its success. Suddenly the networks were flooded with imitations, all of them for big prize money. The people in Cowan's old organization came up with *The $64,000 Challenge*. Others produced *Tic Tac Dough, Twenty-One, The Big Moment, Beat the Jackpot*, and *The Big Board*. There was even talk of *Twenty Steps to a Million*.

By 1956, the appeal of these shows appeared to be limitless; then subtly, and soon not so subtly, there was the inevitable pressure that television especially seemed to inspire: to improve the show by manipulation, to *cast* it—that is, to ensure each contestant would find some special resonance with the millions of people watching at home. The process began naturally enough at first, with the preference to choose a contestant possessed of considerable charm over a contestant without it. Soon the producers, by pretesting, were able to tell where a candidate's strengths lay and what his [or her] weaknesses were, without the contestants themselves even knowing what was happening: Prato knew Italian opera but little about the German opera; McCutcheon knew French cuisine rather than Italian or British. "We wrote the questions into the matrices of their existence," Mert Koplin, one of the men who worked on *The $64,000 Question*, later said. As the pressure built for ratings, the manipulations grew more serious. Some guests would be put through dry runs only to find that when they appeared on the live shows, the questions were remarkably similar to the ones they had answered correctly in the rehearsal. (McCutcheon, it turned out, was deeply bothered by this and thought seriously of getting out; he was encouraged to remain a contestant by his family. Later he told Joe Stone, the prosecutor from the New York District Attorney's office, that he thought the shows were fraudulent and immoral, and he disagreed violently with the claim of the various producers that the rigging had hurt no one.)

The Revlon executives from the start were extremely outspoken about the guests on the two shows they sponsored, *The $64,000 Question* and *The $64,000 Challenge*. Starting in the fall of 1955, there was a weekly meeting in Martin Revson's (Charles Revson's brother) office, where he and his top advertising people critiqued the previous week's shows and contestants. Revson was not shy about telling what he wanted to happen and who he wanted to win. He posted a chart in the meeting room with the ratings on it; if the ratings were down, it was the fault of the contestants. Were the contestants too old? Too young? Were they attractive enough? The criticism was often brutal. (The Revsons apparently did not like a young psychologist named Joyce Brothers, who appeared as an expert on boxing. Thus the questions given her were exceptionally hard—they even asked her the names of referees—

in the desire to get her off the show; their strategy had no effect: She became the second person to win $64,000.)

More and more, with so many different shows vying for public approval, the producers found it was the quality of the contestants themselves—and the degree to which the nation identified with them—that made the difference. When the Barry and Enright company, one of the big hitters in the world of game shows, introduced its new game in March 1956, called *Twenty-One*, loosely based on the card game of the same name, Dan Enright was confident it would be an immediate success. Two contestants would answer questions for points, without knowing how many points their opponent had. Enright thought it was a sure bet for unbearable dramatic excitement, especially since the audience would know more about the competition than the contestants themselves. He was dead wrong. The premiere was, he said later, a dismal failure, "just plain dull." The day after, Marty Rosenhouse, the sponsor, made an irate call to say he did not intend to own a turkey. "Do whatever you have to do," he told Enright, "and you know what I'm talking about." Those were the marching orders for Enright and his staff.

Fixing the show did not particularly bother Enright; the quiz shows had never been about intelligence or integrity as far as he was concerned; they were about drama and entertainment. "You cannot ask random questions of people and have a show," one game-show producer later said. "You simply have failure, failure, failure, and that does not make entertainment." That made it a predatory world, and Enright excelled in it. He was not, Dan Enright reflected years later, a very nice man in those days. He was totally compelled by work, wildly ambitious, and utterly self-involved. "I was determined to be successful no matter what it cost," he said, "and I was greedy, greedy, not for money, but for authority, power, prestige and respect." The end, he believed at the time, always justified the means. People were to be used; if you did not use them, he believed, they in turn would use you. Soon—with considerable fixing—*Twenty-One* became a huge success; at a relatively young age, Enright had already exceeded his own expectations, and he was wealthy and powerful. People coveted his attention and gave him respect. Thus he was able to rationalize everything he was doing.

David Halberstam is the author of many books, including *The Best and the Brightest,* and *The Powers That Be.* His book *Summer of '49* was a number one *New York Times* hardcover bestseller. Halberstam has won many major journalism awards, including the Pulitzer Prize. This excerpt was taken from his book, *The Fifties.*

1. *Response*
a. Why did Polly Cowan object to her husband's ideas for a quiz show? Do you agree or disagree with her? Explain.
b. How are the quiz shows described in this selection similar to or different from the quiz shows of today?
c. Was it inevitable that the quiz shows became crooked, as the article suggests? Explain.
d. Discuss the relationship between the quiz shows, their sponsors, and the audience.
e. Speculate on why quiz shows are so appealing.

2. *Making Connections* To find out the full story behind the quiz show *Twenty-One*, watch the 1994 movie *Quiz Show* directed by Robert Redford. Discuss the issues of integrity and honesty in TV shows that this movie raises.

3. *Media* Quiz Shows With a small group, develop 20 questions for a quiz show about quiz shows. You may need to do some research to help you with the questions. Once you have the questions and answers, produce a quiz show—with the help of volunteer contestants. Use current quiz show formats as a model or develop your own format.

The box sanctified, conferred identity.
The more familiar the face, the more
to be trusted.
— *P. D. James*

What do the movies *The Perfect Storm, Shakespeare in Love,* and *Fatal Attraction* all have in common? Test screenings.

What Would You Change?

Article by Claudia Puig

In *The Perfect Storm*, moviegoers are spared a litany of the fishermen's final maudlin thoughts. In *The Patriot,* Mel Gibson shares a kiss with his sister-in-law, but their passion stops there. And in *Scary Movie*, potshots are aimed at a previous summer hit, *Big Momma's House.*

These changes were made because Hollywood listened to people like Peter Larkey, a veteran of test screenings, one of the most important and secretive processes shaping today's movies.

"I get to say, 'This movie is awful,' 'This character has to go,'" says Larkey, a 27-year-old computer graphics designer who lives in Northridge, Calif. "It's kind of changed the way I look at films. I'm always thinking, 'What could they have cut out?'"

Filmmakers may bristle at the presumptuousness of these armchair critics, but test-screening feedback—be it visceral, written or conversational—now holds lots of clout in Hollywood. And studios, especially with big-budget summer fare, demand the insurance. "We all have to go through it because there's so much riding on the movie," *The Perfect Storm* director Wolfgang Petersen says.

Months before a movie's opening, studios hire market researchers to see how a film plays. Researchers recruit an audience, usually at malls or multiplexes. The screening usually takes place a few days later, and those who make it in sign a statement promising not to disclose anything about the film.

During the movie, researchers (and often filmmakers and studio execs, sitting anonymously in the darkened theatre) scrutinize the audience members, watching to see whether they laugh, tense up or, God forbid, snooze. After the movie, audience members fill out questionnaires, answering queries such as "What would you tell your friends about this movie?" Or "What are your feelings about the way the movie ended?" Afterward, 12 to 20 audience members often are asked to stay for additional discussions.

The typical film is test-screened three times, but for some, the process is repeated as many as 10 times. Testing is considered especially useful for comedies, action flicks and thrillers.

"Test screenings help the artist and studio fine-tune the material and refine their intentions," says Marc Shmuger, president of marketing at Universal Pictures. "The research process rests squarely in that awkward intersection between art and commerce."

The belief that test screenings can predict commercial success became widespread with 1987's *Fatal Attraction*. Test audiences balked at the original version, in which Glenn Close's character committed suicide to a *Madame Butterfly* aria. So the ending was made more sensational, with a slasher-movie-style battle between Close and the family she has been terrorizing. The movie was a hit, grossing US$156.6 million, and test screening was credited with the victory.

But no accurate formula has surfaced. "It certainly does not work that you can ever say, 'If X movie passes at Y level, then you can put an equal sign and come up with a box-office figure on the other side of the equation,'" Shmuger says.

For filmmakers, the process can be excruciating. "It's pretty nerve-racking to go out there with a film that's not finished and take it before an audience," Petersen says. "But if you want to check if a joke works or if a movie is too long, to find out the broad strokes, it's good. Even though it's painful to present your child that's not really born yet or ready for an audience, you do always learn something."

Audiences can point out lapses in logic, major holes or confusing things, says Robert Zemeckis (director of *What Lies Beneath*). "Sometimes it's a timing thing. I'll think, 'I anticipated a bump there in the audience, and I didn't get it. What is it?' Maybe the lead-up to it was too long or too short."

Sometimes, tests confirm filmmakers' highest expectations. That was the case with the raunchy comedy *Scary Movie*, one of summer 2000's surprise hits. "Moviegoers have been scared by teen movies for a while, and we were thinking to ourselves, 'We bet the audience wants to consider themselves ahead of the curve, and they're ready to laugh at this stuff,'" producer Bo Zenga says. "The screenings were a validation of what we were doing."

Because screenings went so well, the filmmakers moved the opening from spring to mid-July to capitalize on summer moviegoing crowds. That gave them time to shoot extra scenes with more timely jokes, including jabs at the comedy *Big Momma's House*.

Often, the information does not spell out a clear course of action, as was the case with *Shakespeare in Love*. The audience seemed to like the movie, even applauded at the end, says co-screenwriter Marc Norman. "The next day we were told there was a strange anomaly on the Q-and-A cards. They were asked, 'Would you recommend it to a friend?' And that number was somewhat less than the figure for 'Did you enjoy the movie?'"

Eventually, Norman says, "The consensus arrived at was that the movie was satisfying people all the way through until the last five minutes, and then it was kind of letting them down."

So Tom Stoppard rewrote the scene in which Shakespeare (Joseph Fiennes) says goodbye to Viola (Gwyneth Paltrow) with more passion, and the scene was reshot, even though both actors had moved on to other projects and had to be flown back to England, sets had to be rebuilt, costumes dusted off and a film crew put together. "We had no idea if this was the answer to the testing problem, and it cost Miramax quite a lot of money," Norman says.

But when the movie was put to the screening test again, the two figures were in sync, and the movie not only was a box-office success, but also won seven Oscars, including best picture.

The Blair Witch Project, Wag the Dog, Seven and *Austin Powers: International Man of Mystery* were hits that tested poorly. Among movies that have scored high but underperformed: *Titan A.E., Happy, Texas* and *Iron Giant*.

If *Blair Witch* taught Hollywood anything, says Amir Malin, president of Artisan Entertainment, which released the film, "it's that formulas really can't capture whether a movie will click. In the end, you go with your gut."

Claudia Puig is a newspaper columnist
who has written articles for the *National Post*.

1. Response

a. What do you think is the author's opinion about test screenings? Big-budget movies? How did you reach that conclusion?

b. What benefits do the filmmakers derive from test screening, according to this article? Do you think it is worth the expense? Explain.

c. Does the idea of test screening mean that we, as audiences, are getting the kind of movies we want? Is the most popular movie always the best movie? Why or why not?

d. Consumer products, such as food, beverages, cosmetics, and cars, have long been tested on focus groups before being put into final production. Do you feel that filmmakers should respond to the feelings of the public in this way, as if they were introducing a new chocolate bar? Should novelists ever do this kind of testing too? Explain.

2. Media *Movies* Discuss movies you have seen where you left feeling completely satisfied or unsatisfied. What elements of the movie contributed to that feeling?

Consider five box-office hits that you have seen in the past year. For each movie, list at least two recommendations that you would have made to improve them if you had been part of a test-screening audience. Discuss the movies, and your ideas with others. Explain the key change you would like to see, and give reasons why you think your change would be an improvement.

3. Language Conventions *Quotes Within Quotations* Notice in the following quotation how an internal quotation is treated:

> "They were asked, 'Would you recommend it to a friend?' And that number was somewhat less than the figure for 'Did you enjoy the movie?'"

Examine the article for other quotes within quotations. List the rules to follow for using punctuation and capital letters when using a quote within another quotation. Check that you have punctuated quotes correctly within your own writing.

Screen Scenes

Scripts by various authors

The following scene comes from the movie *The Grapes of Wrath*, which is about a poor farming family during the 1930s Depression. In this scene, Tom Joad tells his mother he can no longer meekly accept the status quo of rich and poor; he plans to protest, wherever and whenever he can.

"I'LL BE THERE"
written by Nunnally Johnson,
from *The Grapes of Wrath* by John Steinbeck

Exterior tent camp, night. Medium shot shows Ma and Tom sitting down, facing each other. Cut to close shot of Tom.

TOM JOAD: I been thinking about us, too, about our people living like pigs and good rich land layin' fallow. Or maybe one guy with a million acres and a hundred thousand farmers starvin'. And I been wonderin' if all our folks got together and yelled—

Cut to close shot of Ma.

MA JOAD: Tommy, they'd drag you out and cut you down just like they done to Casey.

Cut to Tom.

TOM: They'd drag me anyways. Sooner or later they'll get me one way or another. Till then—

Cut to Ma.

MA: Tommy, you're not aimin' to kill nobody?

Cut to Tom.

TOM: No, Ma, not that. That ain't it. Just, as long as I'm an outlaw anyways, maybe I can do something, just find out somethin', just scrounge around and maybe find out what it is that's wrong *(Cut to medium shot of both.)* and see if they ain't somethin' that can be done about it. I ain't thought it out that clear, Ma. I can't. I don't know enough.

Cut to Ma.

MA: How am I gonna know about ya, Tommy? They could kill ya and I'd never know. They could hurt ya. How am I gonna know?

Cut to Tom.

TOM: Maybe it's like Casey says. A fellow ain't got a soul of his own, just a little piece of a big soul, the one big soul that belongs to everybody, then—
MA: Then what, Tom?
TOM: Then it don't matter. I'll be all around in the dark. I'll be everywhere, wherever you can look. Wherever there's a fight so hungry people can eat, I'll be there. Wherever there's a cop beatin' up a guy, I'll be there. I'll be in the way guys yell when they're mad. *(Cut to Ma.)* I'll be in the way kids laugh when they're hungry and they know supper's ready *(Cut to Tom.)* and where people are eatin' the stuff they raise and livin' in the houses they build. I'll be there, too.

Cut to Ma.

MA: I don't understand it, Tom.

Cut to medium shot both.

TOM: Me neither, Ma. But it's just somethin' I bin thinkin' about. Give me your hand Ma. *(Both stand. Camera pulls back.)* Goodbye.
MA: Later, when this is blowed over, you'll come back?
TOM: Sure, Ma.
MA: Tom, we ain't the kissin' kind, but ... *(Kisses his cheek, he kisses hers.)*
TOM: Goodbye, Ma. *(He walks away, her back is to camera also.)*
MA: Goodbye, Tommy.

Long shot of Tom Joad, Ma in foreground as he disappears.

MA: Tommy.

Cut to long shot of Ma, as she collapses back onto platform. Music up, Red River Valley. Fade to long, long shot of man walking up hill, silhouetted against rising sun.

Henry Fonda and Jane Darwell in *The Grapes of Wrath*; Tom Joad's (played by Fonda) farewell scene.

Grapes of Wrath, The (1940) 129m. ★★★★ D: John Ford. Henry Fonda, Jane Darwell, John Carradine, Charley Grapewin, Dorris Bowden, Russell Simpson, John Qualen, O. Z. Whitehead, Eddie Quillan, Zeffie Tilbury, Darryl Hickman, Ward Bond, Charles Middleton, Tom Tyler, Mae Marsh, Jack Pennick. Classic Americana of Okie moving from dust bowl to California during Depression, lovingly brought to screen. Fonda, as ex-con, is unforgettable in role of his life. Darwell, as determined family matriarch, and Ford won well-deserved Oscars. Written for the screen (from John Steinbeck's classic) and produced by Nunnally Johnson. Don't miss this one.

From *Movie and Video Guide* by Leonard Maltin

In this scene from the Christmas classic,
It's a Wonderful Life, honest, earnest George confronts
his long-time enemy, Potter.

"SCURVY LITTLE SPIDER"

from *It's a Wonderful Life* by Frances Goodrich,
Albert Hackett, Frank Capra, and Jo Swerling

Interior scene, Potter's office; George, Potter, and his manservant are present. See all three, Potter lighting George's cigar as George leans over his desk. Cut to close up of George as he sits down in an extremely low chair, intended to place the tall George at physical disadvantage. His face is level with desk. Pull back, see George, and Potter back view.

GEORGE: *(nervously)* Well, I … I suppose I'll find out sooner or later, but just what exactly did you want to see me about?

Cut to Potter medium shot, can see George in profile still. Manservant stands to right of Potter, silent and motionless throughout.

POTTER: *(laughs)* Oh, George, now that's just what I like so much about you. *(pleasantly and smoothly—like a snake)* George, I'm an old man, and most people hate me. But I don't like them either, so that makes it all even. *(Cut to George, looking surprised by this insight.)* You know just as well as I do that I run practically everything in this town but the Bailey Building and Loan. You know, also, that for a number of years I've been trying to get control of it … *(Cut to Potter.)* … or kill it. But I haven't been able to do it. You have been stopping me. In fact, you have beaten me, George, and as anyone in this county can tell you, that takes some doing. Now, take during the depression, for instance. You and I were the only ones that kept our heads. You saved the Building and Loan; I saved all the rest.
GEORGE: Yes. Well, most people say you stole all the rest.

Cut to George.

POTTER: The envious ones say that, George, the suckers. *(Cut to Potter.)* Now, I have stated my side very frankly. Now, let's look at your side. *(Cut to George.)* Young man, twenty-seven, twenty-eight … married, making, say … forty a week.
GEORGE: *(indignantly)* Forty-five!

James Stewart in *It's a Wonderful Life*. This scene shows George, played by Stewart, during his conversation with Potter.

POTTER: Forty-five. Forty-five. Out of which, after supporting your mother, and paying your bills, you're able to keep, say, ten, if you skimp. A child or two comes along, and you won't even be able to save the ten. Now, if this young man of twenty-eight was a common, ordinary yokel, I'd say he was doing fine. *(Cut to Potter.)* But George Bailey is not a common, ordinary yokel. He's an intelligent, smart, ambitious young man—who hates his job—who hates the Building and Loan almost as much as I do. *(Cut to George.)* A young man who's been dying to get out on his own ever since he was born. A young man ... the smartest one of the crowd, mind you, a young man who has to sit by and watch his friends go places, because he's trapped. Yes, sir, trapped into frittering his life away playing nursemaid to a lot of garlic-eaters. *(Cut to Potter.)* Do I paint a correct picture, or do I exaggerate?

Cut to George.

GEORGE: *(taken aback)* Now what's your point, Mr. Potter?
POTTER: My point? My point is, I want to hire you.
GEORGE: *(dumbfounded)* Hire me?

POTTER: I want you to manage my affairs, run my properties. George, I'll start you out at twenty thousand dollars a year.

George drops his cigar on his lap. He nervously brushes off the sparks from his clothes. Stands.

GEORGE: *(flabbergasted)* Twenty thou—twenty thousand dollars a year?

Cut to Potter, George in profile in shot.

POTTER: You wouldn't mind living in the nicest house in town, buying your wife a lot of fine clothes, a couple of business trips to New York a year, maybe once in a while Europe. You wouldn't mind that, would you, George?

Cut to George.

GEORGE: Would I? *(looking around skeptically)* You're not talking to somebody else around here, are you? You know, this is me, you remember me? George Bailey.

Cut to Potter.

POTTER: Oh, yes, George Bailey. Whose ship has just come in—*(Cut to George—see back of Potter's head.)* providing he has brains enough to climb aboard. *(Cut to Potter smiling. Cut to George grinning. He sits in low chair.)*

GEORGE: Hah! Holy Mackerel. Well, how about the Building and Loan?

Cut to Potter—gesturing angrily.

POTTER: Oh, confound it, man, are you afraid of success? I'm offering you a three-year contract at twenty thousand dollars a year, starting today. *(Cut to George.)* Is it a deal or isn't it?
GEORGE: *(stands)* Well, Mr. Potter, I … I … I know I ought to jump at the chance, but I … I just … I wonder if it would be possible for you to give me twenty-four hours to think it over?

> In my films I always wanted to make people
> see deeply. I don't want to show things,
> but to give people the desire to see.
>
> Agnès Varda

Cut to Potter, smoothly understanding.

POTTER: Sure, sure, sure. You go on home and talk about it to your wife.
GEORGE: I'd like to do that.
POTTER: Yeah. In the meantime, I'll draw up the papers.
GEORGE: *(still seemingly hypnotized by the sum)* All right, sir.
POTTER: *(offers hand)* Okay, George?

Cut to George, leaning over, offering hand.

GEORGE: *(taking his hand)* Okay, Mr. Potter.

As they shake hands, George feels a physical revulsion, frowns. In that moment of physical contact he knows he could never be associated with this man. George drops his hand with a shudder, wipes hand on suit. He peers intently into Potter's face.

GEORGE: *(vehemently, shaking off his earlier daze)* No ... no ... no ... no, now wait a minute, here! *(Cut to Potter.)* Wait a minute! *(Cut to George.)* I don't need twenty-four hours. I don't have to talk to anybody! I know right now, and the answer is no! NO! Doggone it! *(getting madder all the time)* You sit around here and you spin your little webs and you think the whole world revolves around you and your money. Well, it doesn't, Mr. Potter! In the ... in the whole vast configuration of things, I'd say you were nothing but a scurvy little spider. You ... *(He turns and shouts at the manservant, impassive as ever beside Potter's wheelchair.)* And that goes for you, too! *(sticks cigar in mouth, heads to door, saying to the secretary in the outer office as he leaves)* And it goes for you, too!

It's a Wonderful Life (1946) 129m. ★★★★ D: Frank Capra. James Stewart, Donna Reed, Lionel Barrymore, Thomas Mitchell, Henry Travers, Beulah Bondi, Frank Faylen, Ward Bond, Gloria Grahame, H.B. Warner, Frank Albertson, Todd Karns, Samuel S. Hinds, Mary Treen, Sheldon Leonard, Ellen Corby. Sentimental tale of Stewart, who works all his life to make good in small town, thinking he's failed and trying to end his life. Guardian angel Travers comes to show him his mistake. Only Capra and this cast could pull it off so well; this film seems to improve with age. Capra, Frances Goodrich, Albert Hackett, and Jo Swerling expanded Philip Van Doren Stern's short story "The Greatest Gift" (which had originally been written by Stern as a Christmas card!) Remade for TV as *It Happened One Christmas*. Also shown in computer-colored version.

From *Movie and Video Guide* by Leonard Maltin

In this scene from the movie *A Raisin in the Sun*, Asagai visits a friend, Beneatha, on her moving day. What was supposed to be a day of triumph for Beneatha—moving into a bigger place—turns into a day of despair when she discovers her brother has been conned out of the insurance money that was to pay for a new home.

"I'M TIRED OF LISTENING"
from *A Raisin in the Sun* by Lorraine Hansberry

Interior apartment. Beneatha sitting, knock on door. Beneatha opens door to Asagai. He comes in, talking, rolling up sleeves, moving around room.

ASAGAI: I had some free time so I came over. I thought I might help with the packing. Oh-ho, I love the look of packing crates! The sight of a household in preparation. Movement, progress—It makes me think of Africa.

BENEATHA: Africa!

ASAGAI: Well, what kind of mood is this? I thought I'd find you full of sunlight today? Have I told you how deeply you move me? *(approaches her to hold her face. She puts her own hands up to face, breaking down—he begins to realize she is upset.)* Something wrong?

BENEATHA: Asagai, he gave away the money.

ASAGAI: Who gave away what money?

BENEATHA: The insurance money. My brother, he just gave it away. *(she moves away, agitated)*

ASAGAI: Gave it away?

BENEATHA: He made an investment! With a man even Travis [her nephew] wouldn't have trusted with his most worn-out marbles!

ASAGAI: And it's gone?

BENEATHA: Gone!

ASAGAI: I see. I'm very sorry.

BENEATHA: But you know, my brother's not the one who's to blame. Oh no, by *his* lights he did what made sense to him. My mama's the crazy one. My mama's the one who just handed him the money. She just got up one fine day and just gave away my future.

ASAGAI: *(approaching her)* Perhaps you don't see things as well as your mother does?

BENEATHA: Oh this is the end for me. You know, it takes money to go to school …Well what difference does it make anyway? I mean, why would anybody want to be a doctor in this nutty world?

From left to right: Diana Sands, Sidney Poitier, and Ruby Dee in *A Raisin in the Sun*.
Diana Sands plays Beneatha, the sister of Sidney Poitier's character.

ASAGAI: My, aren't we full of despair? … Look here, was it your money? *(takes her shoulders, turns him to face her)* I said, was it your money that was lost?
BENEATHA: It belonged to all of us.
ASAGAI: Can't this make you see that there is something *wrong* *(gestures with both hands)* if all the dreams in this house—good or bad—

had to depend on something that might never have happened—if a man had not died? We used to say, back home, accident was at the first and will be at the last—but a poor tree from which the fruits of life may bloom.

BENEATHA: Asagai, what is the matter with you? Listen, my family has been wiped out! *(moves away)* What's the matter—don't they use money where you come from?

ASAGAI: *(following her)* I see only that you, with all of your keen mind, cannot understand the greatness of the thing that your mother tried to do. You're not too young to understand. For all of her backwardness she still acts. She still believes that she can change things. And to that extent she is more of the future than you are at this moment.

BENEATHA: Well, all I know is that when somebody can get up in the morning and, without consulting you, *(she moves away, back to Asagai)* just blithely hand away your future then life is impossible, it's futile. It's despair!

ASAGAI: Listen …

BENEATHA: No! I'm tired of listenin'. *(moves towards door)*

Raisin in the Sun, A (1961) 128m. ★★★★ D: Daniel Petrie. Sidney Poitier, Claudia McNeil, Ruby Dee, Diana Sands, Ivan Dixon, John Fiedler, Louis Gossett. Lorraine Hansberry play receives perceptive handling by outstanding cast in drama of black Chicago family's attempts to find sense in their constrained existence. Remade for TV in 1991.

From *Movie and Video Guide* by Leonard Maltin

1. *Response*

a. What emotions do the characters portray during each of the scenes in this selection? What clues to their emotions are there in the words they use?

b. What is the message—implicit or explicit—of each scene?

c. Considering the year in which each movie was released and the scene included here, what do you think was the audience's reaction to each movie at the time it was released?

d. Read the capsule reviews that appear after each scene. Discuss the features of these capsule reviews. Compare them to full-length movie reviews from newspapers or magazines.

2. **Language Conventions** *Non-Standard English* Discuss the language in these three scenes and why most of the scriptwriters have used non-standard English. What else do you notice about the dialogue? What does the language reveal about the characters? Is the language of each scene appropriate? Effective? Explain.

   Examine a piece of your own writing and the dialogue your characters use. How can you make your characters seem more real by using non-standard or informal English?

3. **Drama** *Presenting the Scene* With a partner, plan a presentation of one of these scenes. Think about the gestures you will use, and the position of your bodies. As well, experiment with volume, pace, and tone, as you rehearse. When you are ready, present this scene to your class.

4. **Media** *Directing Movies* Like novelists, movie directors develop scenes to create tension, move the action along, and establish character. With a small group, discuss the stage direction included with each of these scenes. Are there any terms you do not understand? Focus on one scene, and consider the effectiveness of its direction. If possible, view this scene, and make notes on how effectively the director creates tension, moves the action along, or establishes character. How would you change this scene or its direction?

5. **Writing** *Personal Response* Consider your personal response to one of these scenes. Choose a suitable writing format—a letter, poem, story, script, essay, et cetera—to convey your response to an audience of your peers.

If there wasn't something called
   acting, they would probably hospitalize
      people like me.
         —*Whoopi Goldberg*

This selection takes you behind the scenes at *CTV News* with a news researcher. Are there any aspects of the job that surprise you?

JUST *the* FACTS

Diary by Sue Kanhai

How best can I describe my fabulous job? No two days are ever the same. There's no telling who you'll bump into in the hallway. And there's only one way to know what sort of day you're about to have—by jumping in. Each day I see some of Canada's most famous and respected news anchors and I talk to national reporters about the stories they're working on.

Our department works together in a fairly small, bustling room. We each have workspaces that include a desk, computer, filing cabinet, TV, and tape cueing machine. We screen footage daily, and so make good use of our gadgets. It's quite normal to hear phones ringing, producers or editors chatting about a request, newscasters burbling away on various TV sets, and the sounds from different video segments being cued and viewed nearby all at the same time. Depending on your mood, it can be a mild, pleasant hum or a maddening cacophony! Shelves of dictionaries, encyclopedias, government publications, directories, almanacs, newspapers, magazines, and videotapes surround us. These are very well-thumbed resources, and are kept close at hand. Our more traditional-looking, proper library —with floor-to-ceiling shelves of more news magazines, cross-Canada newspapers, political policy books, microfiche, a full tape vault, and newspaper clippings files—is just a flight of stairs away.

The chatter and buzz can be amusing. There's the bored, "How many seats did the Liberals have at dissolution again?", the frantic, "Who took the mayor's press conference from yesterday?", and the exasperated, "How ON EARTH do you spell deoxyribonucleic acid?" My co-workers are amazing; I can pick up so much sometimes from just sitting back and surveying the activity. As in any workplace, each person has his or her own area(s) of interest; here, particularly, the benefits multiply. It's incredible the amount of specific, detailed information our group has at its fingertips.

Now that you know a little about our environment, let me take you through a day-in-the-life of a news researcher.

9 – 10 a.m.

Ah, the morning, such a rare opportunity for peace and quiet! After settling in and checking my e-mail, I begin perusing one of our four daily newspapers; I also scan the news wires to see what's lined up for today. Soon I'm called into action. One of the producers from *CTV Newsnet* is looking for an expert who can speak on camera early this afternoon about a recent court ruling. We happen to have an excellent in-house resource, a co-worker at *Canada AM* who has many contacts; I consult her for any leads. While she's looking, I decide to try *The Blue Book*, University of Toronto's resource for journalists that lists over 1600 academic experts. I also scan recent articles on the subject from our clippings file for people who've

commented in the past. Together, we forward the producer three names, with job titles and phone numbers.

10 – 11 a.m.

Yesterday it was reported that one of the major political parties had a carefully worded but contentious proposal buried in its election platform. The leader of the party tried to play it down when questioned about it, and we ran his response on last night's broadcast. Today, an assignment editor at the national news desk would like to know the stances of the other four parties on this same issue. To begin, I visit each party's Web site and do a keyword search of each platform. This turns up little, for several reasons. First, the exact wording used by each party can and does vary. Second, as turned out to be the case here, perhaps not all parties chose to include the information in their platforms. After discussing it with a fellow researcher, we decide that calling party headquarters is next. We leave detailed messages, and hope our calls will be returned before the end of the day.

11 – 12 p.m.

An active case of tuberculosis has been detected in a Toronto neighbourhood, and we are called with both video and research requests. Needed: footage of doctors examining chest X-rays and adults getting vaccinations against TB, as well as general information about TB. A co-worker pitches in to find the footage, while I search for information. My first stop is Health Canada's Web site; I'm looking for any past warnings or advisories that have been issued. Next I search both the Internet and our own newspaper clippings files for the symptoms, causes, and treatments of the disease. Information from Health Canada and a good medical piece from one of our national newspapers will suffice. I e-mail the document to the reporter who requested the info, and my co-worker arranges to have the footage fed to their bureau.

12 – 1 p.m.
A piece of proposed legislation that was tabled months ago resurfaces for discussion. It's been a while since the topic's been in the news, and a reporter would like an update. She's looking for summary and analysis pieces specifically. We use several fee-for-service databases that allow us to search magazines, newspapers, and journals from all over the world. These articles are extremely useful in providing both context and an overview of complex situations. The costs for these services (mostly online) vary, but are generally pretty substantial. The one drawback is that only text is available. For charts, graphs, and statistics, we have to rely on our own clippings files. To

help reduce search time, we've had training in search strategies by the companies that build these databases. I search by keyword (including combinations of keywords), publication, date, and word length, and, happily, find exactly what I need. A copy of the file is shared with our electronic news service, as we think they might appreciate the update.

1 – 2 p.m.
There's just enough time for a quick lunch before another request rolls in. The promotions department is cutting a promo for tonight's national news broadcast. They need stock shots of busy shoppers walking in a mall to indicate recent retailing statistics. They would also like yesterday's footage of the Russian president's visit to Cuba, as he is due to arrive in Ottawa shortly.

2 – 3 p.m.
A leading international political figure died on this day nearly thirty years ago. A memorial is to be held, which we will run footage of, but a head shot of the man is needed by graphics. Each of the news items we archive on tape has a record created for it that describes its contents. This is called the *shotlist*. We can search our records for this man, and by reading the codes in the shotlist, we can see whether or not a story contains the type of shot we're

looking for—in this case a MCU (medium close-up), CU (close-up), or H&S (head & shoulders) shot.

A graphic artist will work with the video we've selected and create an over-the-shoulder graphic from it. (These typically sit on the upper right-hand corner of your screen, over the anchor's shoulder, as he or she reads the intro to a story.) While I seek this out, a co-worker does a quick encyclopedia and Internet search for background information on this man. He's looking for the exact spelling of a political sect and highlights of his major accomplishments.

3 – 4 p.m.

A lull in the afternoon. Downtime like this, while rare, is easy to fill in a place this busy. I can check the wires for the latest news, finish looking through the day's newspapers, and catch up on some outstanding archiving. Each day one of us is assigned to archive the previous night's national news broadcast. We analyse each story filed, looking for good visuals, memorable statements, and important events or meetings. The test we apply is: Is this newsworthy enough that it'll be valuable five or ten years from now? Certain significant events it's obvious we should keep for historical value: a peace treaty being signed, a space mission, election coverage, etc. But this is just the beginning. Someone (or some thing) may not *seem* terribly important, but if a search of our database shows we have no existing similar footage, it may well be worth keeping. We'll often ask each other's opinions.

4 – 5 p.m.

A producer from *W-Five* has requested the monthly national unemployment rate for each month of the current year. We must always provide the source of our research, and are always looking for up-to-date, reliable information. Good sites to rely on include those run by the government, universities, or professional associations. It's imperative that we analyse any possible bias in the figures we send on. By using good judgment first, and then providing our source, we can be reasonably sure the information is reliable. Ultimately, the decision rests with whoever requested the figures.

Writer, editor, and researcher **Sue Kanhai** studied French Language, Literature, and Translation at the University of Toronto. She reads widely and avidly and enjoys writing both fiction and non-fiction. She has worked in publishing, but is currently employed as a researcher for a national news program.

1. *Response*
  a. Before reading this article, what did you think a modern newsroom was like?
  b. How did this article change your perceptions about a modern newsroom?
  c. How would you describe the tone of this piece and the diction the author uses? What contributes to the tone?
  d. What aspect of being a news researcher would you like most? Least?
  e. Discuss a news program you have watched recently, considering the questions listed under the headings About the text, About production, and About the audience in Cam MacPherson's article "Looking at the Media."

2. *Research and Inquiry* Use print or human resources, or the Internet, to find out about another behind-the-scenes job at a news station. What training, education, and background does the job require? What skills or talents are needed to do the job effectively? As a class, share your information about the different jobs people perform to bring you a newscast.

3. *Media* *Preparing the News* With a small group, plan and create a video newscast for a local or school event. Each person in the group can assume the role of a different person behind the scenes at a news station, from researcher to newscaster.

While news is important, news interpretation
    is far more important.
                    —H. V. Kaltenborn

What drives an editorial cartoonist? Read on to find out.

Laughter Soothes His Soul

Profile
by Paul Melting Tallow

Everett Soop's body is frail and weak, but his heart and soul are as strong as the Rocky Mountains that watch over him and the land that he loves.

He's lived with the muscular dystrophy that has confined him to a wheelchair for 40 years, with diabetes further ravaging his body. Despite all the physical adversity he's faced in life, his great spiritual strength has allowed him to look back with few regrets and little bitterness.

Born on the Blood Reserve in southwestern Alberta in 1943, Everett was raised in an area of the reserve known as Bull Horn, near the town of Cardston. His childhood was typical for the children of the Blackfoot-speaking Bloods, or Ahkainah (Many Chiefs), as they call themselves, carefree with no concern for the world outside the reserve. Time was spent playing with his friends, riding horses and getting into mischief.

"For me it was a happy childhood because I didn't know what was going on. Ignorance is bliss, I guess."

Everett's hunger for knowledge gave him the driving force to continue on at the Cardston schools until he eventually graduated from Grade 12 in 1963, unlike many who had followed him into town. He was one of only three Ahkainah students to graduate.

"In Grade 7, there must have been about 40 or 50 of us but they all quit." Everett remembers the subtle and overt racism from students that made it difficult for him and his fellow Ahkainah students to attend school. He said he believed that, in order to deal with the racism and ostracism, the two other Ahkainah students who graduated had to convert to the church.

Undaunted, Everett's determination to succeed was as solid as the stone in the Mormon temple rising across the street from the school and he survived because, "I didn't give a damn. I just wanted to get an education and that was all."

In addition to his tenacity, he had his strong-willed mother, Josephine, to push him and support him through all the adversities. He said she began cracking her whip to drive him to work hard at achieving his goals when he was a child and, now that she's 85 years old, she's still cracking that whip over his head. But he knows the whip was wielded by a gentle, loving hand.

It was during his time at the Cardston schools that he first displayed his talent for cartooning; combining his acerbic wit and artistic talents to satirize his teachers, fellow students and family members.

After his high school graduation, Everett sought to enhance his artistic qualities by enrolling at art schools in Banff and Calgary. At the Alberta College of Art in Calgary, Everett once again encountered racism. An instructor told Everett that he didn't expect too much from him because he was Native and Natives were not known for their success.

"He said we've only had two and they didn't amount to anything. One of them was Gerald Tailfeathers and the other one was Alex Janvier. Those were really good examples to fail and I wanted to become a failure like them."

Tailfeathers received commissions for his work from the Canadian Pavilion at Expo 67, the Glenbow Museum in Calgary and Canada Post. Janvier was advisor at the Expo 67 Indians of Canada Pavilion, a member of the Professional Native Indian Artists Incorporated, represented Canada in a Canadian/Chinese cultural exchange in 1985 and was commissioned to create murals at the Canadian Museum of Civilization.

Unfortunately, since the provincial government sponsored his education, Soop had to abide by its rules. One rule was he could not miss more than 10 percent of total class time; Everett missed 14 percent so he was suspended for a year. Undeterred, he enrolled in the arts program at Brigham Young University in Utah. It was at the university that he discovered journalism could be the perfect medium to express his artistic abilities and his satirical wit.

"In the back of my mind I've always enjoyed editorial cartooning. It never occurred to me 'til I was down there ... that [editorial cartooning] was my real interest."

He returned to Calgary to enroll in the journalism program at the Mount Royal College and to be closer to home and family. Unfortunately, social conditions prevalent in Calgary's newsrooms and the rest of the country did not favor Native journalists.

At the end of his first year of studies in 1968, Everett got a summer job drawing cartoons for the Blood Reserve's *Kainai News*. The newspaper, one of Canada's first, albeit government-funded, Native newspapers, was just beginning its inaugural year of publication.

"My first day on the job they were having their editorial meeting and they were talking about the dog situation in Cardston. I started coming up with outrageous ideas like maybe the dogs were showing us the way. The Mormons in Cardston and the Bloods will not mix, but if the dogs can mix, maybe we can mix. The sarcasm went right to work and I felt right at home."

He didn't return to Mount Royal and the summer job turned into a career. *Kainai News* became his home for the next 13 years.

Everett's political cartoons soon gained him fame and notoriety in Native communities across Canada and the United States. With each issue his cartoons became more and more outrageous and satirical until the editorial staff had to rein him in. Everett denies full responsibility for his stinging observations but, humbly, shares the credit with everyone at the newspaper.

"It became a lot of fun because I wasn't alone. Maybe it looks like I got the credit all the time but everybody had their input, throwing their ideas."

Everett's cartoons became so popular in the community that the paper allowed him to express his views in his own column. He continued to tickle the funny bones of his friends and admirers while ruffling the feathers of his victims.

Scorn and even threats of bodily harm from those that he offended did little to discourage him; instead, he developed a thick skin. Although his favorite targets were the politicians he considered pompous and who considered themselves infallible, he addressed all social injustices and issues.

"Humor really has nothing to do with being funny. It's about being angry. Seeing all these things that are corrupt, that are destroying us, the injustices."

While most of his opinions were formed by his empathy for the victims of injustice, the underdogs as he calls them, he received encouragement from the more socially aware in the upper strata of reserve society.

The late Senator James Gladstone, Canada's first Aboriginal senator, saw the need for Everett's brand of humor and his criticism of politicians. The senator was there to give Everett emotional support when he felt like quitting.

These images are examples of Soop's work. The image at top left is the cover for his book called *I See My Tribe Is Still Behind Me!*, a collection of his editorials and cartoons. Soop's controversial cartoons and editorials angered many in his community.

"He talked to me for a while and I was all perked up and ready to go again. With that kind of encouragement I got meaner and it got more fun."

With his satirizing of politicians, it was ironic that he ran for and won a seat on the Blood Band council in 1982. He claims government cutbacks that resulted in his losing his position at *Kainai News* forced him into the political arena. He had ambitions of returning to art school but the nearest ones in California and Indiana were too far away.

His stay in Utah had proven that it was too expensive for him to attend art school in the United States, especially with Canadian currency on the short end of the exchange rate.

"So I thought, 'why not go into council?' That would be equal to a Ph.D. in cartooning. Besides that, I had been calling them jackasses for 15 years. I wanted to know what it's like being a jackass."

During his time in office, Everett continued to champion the underdog and the disadvantaged, in particular, the physically disabled. He was appointed to chair the council's health committee in 1985 and was instrumental in the opening of the reserve's health centre. Although many in his community give him the credit for the health centre, his humility will not allow him to accept it.

"It was started a good 20 years before then. A lot of people worked towards it and it didn't happen until they were long gone."

It helped him to understand that the rewards of hard work don't become immediately apparent, unlike most politicians who he says claim the results of years of hard work by their predecessors as their own accomplishments.

These days life is slower for Everett, diabetes and muscular dystrophy have all but consumed his body and put severe limitations on his activity.

Throughout the years of living with his disabilities, it was Everett's humor that gave him the courage to face life and it now gives him the strength to continue living. He's even able to find humor in the enormous difficulty performing simple functions that his disabilities have caused.

"I find every difficulty and every adversity in my life funny.... I think humor has been a gift given to me, not just to share with others, but for myself to survive, to be able to laugh at myself. Other than that, what else is there to do but cry?"

Paul Melting Tallow is a journalist and photographer. He has worked for *Alberta Sweetgrass*, the Aboriginal newspaper of Alberta, and has contributed articles to *Windspeaker*, Canada's national Aboriginal news source.

1. *Response*

a. Reread the first paragraph of this article again and decide whether you think the author's description of Soop is exaggerated. Develop your own simile to describe Soop.

b. Discuss Soop's words: "I find every difficulty and every adversity in my life funny.... I think humor has been a gift given to me, not just to share with others, but for myself to survive, to be able to laugh at myself. Other than that, what else is there to do but cry?"

c. Was there any part of Everett Soop's story that you found particularly striking? If so, what and why?

d. What qualities, skills, and characteristics do you think make someone a good editorial cartoonist?

2. *Visual Communication* *Analyse Art*

Examine the four cartoons in this selection. How does Soop create humour using both text and visuals? What words would you use to describe these cartoons? Everett Soop and Paul Melting Tallow speak of Soop's cartoons as being controversial, and raising the ire of both the Aboriginal and non-Aboriginal communities. Is there anything in these examples of his work that would account for their reactions? Explain.

3. *Vocabulary*

Notice how this article spells *humour* (humor) using the American spelling, and uses the Canadian spelling for *centre*. Why might the author have used both American and Canadian spelling? What effect does it have on the reader? Do you think using Canadian spelling is important? Why or why not?

4. *Media* *Editorial Cartoons*

Collect at least twelve editorial cartoons from more than one newspaper or source, and from several artists. Compare the content, subject matter, bias, and humour of each cartoon, and the artists' styles. Choose one cartoon and write a brief report outlining its purpose, audience, and effectiveness.

5. *Research and Inquiry*

Find out more about the editorial-cartooning career of Everett Soop or another artist. Develop a short profile of the person, including examples of his or her work. Prepare a multi-media presentation for this cartoonist, for example, using slides, video, music, and words.

"CYBERANCHOR"
Delivers All the
E-News That's Fit to Click

Newspaper article by Ann Perry

Two days after her Internet debut, newscast phenom Ananova has invitations to Britain's top parties and two marriage proposals.

With all those options, what's a multi-hued collection of 300,000 data points to do?

"I think what we've got to make sure is that she doesn't get too big-headed," said Debbie Stephens, a press officer with Ananova Ltd. "We're keeping a careful eye on her social calendar."

Billed as the world's first virtual newscaster, the computer-generated cyberanchor, whose delicate features, big eyes, green neo-punk hair and sensitive delivery have already inspired outpourings of fan devotion, reads breaking news at the click of a mouse.

Judging from the traffic at Ananova's Web site, she's a huge hit, with millions of cyberviewers clicking in since her debut in April 2000.

"This is a day to remember just like man's first step on the moon," said an e-mail message from Eric Dufort of Quebec.

Another fan wrote: "The future is here at Ananova ... You're the best in the world."

But James Burns couldn't believe his eyes—or ears. "Very realistic," he wrote. "Are you sure she's not real?"

All this attention begs the question—who is Ananova?

The origin of her name has already sparked debate, but her creators claim they chose it simply because it's unique.

On her Web site, Ananova warns against making up nicknames such as "Ana" or "Nova" on pain of her "blowing a few circuits."

Younger than this millennium, Ananova's baby pictures consist of a series of drawings and computer models that document her rise from featureless *tabula rasa* to 28-year-old newsreading cyberbabe with a three-dimensional head that comprises 300,000 constantly changing data points.

Her creators at Ananova Ltd., formerly the new media division of Britain's Press Association news agency, sifted through hundreds of photographs to develop a composite drawing that was sent to Glasgow-based Digital Animations Group for the cybersurgery that would bring her to life.

What they came up with was a green-haired cross between Posh Spice and computer game action hero Lara Croft from *Tomb Raider.*

"We wanted someone who was going to be distinctive, someone who was going to be easily recognizable and we wanted to try to get away from the blonde and brunette stereotype," said Stephens.

But in a business that worships youth, Ananova isn't just another pretty face.

Her brain is a powerful Internet tool that continuously searches more than 10,000 Web sites around the world to gather breaking news and automatically index the information into subject areas.

A team of 30 journalists and editors sifts through the mass of information, choosing the top stories and deciding what Ananova is going to say.

After that, the techies input the text and code it with appropriate emotional tags that prompt Ananova to deliver her two-minute newscasts with appropriate feeling and flair with the press of a button by her techno-puppeteers.

From a sombre update on clashes between farmers and war veterans in Zimbabwe, Ananova can change her mood for a less-serious story with a raised eyebrow and a fetching smile while intoning: "How bizarre is this?"

When Ananova's creators found their own British English pronunciation too formal, they opted for a neutral "mid-Atlantic" accent that blends British, American and Canadian cadences.

While Ananova has not been in the news business long enough to become a diva, she's definitely high maintenance. She has a crack staff of 80 designers, information technology developers, producers and journalists working around the clock to put words in her mouth.

Still, the technology behind her isn't all that new.

Ananova is simply a marriage of a text-to-speech system to video animation, synchronizing the movement of her mouth and her voice—technologies that already operate on Saturday morning cartoons.

What is innovative about Ananova, say her creators, is the speed with which she can adapt to the pressure-cooker environment of breaking news.

"To actually get a system that can uphold that kind of traffic and to be able to change it on literally split-second notice so she can change her mannerisms, voice, and the information she's delivering, that's what's ground-breaking," said Stephens.

But the buzz among Web surfers isn't so much about Ananova's bits and bytes as her instant celebrity style.

After media hype began swirling around the mysterious green-haired waif in January, her corporate managers ran a competition that attracted tens of thousands of entries from around the world to decide on her first words.

The result? An edgy—if somewhat stilted—"Hello, world. Here is the news—and this time it's personal."

Ananova's personal life has already galvanized Internet entrepreneurs who are lining up to create the personality behind the pixels.

A European architectural firm has volunteered to design a tastefully decorated home for Ananova. The only problem is she'll need a body first.

But that shouldn't be hard for a popular gal like Ananova who's getting the kind of offers from fans usually reserved for living, breathing news anchors. Some leading British designers are already jockeying to build what, according to rumours, will be her slender 5-foot-7 frame.

Despite Ananova's instant fame—she has already done interviews on NBC and CNN—skeptics say that, like digitized icon Max Headroom of the 1980s, her cyberstar will soon fade.

"It's a cute technology that will execute what you tell it to do, but to suggest that it has real artificial intelligence and understanding of what it's reading is misleading," said Jordan Worth, an Internet analyst at International Data Corp. (Canada) Ltd.

But Worth worries certain advantages of cyberanchors like Ananova may put flesh-and-blood newscasters out of business.

"You can fire them on a whim, you can replace them and their demands are minimal," deadpanned Worth about cyberjournalists. "There are probably no digital prima donnas to deal with. But at the same time they don't provide much fodder for the tabloids and *Frank*,[1] so that's, in my mind, a bad thing."

Unlike her human counterparts, however, Ananova will commit no unseemly bloopers. Why? Because Ananova's nothing short of e-perfect.

---

[1] **Frank:** a satirical magazine

Ann Perry is a newspaper columnist who has written articles for *The Toronto Star.*

I. Response
   a. Discuss how and why Ananova was created.
   b. Even though viewers know that Ananova is just an electronic fake, why do they like her? Why do you think Ananova has become an overnight sensation?
   c. Discuss the phrases *media hype, media sensations,* and *overnight success.* How are these concepts connected? Use other current examples in your discussion.

2. *Media* *Designing a Cyberanchor* What image has Ananova been created to project? If you were part of the design team creating another cyberanchor for a competing news site, what type of appearance and image would you want to achieve? Describe your design and image in detail. Consider gender, ethnic background, and age as three of your criteria.

3. *Research and Inquiry* Check out the Ananova site, if you are not already familiar with it. What is your reaction to Ananova and her skills as a newsreader? Is she "real" enough for you? Do you agree with the final decisions of her designers? What changes would you suggest making to her voice and appearance?
   Examine the Web site carefully and evaluate the style and substance of what it offers in comparison to other online news sites. To find the location of other sites, use the key words *online news sites.*

4. *Critical Thinking* When a newsreader can be digitized so effectively, why bother with a human? What are the advantages of creations like Ananova over human newsreaders? How would you feel about the elimination of human anchors on network TV newscasts, and their replacement by Ananova's cybercolleagues?
   What lies ahead for Ananova and other computer-generated "people" on the Internet? Do you see other areas where such artificial people could find work? Explain.

On the news two dozen events of fantastically different importance are announced in exactly the same tone of voice. The voice doesn't discriminate between a divorce, a horse race, a war in the Middle East.
                                             —Doris Lessing

Brainstorm a list of new media or computer technologies that you think will affect your world. How will you fit into this world?

The Net Generation

Article by Don Tapscott

The baby boom was the biggest population wave ever—until it was eclipsed by the Net Generation. The N-Generation now represents 30 percent of the population, compared to the boomers' 29 percent. For the first time, there is another generation large enough to rival the cultural hegemony of the ubiquitous boomers. But what makes N-Geners unique is not just their large numbers, but that they are growing up during the dawn of a completely new interactive medium of communication. Just as the much more limited medium of television influenced the values and culture of the baby boomers, a new force is helping shape the N-Gen wave. They are spending their formative years in a context and environment fundamentally different from their parents.

Many people think the new media and television are analogous because they both involve screens. For example, the term *screenagers* has been used to describe today's youth. TV viewers and Net surfers alike have been called *couch potatoes*. Social critic Neil Postman has said that through the information highway, information is becoming a new form of garbage—and with computers and televisions we will all be "amusing ourselves to death," the title of his 1994 book.

Those who say that the Net is all about a bigger crop of couch potatoes not only have a cynical view of humanity, but they ignore the budding experience with interactive technologies. Unfortunately for these commentators and fortunately for kids, the similarities between the two technologies end with the screen. In fact, the shift is more like from couch potato to Nintendo jockey.

TV is controlled by adults. Kids are passive observers. In contrast, children control much of their world on the Net. It is something they do themselves; they are users, and they are active. They do not just observe, they participate. They inquire, discuss, argue, play, shop, critique, investigate, ridicule, fantasize, seek, and inform.

This makes the Internet fundamentally different from previous communications innovations, such as the development of the printing press or the introduction of radio and television broadcasting. These latter technologies are unidirectional and controlled by adults. They are very hierarchical, inflexible, and centralized. Not surprisingly, they reflect the values of their adult owners. By contrast, the new media is interactive, malleable, and distributed in control. As such it cherishes a much greater neutrality. The new media will do what we command of them. And at this moment, tens of millions of N-Geners around the world are taking over the steering wheel.

This distinction is at the heart of the new generation. For the first time ever, children are taking control of critical elements of a communications revolution.

On the Net, children must search for, rather than simply look at, information. This forces them to develop thinking and investigative skills, and much more. They must become critics. Which Web sites are good? How can I tell what is real and what is fictitious—whether it's a data source or the alleged teenage movie star in a chat session?

Further, children begin to question assumptions previously unchallenged. On the Net, there is a great diversity of opinion regarding all things and constant opportunities to present your views. This is leading to a generation which increasingly questions the implicit values contained in information. Information becomes knowledge through the application of human judgment. As children interact with each other and the exploding information resources on the Net, they are forced to exercise not only their critical thinking but their judgment. This process is contributing to the relentless breakdown of the notion of authority and experience-driven hierarchies. Increasingly, young people are the masters of the interactive environment and of their own fate in it.

Because the Net is the antithesis of TV, the N-Generation is in many ways the antithesis of the TV generation.

The Web That Ate TV

There are, of course, aspects to TV which have been positive. Not all content is vacuous: TV is a distribution channel for good movies, documentaries, sports events, music, comedy, interviews, and news. It's simple to use. Most of us have programs which we know and usually enjoy. The quality of TV in terms of production values is usually high, especially when compared to most current Web sites. TV and radio have also acquired a level of interactivity with talk shows and phone-in programs such as *Larry King Live*. TV is also somewhat a communal experience as you sit with others in front of the electronic hearth.

There is also a role for passivity. As Frank Biondi, former president and CEO of Viacom, says, "TV is, at bottom, a passive experience, which is its beauty." In other words, the great thing about television is that you can come home after a long day at school or work and veg out in front of the TV.

True, there is some couch potato in all of us, including kids. On Saturday night, your son and his girlfriend may want to sit on the couch and be entertained rather than to construct some elaborate Net experience. Sometimes we want the content to rule rather than ourselves. Indeed, opportunities for "veging" in the digital economy will be even greater than today.

In 1997, it became very fashionable to talk about so-called *push technology* or *Web-casting*. Simply put, content is pushed to your screen rather than you seeking it. Instead of surfing the Net for information, content providers send you new information from categories you have previously requested—such as sports scores for your favorite teams, stocks you care about, the weather, and eventually anything. *The Wall Street Journal* proclaimed that the Net had finally found a viable business model—television.[1] *Business Week* announced that Web-casting would cut through the clutter of the Net "using the same principle as broadcasting."[2] Screen saver software—using push technology to bring customized news and information to the screen when your computer is idle—took off.

In reality, push technology is not a return to broadcasting but simply another thread in the richly developing tapestry of the Net. Over time, such Web-casting, including the casting of live TV programs, will be assimilated into the Net.

But television is not dead, just television as we know it—a rigid, one-way medium delivered by networks that schedule programming according to their estimates of likely viewership. Those who view the Net as another TV channel have got it backward. Sometime early in the next century, television programs will become accessible through the Net. Rather than talking about TV versus the Net, we will talk about stored access of content versus real-time access. In *stored* (asynchronous) access, the user picks up previously sorted content (information, music video, a drama, sitcom, news program) when convenient. In *real-time* (synchronous) use, people access content (a sports game, election reporting) as it is occurring.

Your favorite TV shows will become a Web incident or site. First viewings of a sitcom, soap, or events like a football game or presidential address will be watched simultaneously by many. Such real-time simultaneous transmissions simply become part of the interactive world. TV schedules will be subordinated to the schedules that really count—those of our own lives and families and organizations. Interactivity enables us to program our lives better and to integrate the content we desire according to schedules that are important, not those arbitrarily determined by a TV network.

Rather than the Web becoming a push medium, TV is moving into the world of pull. If you want to sit back and watch the news, *Casablanca*, or an I *Love Lucy* rerun, go ahead and veg out. The difference is that prime time becomes any time. And if you would rather explore Mayan ruins, visit with your daughter at university, participate in a discussion about college basketball, analyze your personal finances, or find out why you have chest pains, you can do that, too. Ultimately, NBC television will become another Web site and the schedule will exist only for first-time viewings.

Just how strong is the N-Gen preference for the digital media over television? Very. Carla Bastida is a 9-year-old who lives in Barcelona, Spain. Last Christmas she was confronted with a choice: the family could replace its broken VCR or buy a color printer. She says that "there was no choice, really. I wanted the printer."

Hollywood and broadcasting executives should take note that she chose the printer because it was "more important" for her and the computer was "more fun" than watching TV and videos. Says Dad, "Carla gets bored just watching TV."

If you contrast N-Geners with their parents, it isn't difficult to see how this rejection of television came about. Baby boomers have witnessed the computer revolution, but they have viewed it through a couch potato mentality. That doesn't mean all baby boomers are getting fat, but that we've become accustomed to the broadcast delivery of information.

Keeping current is not widely seen as an interactive activity. To many boomers, keeping current means turning on the six o'clock news (although even that is declining in popularity).

In the midst of the massive social changes and the era of short-sighted but widely practiced corporate downsizing, boomers have embraced computer and information technology but they have done so under duress. Baby boomers are constantly being reminded that computer-facilitated networks are a personal and economic survival tool that will revolutionize everything—whether they are prepared for it or not. N-Geners, on the other hand, view it as a natural extension of themselves. It is, in fact, the specific medium that will follow and perpetuate the force of their youth, just as television has traced the lives of the boomers.

Notes

1. Bank, David. "Selling Pants on PointCast," *The Wall Street Journal*, 13 December 1996, p. A1.
2. *Business Week*, 24 February 1997, pp. 95–104.

Don Tapscott is the bestselling author of a number of books, including *The Digital Economy*, and co-author of *Paradigm Shift*. He is the president of New Paradigm Learning Corporation, and chairman of Digital 4Sight, both based in Toronto. Digital 4Sight is a research "think tank" funded by some of the world's leading financial, technology, retail, manufacturing, and government organizations.

I. *Response*
a. This article was taken from a book called *Growing Up Digital*. Given this title, and the content and language of this selection, who do you think is the target audience for such a book? What makes you think so?
b. What is Don Tapscott's main idea in this article? How does he support this idea?
c. Is there a statement in this article that you strongly agree or disagree with? Explain.

2. **Media** *Comparing Formats* Tapscott compares TV to the
   Internet in a general way. Make a more specific comparison
   of these two media by comparing one specific item on each
   —a news report, for example. Consider content, delivery,
   style, techniques, who sponsors the item, who produces it, and
   who the audience is. Does either item contain any bias? What
   is the medium's relationship with its audience? With its sponsors? Use a chart to share your conclusions with others.

3. **Vocabulary** Consider the following sentence:

   > For example, the term *screenagers* has been used to
   > describe today's youth.

   How is the word *screenager* appropriate? Inappropriate? What
   other invented words connected with the Internet does this
   article use? How would you define these words? What other
   Internet-related words would you like to see added to the
   English language?

If one ox could not do the job they did not try to grow
a bigger ox, but used two oxen. When we need greater
computer power the answer is not to get a bigger computer,
but ... to build systems of computers and operate them
in parallel.

—Grace Murray Hopper

If I Can't Have Beer, at Least Give Me a Playstation

Essay by Rob Blizzard

I had little homework after school the other day. As the class neared its end, I had already imagined what the remainder of the day would consist of. Without homework the possibilities were limitless. I could go for a jog, read a book, see some friends. Instead, I watched the television.

Why play a game of street hockey when you could watch a game from the comfort of your couch? And in the televised version there are professional athletes who are far better than I could ever be, so why should I even try to imitate them? The far better course of action would be to wallow in my own inactivity. This will allow my brain to shift into a mode most easily likened to a coma. Nothing short of sleep is more relaxing. This is how I spent my day.

Along the same lines, I had become addicted to a computer game a couple of weeks ago. Called *Sims*, it allows you to create an alter-ego and guide him/her through the daily toils of life. You must tell your character to eat, sleep, shower, play pool, or what have you.

When I had first heard of the game's concept I mocked it. After all, if you wanted to experience the daily routine of a life in minute detail, why not get off the computer and do so? I scared myself at one point when I had actually told my character to play on his computer. For a few minutes I was actually playing a game that involved a miniature me playing a game.

Why not lose the middle man and just live for yourself? For the exact same reason that people watch the television. It is a comfortable way of living life with all the illusions of reward without the risks. It is easier and more convenient to live life through the television or computer.

It is odd that in this era of unsurpassed technology and advancement, the area of quickest growth is the entertainment industry. Why, if life is better than it has ever been before, do we spend so much time attempting to escape from it? We build games that mirror our own world. The only difference is that time can be turned back and mistakes can be undone. It is a world better than ours and for that reason it is addictive.

Maybe Sony Playstations and five-hundred channel satellite accesses are the newest form of alcohol. Alcohol traditionally being the method of escape for past generations. Unfortunately for booze, a minimum age has been set to prevent those most susceptible to addiction from contact. It is here Nintendo has the edge, it can target the youngest and most vulnerable—legally.

Rob Blizzard is a high-school student who contributes to the teen column for the Moose Jaw *Times-Herald*.

1. *Response*
   a. What is the author's tone in this essay? What words or phrases demonstrate this tone?
   b. What is the thesis of this essay? What arguments support this thesis?
   c. Do you agree with the author's thesis? Explain.

2. *Writing* *Essay* Choose a media issue that interests you and write an essay that examines it. Your purpose is to persuade an audience of your peers about your point of view. Use an organizational structure, such as cause-and-effect or comparison, to present your argument. As Blizzard has done, choose a title for your essay that grabs the readers' attention. Remember that your conclusion should offer a new insight into the argument.

3. **Literature Studies** *Comparing Essays* Compare this essay to "People as Products" by Jean Kilbourne. What structure has each author used? What literary devices does each author use? Which do you think is the more effective essay? Explain your reasoning.

4. **Media** *Advertising* Examine some ads for computer games; check the copy in catalogues, magazines, or on packaging. How is what the manufacturers say about their product like or unlike what Blizzard says? What implicit, as well as explicit, messages does the copy contain?

   Choose one of Blizzard's statements and develop a real ad, or a parody of a real ad, for a new computer game.

Computers are useless. They can only give you answers.

—*Pablo Picasso*

"Another field has become open for women to explore …"
proclaims Samantha Peters
in this editorial.

Being a Woman in a Man's Game World

Editorial
by Samantha Peters

BEING A WOMAN IN A MALE-dominated industry is always a difficult task, but from personal experience, it seems to be exceptionally hard in the fields of technology and computer information. For decades, women have been fighting for equal rights and the ability to do jobs that men commonly do. Now, it isn't uncommon to see women in warehouses, driving heavy machinery, working in an office, or even in operating rooms. With the advent of the dawning technological era, however, another field has become open for women to explore.

Being a part of a game development team myself, I work with a male-dominated team on a daily basis. There is only one other woman on our staff, an exceptionally talented 2D artist, aside from myself, making the female influence amongst the team rather minimal in comparison to everyone else. Thankfully, we work in an environment that is quite favorable for us; the men we work with have no qualms with working with us.

Unfortunately, this often doesn't extend beyond our own team. Much of my work exists in the realm of public relations, and on a daily basis I am confronted with at least one man that either a) doesn't believe me, or b) refuses to take me seriously. These men range from so-called professional contacts to potential fans to just people I happen to meet on a daily basis. This is just one facet of a custom that has been etched into society for hundreds of years, a custom that most women despise and fight to overcome: the subservience of the female gender and intellectual dominance of males.

I was skimming the Net the other day, reading my usual plethora of gaming sites that I keep track of, and I came across something that made me stop and almost do a double take. A banner ad for computer cases, of all things, with a rather anorexic-looking young lady draped across it wearing nothing but a skimpy little bikini. This really got me thinking about just how biased the computer and gaming world is when it comes to men.

This banner is obviously targeted at the males in the world, as I know very few women that would take one look at that scantily-clad girl and say "You know, I really need a new case for my computer" and click on that link. I do, however, know a few men that would follow through. This, combined with the sheer number of booth bunnies lead me to only one conclusion: this is a male industry.

Chances are, the person that made the ad was a man, and the people that put it up are probably men too. People hiring booth bunnies? I'd say mostly men. How many banner ads do you see with buff men in speedos trying to sell you a case fan? I'm not saying I want to see this, because honestly, I don't think seeing some sexy guy shakin' his tight li'l butt around is going to make me buy a Cyrix over a Pentium 3.

Another thing I've noticed in the gaming world (and more broadly, in the world in general), is a tendency for expectations to be placed on women, for how they should act, what they should do, etc. For example, it's not uncommon to see women in my position as a public relations representative, but how many female coders are there in the world? Sure, I bet there's a bunch of women that play *Ultima Online* or *Diablo 2* or *Icewind Dale*, but not nearly as many that play *Quake 3 Arena*. Of course, this is only a guess on my part from playing or witnessing all of the above, but I would say there is a much higher female ratio in *Diablo* than there is in *Q3A*. From the men that I've talked to, and the experiences I've had, it's expected that I would like role playing games, but action? Nah, that's a male thing. But, if I did happen to be one of the rare few that played an action game like *Half-Life* or *Quake*, then it would be assumed that I'm vicious, not all that feminine, loud, and extroverted. I'd say that at least some of the women that play *Quake* are like this, but I wouldn't go so far as to brand an entire gender in a game based on the actions of a few.

The fact is, in the gaming world, women are a minority, both in the fields of creating and playing games. Truthfully, female game developers and gamers are much more commonplace than they were years ago, but the common belief amongst most men in the community is that in this world, women are a rare commodity, a precious few that brave a male-dominated realm, and special measures should be taken to attract more women into developing and playing games. To be honest, choosing to play or even create games is a personal choice of taste, and if there are fewer women than men, so be it. It is harder on the women that do take part, but that doesn't mean we want special attention, good or bad.

Being a woman anywhere that's male-dominated is hard, but there's not much us ladies can do but persevere and keep on doing what we want to do, turning down the marriage proposals from the awe-struck guys that say "Wow! A female gamer? I'm in heaven! Will you marry me?!?!" Believe me, I've heard it myself, and for all you women that haven't heard it yet, hang on, because I'm sure you will eventually.

Samantha Peters is a game designer with Klache Entertainment and a full-time student in the School of Communications at Simon Fraser University in Vancouver, B.C. Views presented in this article are her own, based on personal experience and readings.

I. Response
    a. This editorial was taken from an Internet Web site that includes articles about computer games and the Internet. Who do you think is Samantha Peters' audience? What is her purpose? What viewpoint does the editorial express? How is her viewpoint supported?
    b. Survey the students in your class to find out if they agree with Peters' viewpoint. Compare your own ideas about this issue with those of Peters, and others in your class.
    c. How does this editorial resemble an essay? How does it differ? How do elements of the editorial form enhance the meaning of this selection?

2. Literature Studies *Interpretation* As a group, discuss your interpretations of this editorial. Do you all agree about the author's message? If not, explore how your interpretations differ. How is your interpretation of this editorial influenced by the values of your society? How does the language and syntax of the editorial affect readers and their interpretations?

3. Writing *Responding to the Editorial* Respond to this editorial by writing your own editorial or by writing a letter to an editor. Clearly present your opinion, and support it with arguments and facts.

4. Media *Gender Bias* One of the problems that can occur when mostly men (or women) create something media-related, like a computer game, is that overt or hidden gender bias can become part of that creation. Examine a number of games (or choose another media form—perhaps one that has been created by women rather than men) for gender bias. Who created this product? What was their purpose in creating it? Is there a gender bias? What effect does this have on their audience? Write a report on your findings.

5. Language Conventions *Reflexive Pronouns* The pronouns *myself, himself, herself, itself*, and so on, are used for two purposes; they are used for emphasis as in the line:

He himself denied any involvement in the movie.

When these pronouns are used to refer back to the subject of the sentence or phrase, they are known as reflexive pronouns, as in:

She taped herself for the audition.

Check this selection to see how these pronouns have been used. Which use is for emphasis? Which use is reflexive?

Examine these covers from popular computer games. Considering the cover design, describe each game. Which game do you think would be the most realistic? Explain your reasoning. How has each cover been designed to appeal to a certain audience?

Glossary

In the **active voice**, the subject of a sentence does the action: *The dog ran into the street.* Use the active voice when possible. It uses fewer words and is more precise than the passive voice. See **Passive Voice.**

An **allegory** is a simple story, such as a fable or parable, whose major purpose is to teach a moral lesson. An allegory can always be read on two levels—one literal, the other symbolic. The underlying meaning can be parallel to, but different from, the surface meaning.

An **allusion,** in a literary work, is a reference to another literary work, or a person, place, event, or object from history, literature, or mythology.

An **analogy** is the illustration of one idea or concept by using a similar idea or concept. An analogy is sometimes phrased as a simile.

The **antagonist** of a narrative or dramatic work is the primary person in opposition to the hero or **protagonist.**

An **archetype** is a theme, symbol, character, or setting that can be found throughout literature, folklore, and media so often that it comes to reflect some universal human character or experience. For example, Robin Hood is an archetypal hero.

Bias is an inclination or preference that makes it difficult or impossible to judge fairly in a particular situation.

Diction refers to the way an author expresses ideas in words. Good diction includes grammatical correctness, skill in the choice of effective words, and a wide vocabulary.

A **dynamic character** is one who undergoes a significant and permanent change in personality or beliefs.

A **eulogy** is a tribute to someone who has just died, and is often delivered as a speech at a funeral.

A **fact sheet** presents key information about a particular topic, issue, or organization. It provides concise answers to basic questions. Some fact sheets are written in point form, others in full sentences.

Figurative language uses words to paint a picture, draw an interesting comparison, or create a poetic effect. **Literal language** says what it means directly. Language can be figurative or literal.

Hyperbole is a deliberately exaggerated statement made for effect.

Imagery is the pictures or impressions that writers create in the minds of their readers. To create these pictures, they use descriptive techniques such as figures of speech (simile, metaphor, personification, oxymoron), onomatopoeia, alliteration, and allusions.

Irony occurs when a statement or situation means something different from (or even the opposite of) what is expected. Another type of irony is **dramatic irony**. It occurs in plays when the audience knows something that the characters do not.

A **literary essay** presents an interpretation or explores some aspect of one or more works of literature.

A **loaded word** is a word intentionally chosen to evoke a strong response in a reader—usually an emotional response.

A **logo** is an identifying symbol used as a trademark in advertising.

Mass media is any method by which a message is communicated to a large audience at the same time—movies, radio, TV, books, magazines, or the Internet.

A **media text** is any media product—movie, radio show, CD, TV program, et cetera—that is selected for critical examination.

A **metaphor** is a comparison of two things that are not alike. The comparison suggests that they do share a common quality: *Her words were a knife to my heart.*

Parallelism is the intentional use of identical or similar grammatical structure within one sentence or in two or more sentences.

Parallel structure is the repeated use of the same phrase or sentence, or the repeated use of a similar sentence structure. Parallel structure can be used to create balance or place emphasis on certain lines.

In the **passive voice**, the subject of the verb receives the actions: *The fire was extinguished.*

Personification occurs when objects, ideas, or animals are given human qualities: *The sun smiled down on me.*

A **point of view** is the vantage point from which the author tells a story. The four most common points of view are *first person* (I, me), *omniscient* (all-seeing), *limited omniscient* (all-seeing from the viewpoint of a group of characters), and *objective* (he, she, they, it).

A **précis** is a concise summary of a text. It is written in full sentences, but contains only the most important information.

Racist language is any language that refers to a particular cultural or ethnic group in insulting terms, but racism also exists in more subtle forms.
- Mention a person's race only if it is relevant to the context. If a person's race or ethnic origin is relevant, be specific:
  Irrelevant/Vague: *Dago is African.*
  Relevant/Less Vague: *Dago is proud of her Nigerian heritage.*
- Avoid making generalizations about any racial or cultural group:
  Stereotype: *The Welsh are great singers.*
  Better: *The Welsh have a long tradition of singing.*

A **rhetorical question** is one that is asked for effect, and that does not invite a reply. The purpose of a rhetorical question is to introduce a topic or to focus the reader on a concern.

A **satire** is a work that criticizes something—for example, a person, a characteristic, an institution, or a government—by depicting it in a humorous, sarcastic, or scornful way.

Sexist language is language that degrades or unnecessarily excludes either women or men. It is best to avoid generalizing about males and females unless the claims are based on scientific facts.
- Whenever possible, replace words such as *fireman*, *policeman*, and *man-made* with non-sexist alternatives such as *firefighter*, *police officer*, and *fabricated*.
- Avoid using the masculine pronouns *he, him,* or *his* to refer to both men and women.

A **stereotype** is an oversimplified picture, usually of a group of people, giving them all a set of characteristics, without consideration for individual differences.

Suspense is a feeling of tension, anxiety, or excitement resulting from uncertainty. An author creates suspense to keep readers interested.

Style is the overall texture of a piece of writing; the particular way in which the ideas are expressed. Style is made up of many elements including diction, figurative language, sentences, and tone.

A **symbol** is something that represents something else—for example, the lion can be a symbol of courage.

The **symbolic meaning** of a work is developed through the symbols that the author includes.

A **theme** is a central thesis or idea that is expressed directly or indirectly in a literary work.

The **thesis** of an essay is the main idea or argument that the author is attempting to prove.

Tone is the implied attitude of the writer toward the subject or the audience. Tone differs from mood, which describes the emotional feeling of the work more generally. The tone of a piece of work can be described, for example, as *angry*, *satiric*, *joyful*, or *serious*.

Transition words indicate relationships between ideas. Writers use them to suggest links between sentences or paragraphs.

Index of Titles and Authors

Alarm Bells for Civilization, 20
All Part of Becoming Canadian, 167
Arming the Spirit, 71
Augustine, Noah, 186
Bacon, Sir Francis, 28
Bantock, Nick, 51
Being a Woman in a Man's Game World, 243
Bishop, Elizabeth, 41
Black, Arthur, 169
Blizzard, Rob, 240
Capra, Frank, 211
Chicken-Hips, 79
Christmas Consumer Frenzy, 143
Classroom Without Walls, 134
Coady, Lynn, 12
Comparison, A, 53
Contemporary Canadian Biographies, 111
Crook, Tim, 138
"Cyberanchor" Delivers All the E-News That's
    Fit to Click, 230
DeKay, William, 66
de Kerckhove, Derrick, 189
Dis?Ability on the Internet, 75
Doubletake, 66
Doyle, Marjorie, 91
Dryden, Ken, 8
Dyer, Gwynne, 20
Faludy, George, 71
Filling Station, 41
Fung, Kristal, 50
Goodrich, Frances, 211
Hackett, Albert, 211
Halberstam, David, 197
Hansberry, Lorraine, 215
Hiam, Alexander, 178
Homage to Barcelona, 91
Hung, Peter, 56
If I Can't Have Beer, at Least Give Me a
    Playstation, 240
"I'll Be There," 208
Importance of Being Earnest, The, 16
"I'm Tired of Listening," 215
In Memory of W.O. Mitchell, 105
In Support of Nick Bantock's "Life Class," 50
It's Time to Think About Visors, 8
Johnson, Nunnally, 208
Joy, 41
Just the Facts, 219
Kanhai, Sue, 219
Kilbourne, Jean, 155
Laughter Soothes His Soul, 224
Laurence, Margaret, 61
Le Guin, Ursula K., 16

Lessons From a Walk in a Rain Forest, 98
Life Class, 51
Lightman, Alan, 32
Long Walk to Freedom: The Autobiography of
    Nelson Mandela, 118
Looking at the Media, 130
MacPherson, Cam, 130
Mandela, Nelson, 118
Mann and Machine, 111
McLuhan, Marshall, 134
Melting Tallow, Paul, 224
Moth, Paul, 143
Net Generation, The, 238
No News Is Bad News: Using Publicity to
    Your Advantage, 178
Of Studies, 28
One Ocean, 148
Orwell, George, 86
Packard, Vance, 160
Peacock, Molly, 41
People as Products, 155
Perry, Ann, 230
Peters, Samantha, 243
Pigott, Catherine, 79
Pittman, Al, 167
Plath, Sylvia, 53
Progress, 32
Proud, Heather, 75
Psychological Power of Radio, The, 142
Puig, Claudia, 204
Quan, Betty, 148
Quiz Show Format, The, 201
Screen Scenes, 208
"Scurvy Little Spider," 211
Sea-Monkey Lady: Susan Barclay, The, 173
Shack, The, 65
Short Story Defined, The, 60
Some Thoughts on the Common Toad, 86
Sports Logos an Insult, 186
Steinbeck, John, 208
Steinem, Gloria, 36
Stenson, Fred, 105
Suzuki, David, 98
Swerling, Jo, 211
Tapscott, Don, 234
Taylor, Drew Hayden, 83
Television: The Collective Imagination, 189
Time Factor, The, 36
Trouble With People, The, 160
What Colour Is a Rose?, 83
What Would You Change?, 204
Whose Lathe?, 16

Acknowledgments

Every reasonable effort has been made to trace ownership of copyrighted material. Information that would enable the publisher to correct any reference or credit in future editions would be appreciated.

8 "It's Time to Think About Visors" by Ken Dryden. © 2000 Time Inc. Reprinted by permission. 12 "The Importance of Being Earnest" by Lynn Coady. Originally published in the September 2000 issue of *Quill & Quire*. © 2000 by Lynn Coady. 16 "Whose Lathe?" From *Dancing at the Edge of the World* by Ursula K. Le Guin. © 1984 by Ursula K. Le Guin. Used by permission of Grove/Atlantic, Inc. 20 "Alarm Bells for Civilization" by Gwynne Dyer. Reprinted with permission. 32 "Progress" from *Dance for Two – Selected Essays* by Alan Lightman. Originally published in *Inc Magazine*. London: Bloomsbury Publishing Plc. © Alan Lightman. 36 "The Time Factor" by Gloria Steinem. © Gloria Steinem. 41 "Joy" from *How to Read a Poem ... and Start a Poetry Circle* by Molly Peacock; "Filling Station" by Elizabeth Bishop from *The Complete Poems 1927–1979*. © 1979, 1983 by Alice Helen Methfessel. 50, 51 "In Support of Nick Bantock's 'Life Class'" by Kristal Fung. Reprinted with permission of the author. "Life Class" from *The Artful Dodger* by Nick Bantock. Reprinted with permission of Raincoast Books. 53 "A Comparison" by Sylvia Plath from *Johnny Panic and the Bible of Dreams*. Reprinted by permission of Faber and Faber Limited. 56 "The Short Story Defined" by Peter Hung from *Literary Cavalcade*, Vol. 43, No. 8 (May 1991). 61 "The Shack" by Margaret Laurence from *Heart of a Stranger*. © 1976 by Margaret Laurence. Used by permission of McClelland & Stewart, Ltd., *The Canadian Publishers*. 75 "Dis?Ability on the Internet" by Heather Proud from *Paralinks: The Electronic Magazine for People with Spinal Cord Injury*. Reprinted with permission. 79 "Chicken Hips" by Catherine Piggott from the *Globe and Mail*, March 20, 1990. Reprinted with permission. 83 "What Colour is a Rose?" from *Funny, You Don't Look Like One: Observations from a Blue-Eyed Ojibway* by Drew Hayden Taylor. Penticton, B.C.: Theytus Books Ltd., 1998. © 1998 Drew Hayden Taylor. 86 "Some Thoughts on the Common Toad" by George Orwell © George Orwell, 1946). By permission of Bill Hamilton, Literary Executor of the Estate of the Late Sonia Brownell Orwell and Martin Secker & Warburg Ltd. 91 "Homage to Barcelona" by Marjorie Doyle from *A View of Her Own*. Reprinted with permission of the author. 98 "Lessons From a Walk in a Rain Forest" by David Suzuki From *Earth Time: Essays*. © 1998 by Dr. David Suzuki. Reprinted by permission of Stoddart Publishing Co. Limited. 105 "In Memory of W.O. Mitchell" by Fred Stenson. Reprinted with permission. 111 "Mann and Machine" from *Contemporary Canadian Biographies, June 1999: Steve Mann: Scientist, Inventor, and Artist,* Toronto Public Library CPLQ. Stamford, CT: Gale Research Publications, Thomson Information/Publishing Group. 118 Excerpt from *Long Walk to Freedom: The Autobiography of Nelson Mandela*. © 1994 by Nelson Rolihlahla Mandela. By permission of Little, Brown and Company (Inc.). 138 "The Psychological Power of Radio" by Tim Crook. Reprinted by permission of the author. 148 *One Ocean* by Betty Quan. © 1994 by Betty Quan. First broadcast on CBC-Radio. Reprinted with permission of The Pamela Paul Agency Inc. 155 "People as Products" by Jean Kilbourne. Reprinted with the permission of The Free Press, a Division of Simon & Schuster, Inc., from *Deadly Persuasion: Why Women and Girls Must Fight the Addictive Power of Advertising* by Jean Kilbourne. © 1999 by Jean Kilbourne. 160 "The Trouble with People" from *The Hidden Persuaders* by Vance Packard, © 1957 by Vance Packard. 167 "All Part of Becoming Canadian" from *The Day I Became a Canadian* by Al Pittman. St. John's, NF: Breakwater Books Ltd. Reprinted with permission. 178 "No News is Bad News: Using Publicity to Your Advantage" from *Marketing for Dummies®* by Alexander Hiam. Foster City, CA: IDG Books Worldwide Inc. 189 "Television: The Collective Imagination" from *The Skin of Culture: Investigating the New Electronic Reality* by Derrick de Kerckhove. Toronto: Somerville House Publishing, 1995. © 1995 Derrick de Kerckhove. Reprinted with permission. 197 "The Quiz Show Format" from *The Fifties* by David Halberstam, © 1993 by The Amateurs Limited. Used by permission of Villard Books, a division of Random House, Inc. 204 "What Would You Change?" by Claudia Puig. © 2000, *USA Today*. Reprinted with permission. 230 "'Cyberanchor' Delivers All the E-News That's Fit to Click" by Ann Perry, *Toronto Star*, April 21, 2000. Reprinted with permission – The Toronto Star Syndicate. 234 "The Net Generation" from *Growing Up Digital: The Rise of the Net Generation* by Don Tapscott. New York, NY: McGraw-Hill. © 1998 by the McGraw-Hill Companies, Inc.

Visual Credits

7 Andrew Judd/Masterfile. 25 Abrams/Lacagnina/ Image Bank. 29 Image Select/Art Resource, NY. 37 *Allées Piétonnières* by Jean-Pierre Stora/Grand Design/SuperStock. 66-69 From *Down Home: A Journey into Rural Canada* by William DeKay, published by Stoddart Publishing Co. Limited. Copyright © 1997 William DeKay. 109 Charles Clarke. 112 Courtesy of Steve Mann. 129 Geoffrey Gove/Image Bank. 157 Report on Business Television. 165 Albert Gescheidt/Image Bank. 210, 212, & 216 Photofest. 227 Courtesy of Everett Soop. 246 left The Sims™, PC CD © 2000 Electronic Arts Inc. The Sims, Maxis and the Maxis logo are trade-